Competitiveness
and the Management Process

Competitiveness and the Management Process

Edited by
Andrew M. Pettigrew

Basil Blackwell

Copyright © Basil Blackwell 1988

First published 1988

Basil Blackwell Ltd
108 Cowley Road, Oxford, OX4 1JF, UK

Basil Blackwell Inc.
432 Park Avenue South, Suite 1503
New York, NY 10016, USA

British Library Cataloguing in Publication Data
Competitiveness and the management process.
  1. Management
  I. Pettigrew, Andrew M. (Andrew Marshall),
  1944–
  658

  ISBN 0–631–16465–0

Library of Congress Cataloging in Publication Data
Competitiveness and the management process / edited by Andrew M.
  Pettigrew.
     p.   cm.
  Selected papers from the inaugural conference of the British
  Academy of Management, Sept. 13–15, 1987.
  ISBN 0–631–16465–0
  1. Management—Congresses. I. Pettigrew, Andrew M. II. British
  Academy of Management.
  HD29.C635 1988
  658—dc19   88–14606
                                                                        CIP

Typeset in 10 on 12 pt Plantin
by Columns of Reading
Printed in Great Britain by
T.J. Press Ltd, Padstow, Cornwall

Contents

About the authors

Simon Archer is Senior Lecturer, Department of Accounting and Finance, School of Management, University of Lancaster

Michael Baker is Professor and Head of the Department of Marketing, University of Strathclyde

Patrick Barwise is Senior Lecturer in Marketing, London Business School

Andrew Campbell is Director, Ashridge Strategic Management Centre

Nigel Campbell is Lecturer in Strategic Management, Manchester Business School

Cary L. Cooper is Professor of Organizational Psychology, Manchester School of Management, UMIST

Arthur Francis is at The Management School, Imperial College, London

Michael Goold is Director, Ashridge Strategic Management Centre

Rob Grant is Professor, Management Department, California Polytechnic State University

Peter Grinyer is the Esmée Fairbairn Professor of the Economic (Finance and Investment) Programme, Chairman of the Department of Management, University of St Andrews

Peter McKiernan is Senior Lecturer, Warwick Business School, University of Warwick

Iain L. Mangham is Professor of Management Development, Head of the School of Management, University of Bath

Paul Marsh is Faculty Dean, Professor of Management and Finance, London Business School

David G. Mayes is Head of Economics and Statistics, National Economic Development Office

Andrew M. Pettigrew is Professor of Organizational Behaviour, and Director, Centre for Corporate Strategy and Change, University of Warwick

Sudi Sharifi is a contract researcher in the Innovation Design and Operations Management Research Unit, Aston University Management Centre

Howard Thomas is the James Towey Professor of Business Administration, Department of Business Administration, University of Illinois

Kathryn Thomas is Consultant with the Centre for Business Strategy, London Business School

Robin Wensley is Professor of Marketing and Strategic Management, Warwick Business School, University of Warwick

Diana Winstanley is at The Management School, Imperial College, London

Preface

This volume has developed from the Inaugural Conference of the British Academy of Management hosted by Warwick University between 13 and 15 September 1987 and chaired by the editor of this book. The British Academy of Management has been formed as a learned society to assist the generation and dissemination of knowledge from all the management subjects. The Academy has the following objectives:

(1) to encourage the sharing and development of a research–knowledge base for all the management disciplines;
(2) to act as a forum for the various disciplines in management and to encourage the development of an integrated body of knowledge commensurate with management as a profession;
(3) to encourage and promote interdisciplinary research and collaboration among the various management disciplines;
(4) to further the development of management education in the UK.

The content and style of the conference was designed to reflect the multidisciplinary aims of the British Academy of Management. All five keynote speakers were asked to present papers describing existing or prospective research on multidisciplinary problem areas. Four of these papers are published in this volume together with the Presidential Address given by Professor Cary Cooper. In addition to the keynote speakers the conference was divided into six subthemes. These themes paralleled the five keynote presentations, and were respectively strategy and performance; strategic decision-making; managerial activities; competences and learning; the new frontiers for British marketing; and the management of technology. The sixth theme was epistemological and methodological issues in management research. The papers presented in the subthemes were selected from a large body of synopses, and the best paper from each subtheme was in turn chosen for publication in this volume. I am grateful to Professor John Bessant, Professor John Burgoyne, Professor Gerry Johnson, Professor Paul Marsh, Professor

Roy Payne and Professor John Saunders for their assistance in organizing the subthemes in the conference and, with their colleagues, in choosing the best papers for this book.

At the time of preparation of this volume (February 1988) the British Academy of Management is just 18 months old. Thus far we have 55 founding institutional members, representing nearly all the major university, polytechnic and further education schools of management and business in the UK and Ireland. Our individual membership is now in excess of 500, and our first major conference attracted 180 participants from most of the disciplines and functions of management. This kind of progress is a great credit to the first Executive Committee of the Academy and I would like to record my appreciation of their support here.

Finally I would like to recognize the marvellous support given to the British Academy of Management by Gill Drakeley of the Centre for Corporate Strategy and Change, University of Warwick. Whilst I have been Chairman of the Executive Committee of the British Academy of Management the administrative office of the Academy has been at Warwick and Gill Drakeley has done a superb job of setting up and running the secretarial and administrative systems of the Academy. I would like to express my gratitude for this support and for Jeanette Whitmore's assistance in preparing for the conference.

Andrew M. Pettigrew
Centre for Corporate Strategy and Change
Warwick University
February 1988

Introduction

Andrew M. Pettigrew

What have been and still are some of the key management problems of the 1980s? Without doubt change has been a critical area of management experience. Firms have been influenced not only by the post-1980 international economic environment, but also by consequential adjustments in the fortunes of their own and related industry sectors. The pattern for many North American and European firms is for a dramatic stiffening of competitive environment since 1980, often a loss of competitive advantage, and rapid changes in business strategy, structure and human resources.

The survivors of the post-1980 era of radical change are now pursuing multiple paths to regeneration. These paths include reducing fixed costs, technological change, new product developments and significant divestments, internationalizing activities, changing customers and channels of distribution, and in some cases major changes in human resource policies and practices. Alongside product market, service and technological changes firms have also made significant organizational and cultural adjustments. Firms have looked to replace their top leaders, and in turn the style with which the top executives run the business. There has been a trend to decentralize responsibilities to more sharply accountable business units and, associated with that, energetic and persistent attempts to introduce performance-orientated and quality-orientated cultural change. For some managements there has come a realization that managerial competences have to change and, together with that, a new priority to create an atmosphere and the will for a series of interrelated changes to occur more or less continuously (Pettigrew et al., 1988).

If the theme of change captures an important piece of the experience of management in the 1980s, how was the change theme built into the interdisciplinary topic areas of the first British Academy of Management conference?

Structure of the book

The structure of this book directly reflects the priority topic areas of the conference. Six themes provided a focus for the conference:

competitive strategy and performance;
strategic decision-making;
managerial activities, competences and learning;
new frontiers for British marketing;
the management of technology;
epistemological and methodological issues in management research.

This book contains four of the five keynote presentations of the conference and the six best papers from each of the themes. Thus chapter 2 by Grinyer, Mayes and McKiernan was the keynote presentation for the competitive strategy and performance theme, and chapter 3 by Grant and Thomas was the best paper presented under that theme. Chapter 4 by Marsh, Barwise, Thomas and Wensley was the keynote paper on strategic decision-making, and the paper by Campbell and Goold was the best presentation in the decision-making category. Mangham (chapter 6) gave the keynote presentation in the managerial competence area, and Sharifi's paper was chosen to represent the conference papers on managerial activities, competences and learning. Chapter 8 by Baker and chapter 9 by Campbell were the equivalent papers in the marketing theme. Chapter 10 by Francis and Winstanley and chapter 11 by Archer were respectively the best papers chosen from the management of technology and the epistemology and methodology sections of the conference. Appropriately, Cary Cooper's presidential address to the inaugural conference is published here as chapter 1.

Between them these chapters convey important aspects of topical and continuing management problems. How and why are some firms able to make dramatic improvements in competitive performance? What is the reality of how firms make major strategic investment decisions? How and why are the corporate centres of large diversified firms responding to environmental change? What do we know of the executive process at the very top of organizations, and how and why must marketing strategies change to reflect the globalization of markets and the apparent success of Japanese marketing methods and styles? What is the significance of engineering design in the competitive process, and what are some of the challenges in more effectively linking technical and professional staff to the broad performance objectives of the firm? Aside from relevance and topicality, what is also common to the above questions is their clear interdisciplinarity. None of them is containable, analysable or answerable within the myopia of any particular management discipline. Equally well, their study will require novel methodologies and research data, often using qualitative approaches. Chapter 11 by Archer makes an important contribution in exposing some of the epistemological problems of qualitative research.

Chapter 1 by Cooper draws together some of the recent research on the causes of stress in the workplace and its direct and indirect costs. Aside from discussing well-known literature on features of role, career development, organization context and the home–work interface as contributors to stress, Cooper also dwells on recent findings on the links between redundancy and stress. His chapter concludes by discussing the various mechanisms available to manage stress at work.

The chapter by Grinyer, Mayes and McKiernan reports on an important UK study of the process by which companies which had been in relative decline reversed this process and achieved sustained superior performance. Grinyer et al. call such companies 'sharpbenders', the point at which their performance turned upward dramatically the 'sharpbend' and the process followed 'sharpbending'. Using a range of quantitative and qualitative data and with a research sample which included sharpbenders and a number of comparable control companies, the authors explore causes of firm decline and triggers for and actions taken to sharpbend, as well as continuing characteristics of sharpbenders. They point to a number of qualities or characteristics of sharpbending firms. These include features of top team leadership and a shared sense of excitement and commitment for improvement. Crucially, Grinyer et al. argue that qualities are only part of the story. The significant issues about sharpbending are to do with the management of the processes through which experience is achieved. This is a theme in several papers in this book and is an important phenomenon to return to when we discuss an agenda for management research in the 1990s at the end of this introduction.

In chapter 3, Grant and Thomas report on the results of an empirical study of how diversification has affected corporate performance in 304 large manufacturing companies. The findings indicate that, in general, multinational diversification is more profitable than product diversification, and that once a high level of product diversity is reached increased diversity is associated with lower levels of profitability. The authors further conclude that the nature of the relatedness between a firm's business activities is a key determinant of the success of diversification: corporate-level relatedness is easier to manage than operational relatedness.

In chapter 4 Marsh et al. discuss part of the results of a three-year study of three strategic investment decisions in major British companies.

The authors note that in large diversified firms most organic development consists of strategic investment decisions (SIDs) initiated by, and later implemented by, divisions or business units. Marsh et al. explore the ways in which such SIDs are managed by corporate senior management. These include formal systems for planning and capital budgeting, direct involvement by top management in particular SIDs and the wider organizational context. Like Grinyer et al., Marsh et al. take a process perspective, seeking to examine the intermingling of formal analytical and more informal features of decision-making. While the authors' findings are similar to those of earlier studies of strategic investment decision-making, their results suggest a more significant direct role for top management.

Further weight is given to the empirical character of this book by Campbell and Goold's chapter on strategic management styles. However, a new dimension is added to the data in chapter 5 by the authors' freedom to use the proper names of the companies they study. Campbell and Goold's concern is with the role of top and central management in guiding and directing the businesses they control. From a database of 16 multibusiness companies in the UK, the authors are able to identify three major different sorts of relationship between central managers and business unit managers, i.e. three strategic management styles for the centre. Campbell and Goold conclude that these three styles – strategic planning, strategic control and financial control – each have their strengths and weaknesses and that there is no single ideal way for the centre to manage a diversity of business units.

The nature of top management behaviour, and in particular the effectiveness of the top team executive process, is Mangham's preoccupation in chapter 6. Mangham's central point is how little we know about what top managers do. Fifty years after the publication of Chester Barnard's *The Functions of the Executive* we know still less about executive function and process. A way of filling these knowledge gaps, contends Mangham, is to study matters of authority and fraternity at the executive level. Nearly all action at senior level is informed by these twin referents which are, in turn, the source of a large amount of emotion.

In chapter 7 Sudi Sharifi continues the theme of managerial work by offering a critical review of the empirical research and conceptual writing on managerial behaviour. Bound by the limited research in this area (mostly at middle and junior levels of management), Sharifi argues that much work on management is unidimensional and acontextual. Time and contact management are the preoccupations of the activity or 'work study' school of writers about managerial behaviour. In their concern to expose managerial activities the 'work study' writers thereby fail to bring out the manager as a strategic and analytical thinker and as a politician inside the firm. Recognizing managers as strategists, analysts, and internal and external politicians is critical to the design and development of management learning and training experience.

Baker's keynote paper, presented as chapter 8, returns to the theme of competitive success and asks the straightforward question: what is the role of marketing thinking and expertise in contributing to the performance of firms in the late 1980s? After a broad review of some of the changes in economic, market and customer conditions over the past 20 years, Baker discusses the research by Baker and Hart on marketing and competitive success. Baker and Hart understandably do not impute success or failure to marketing alone but blend marketing into a mixture which includes environmental, organizational, strategic and managerial factors contributing to business performance. Baker, like Grinyer et al., is careful to include high performers and lesser performers in his sample. Also like Grinyer et al., he concludes that, while it is possible to identify certain factors more associated with higher-performing firms than with lesser performers, the key issue is often the quality of implementation of given strategies rather than the presence or absence of techniques of management, which are at best only aids to performance.

Chapter 9 by Campbell nicely dovetails into the competitiveness theme, but this time by pointing to the success of the Japanese approach to relational marketing. Relational marketing is defined as the management of the set of relationships external and internal to the firm which are critical to the marketing process. Thus externally the firm is seen in the context of a network of linkages with manufacturers, suppliers, customers and agents, and internally issues of internal coordination, team spirit and common values and shared assumptions become critical to the successful implementation of marketing plans. These factors are illustrated by data collected from 15 Japanese manufacturing firms and their UK subsidiaries.

The chapter by Francis and Winstanley was chosen to represent recent UK research on the management of technology presented at the British Academy of Management conference. The focus of this chapter is on the organization and management of engineering design, and more generally on the integration of technical and professional staff into the competitive purposes of the firm. Chapter 10 moves easily and appropriately through various levels of analysis, discussing in turn the role and place of occupational groups, such as engineers, in UK society and in the large enterprises where they customarily work. A key part of the chapter is the discussion of the various mechanisms of control and coordination (occupation, managerial, market and corporatist) used to exploit the knowledge and competences of engineering designers.

In the main the first 10 chapters in this book tackle large unstructured research problems which represent the reality of management experience in the late 1980s. Such research problems not only tax the interdisciplinary inclinations and competences of the scholars who work on them, but also make great demands on the practical research skills of those who wish to study them in field situations. Recognizing a move to qualitative research approaches in several of the management disciplines, Simon Archer, in his thoughtful and scholarly chapter, asks some penetrating philosophical questions about the nature of knowledge and the character of the assumptions underpinning so-called qualitative research. What is the rationale for conducting qualitative research? What are the dangers of the particular brand of *ad hoc* theorizing often associated with inductivism? How can significance, stability and invariance be achieved in research reports developed from qualitative research approaches? How are proto-theories to be developed to guide research on novel and significant research problems? These are, of course, deep and perennial questions. They are also questions which can attract only approximate answers even for those who are sufficiently aware to pose them in the first place. However, they are certainly questions which ought to be asked by any researchers challenged by the research agenda which follows.

Management research in the 1990s: some research themes

After the British Academy of Management Conference in September 1987 all the authors were asked to include in their revised chapter a statement of future research themes and questions for their area of research interest. To varying degrees and more or less explicitly each provides a statement of future research for the 1990s. Some of the chapters, for example those by Mangham and Sharifi, are review essays which clearly point to research gaps and encourage us to fill them. Other chapters, for example those by Grinyer et al., Marsh et al. and Campbell, pose the question 'What next?' from the starting point of the unanswered questions of their current research. Looking at the range of responses to this question in management research, and allowing for the editor's perspective, the following research agenda emerges.

Competitive performance and the management process

Given the interests of the authors in this book, the themes of the conference and the national concern on both sides of the Atlantic with competitiveness, it is not surprising that this theme should emerge so clearly.

Grinyer et al. and Baker have, of course, chosen to pursue the issue of competitive success in their 1980s work. They both signal that the so-called excellence literature (Peters and Waterman, 1982: Peters and Austin, 1986) is methodologically flawed not only because of the exclusive choice of the successful for analysis but also because it tells us nothing about *how* performance improvements are achieved and sustained. Baker concludes from his work that future research should concern itself with the quality of management implementation as a determinant of performance. The results obtained by Grinyer et al. point to some of the difficult and intangible areas of management practice such as building a high energy, high commitment climate for improvement as critical to turnaround. They argue that such heady potions are produced by leaders instilling qualitatively different top management processes and extracting from such top team behaviour shared visions for the future.

Studies of top-level managers and executive processes

Even without the connection to competitive performance, which clearly cannot be explained just by firm-level phenomena (Whipp et al., 1987), there is a strong message in this book that we know very little about the behaviour of senior executives as individuals or about what happens when they meet in teams to make strategic investment decisions. Mangham, Marsh et al. and Campbell and Goold all point to top management behaviour as a sorely neglected area of management research. For Campbell and Goold there is a paucity of research on the management process of the corporate centre of firms. Part of Marsh et al.'s future research agenda is more detailed research on the process of analysis of how strategic investment decisions are made. A key role for future empirical work is to help inform theoreticians about the true nature of the decision-makers' problems as seen from the perspective of the actors. Get close to the action, the reality of how top-level decision-making occurs, is a plea from Marsh et al., although they admit that access problems and the sheer complexity of such fine-grained work will invariably mean that it will be a minority taste.

How many empirical studies of the behaviour of top executive teams are available now in 1988? For all the embellishing of the words 'change', 'leadership', 'decision-making' and 'planning' with the magic prefix 'strategic', where are the detailed longitudinal studies of such executive processes? As Mangham rightly argues, 50 years after Barnard's classic *The Functions of the Executive* there is little theorizing about top-level executive processes and even fewer empirical studies. And this is from a population of management teachers and researchers who lay claims to be teaching senior managers about the nature of management. The study of top-level managers and executive processes must be on any research agenda for the 1990s.

Process knowledge

Significant contributions by management researchers have often been in clarifying the what and the why of some phenomena or problems. What do middle managers do? Why are certain organization structures more or less appropriate for different product market conditions? What is the nature of market segmentation? Why may certain diversification strategies impair or facilitate profitability? We have little knowledge about how things are achieved or not achieved in management, and yet the essence of management is supposed to be about achieving results. This absence of process knowledge about the how of management is well exemplified in the pleas for 1990s research in this volume. For Grant and Thomas the issue is about more research on how diversification strategies are pursued. Francis and Winstanley want to know more about the processes of transforming scientific and technical knowledge from the laboratory to design and production areas. For Grinyer et al. the key issue is how to achieve performance improvements, and for Cooper it is the management of stress, which is now an urgent preoccupation, and not just the further refinement of the list of factors which cause stress. All this suggests that process knowledge about the how of management is a crucial area of research and human development in all organizations in the present era of change.

References

Peters, T.J. and Austin, N. (1986). *A Passion for Excellence: The Leadership Difference*. London: Fontana.
—— and Waterman, R.H. Jr. (1982). *In Search of Excellence*. New York: Harper & Row.
Pettigrew, A.M., Hendry, C. and Sparrow, P. (1988). *The Role of Vocational Education and Training in Employers' Skill Supply Strategies*, Research Report, Centre for Corporate Strategy and Change, University of Warwick.
Whipp, R., Rosenfeld, R. and Pettigrew, A. (1987). 'Understanding strategic change processes: some preliminary British findings'. In *The Management of Strategic Change* (ed. A.M. Pettigrew). Oxford: Blackwell.

1
Stress in the workplace: recent research evidence

Cary L. Cooper

Introduction

Studs Terkel in his acclaimed book *Working* suggests that work

is, by its very nature, about violence – to the spirit as well as to the body. It is about ulcers as well as accidents, about shouting matches as well as fistfights, about nervous breakdowns as well as kicking the dog around. It is, above all (or beneath all), about daily humiliations.

It is true that this definition is disheartening, gloomy and pessimistic, but unfortunately in terms of its consequences to the human resource or human capital in the workplace, stress is a fact of everyday life. The US government's National Institute for Occupational Safety and Health has recently published a national strategy document on psychological disorders at work (which incidentally have been designated as one of the 10 top occupational diseases), which highlights the appalling costs of stress to the individual, organizations and the US economy at large (see table 1.1). In addition to the direct costs of alcoholism, drug abuse and mental ill health to industry, there were enormous indirect costs to employers and to the society in general. The National Council of Compensation Insurance, for example, reported that stress at work now represents 11 per cent of all occupational disease claims, and is still

Table 1.1 Costs of psychological disorders in the workplace (in US $ billion)

	Alcohol	Drug abuse	Mental illness
Decreased productivity	51	26	3
Lost employment	4	1	19

Source:National Strategy for the Prevention of Psychological Disorder in the Workplace. Cincinnati, OH: National Institute of Occupational Safety and Health, 1987.

increasing while all other claims are in decline. The Social Security Administration reported that stress or psychological disorder was the third most disabling condition in terms of disability allowance. Finally, psychotherapeutic or stress-relieving drugs were the most common GP prescriptions, representing a quarter of all out-patient prescriptions in the USA.

It is with these figures in mind that research in the field of occupational stress has burgeoned over the last decade. It is the purpose of this paper to highlight some of the sources of work stress, followed by a few suggestions about how stress might be managed by British industry.

Sources of work stress

Seven major sources of occupational stress have been defined in the literature: (1) factors intrinsic to the job; (2) role in the organization; (3) career development; (4) relationships at work; (5) organizational structure and climate; (6) home–work interface; (7) being redundant (see figure 1.1).

Factors intrinsic to the job

Sources of stress that are intrinsic to the job itself across a variety of occupations include (1) poor physical working conditions, (2) shift work, (3) work overload, (4) work underload and (5) physical danger.

Poor physical working conditions   Poor physical working conditions can enhance stress at work. For example, Otway and Misenta (1980) believe that the design of the control room itself is an important variable in the stress experienced by nuclear power plant operators. They propose that control room designs need to be updated, requiring more sophisticated ergonomic designs. As an example they refer to an important stress factor that was highlighted in the Three Mile Island accident – the distraction caused by excessive emergency alarms. In a study carried out by Kelly and Cooper (1981) on the stressors associated with casting in a steel manufacturing plant, poor physical working conditions due to heat and danger were found to be major stressors, leading to negative individual, health and performance outcomes.

Shift work   Numerous occupational studies have found that shift work is a common occupational stressor, affecting neurophysiological rhythms such as temperature, metabolic rate and blood sugar levels. Mental efficiency and work motivation are both directly and indirectly affected.

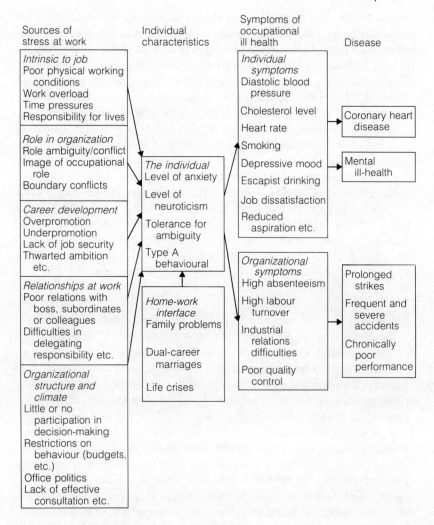

Figure 1.1   A model of stress at work.

A study by Cobb and Rose (1973) involving air traffic controllers (a particularly demanding occupation) demonstrated that hypertension was four times more prevalent among the subjects than in the control group of enlisted men in the military. The air traffic controllers also had a higher prevalence of mild diabetes and peptic ulcers than the control group. Although other job stressors were identified, a major job stressor was reported to be the shift work.

Job overload   French and Caplan (1972) classify work overload as either quantitative (i.e. having too much to do) or qualitative (i.e. being too difficult). Others have associated certain behaviour malfunctions with job overload. For example, the French and Caplan study indicated a relationship between quantitative overload and cigarette smoking (an important behaviour in the development of coronary heart disease). Margolis et al. (1974), in their sample of 1500 employees, found that job overload was associated with such strains as low self-esteem, low work motivation and escapist drinking. In a study by Cooper et al. (1982) of stress among British police officers, it was found that work overload was a major stressor among the lower ranks, particularly police sergeants. In particular, sergeants who scored high on the depression scale of the Crown Crisp Experiential Index tended to be older operational officers who believed they were overloaded and perceived a number of bureaucratic and outside obstacles to effective police functioning. They complained about the long hours and heavy work load, as well as the increased paperwork, lack of resources and the failure of the courts to prosecute offenders.

Job underload   Job underload involves repetitive, routine, boring and understimulating work environments. Machine-paced assembly lines provide an example of such a work environment and have been associated with ill health (Cox, 1980). Moreover, in certain jobs, such as policing and operating nuclear power plants, periods of boredom must be endured simultaneously with maintenance of sufficient alertness to respond to potential emergency situations (Davidson and Veno, 1980). This is difficult to do and is made all the more stressful by awareness of the costs of an ineffective response to an emergency.

Physical danger   There are certain occupations which are known to involve high risk in terms of physical danger (e.g. police officers, mine workers, soldiers and firemen) (Kasl, 1973). However, stress induced by the uncertainty of physically dangerous events is often substantially relieved if the employee feels adequately trained and equipped to cope with emergency situations (Cooper and Smith, 1985).

Role in the organization

The role or roles that a person is supposed to fulfill at work can be stressful when they are unclear or ambiguous, or when the different roles are in conflict. Responsibility for people has also been demonstrated to be a major organizational stressor (Cooper and Marshall, 1976). Authors such as French and Caplan (1972), Beehr et al. (1976) and Shirom et al.

(1972) have related role ambiguity and conflict to such stress-related illnesses as coronary disease. Furthermore, Cooper and Marshall (1976) conclude that less physically involving occupations, such as managerial, clerical and professional positions, are more prone to role conflict.

The problems that role conflicts can generate were amply demonstrated by Cooper et al. (1978) in their investigation of the work stress experienced by dentists. It was found that the variables that predicted abnormally high diastolic blood pressure among dentists were factors related to the role of the dentist. These included the view that the dentist was 'an inflictor of pain' rather than a 'healer', that he or she had to assume the sometimes conflicting roles of administrator, businessperson and clinician and that work role was in conflict with personal life, primarily in terms of time commitment.

Career development

The next group of stressors in the work environment is related to career development which, Cooper and Marshall (1976) maintain, refers to 'the impact of overpromotion, underpromotion, status incongruence, lack of job security, thwarted ambition . . . '. Career development blockages are most notable among women managers, as a study by Cooper and Davidson (Cooper and Davidson, 1982; Davidson and Cooper, 1984) revealed. In this investigation, the authors collected data from over 700 female managers and 250 male managers at all levels of the organizational hierarchy and from several hundred companies. It was found that women suffered significantly more than men on a range of organizational stressors, but the most damaging to their health and job satisfaction were those associated with thwarted career development and allied stressors. These stressors included, for example, sex discrimination in promotion, inadequate training, more favourable treatment of male colleagues and inadequate delegation to women.

Relations at work

Both the quality of an individual's work relationships and the social support available from one's colleagues, boss and subordinates have been related to job stress (Payne, 1980). According to French and Caplan (1972), one mechanism for the development of poor relationships with other members of an organization may be role ambiguity in the organization. This lack of clarity may produce other psychological strains in the form of low job satisfaction. Moreover, French et al. (1982) found that strong social support from peers relieved job strain and also served to mediate the effects of job stress on cortisone, blood pressure, glucose and the number of cigarettes smoked, and was related to the cessation of cigarette smoking. It is interesting to note that, in the case of air traffic controllers, greater help and social support were provided by friends and colleagues than by those in supervisory positions (French and Caplan, 1972).

Organizational structure and climate

Another potential source of occupational stress is related to organizational structure and climate, which includes such factors as office politics, lack of effective consultation, lack of participation in the decision-making process and restrictions on behaviour. Margolis et al. (1974) and Cooper (1981b) found that greater participation led to high productivity, improved performance, lower staff turnover and lower levels of physical and mental illness (including stress-related behaviour such as escapist drinking and heavy smoking).

Home–work pressures

Another cost of the current economic situation is the effect that work pressures (such as fear of job loss, blocked ambition, work overload and so on) have on the families of employees. When there is a career crisis (or stress from job insecurity as many employees in Europe are now facing), the tensions that workers bring with them into the family affect the wife and home environment in a way that may not meet their 'sanctuary' expectations. It may be very difficult, for example, for parents to provide the kind of supportive domestic environment children require at a time when they are beginning to feel insecure and when they are worried about the family's economic, educational and social future.

Dual-career stress   The response of many families to these pressures has been for the wife to become an income earner. Women are increasingly taking on additional roles, often relieving financial pressures but adding to the demands on every family member. According to the US Department of Labor, the 'typical American family', with a working husband, a homemaker wife and two children, now makes up only 7 per cent of the nation's families. In fact, in 1975, 45 per cent of all married women were working, as were 37 per cent of women with children under six; in 1960 the comparable figures were 31 per cent and 9 per cent respectively. Today about half of all US women with children under six are working outside their homes. It is claimed by many psychologists and sociologists that the development of the dual-career family is the primary culprit in the very large increase in the divorce rate over the last 10 years in the USA and Western Europe (Cooper and Davidson, 1982).

Not only are these stressors numerous and diverse, but at one time or other the majority of workers confront them. Furthermore, most people cope with the stress of work fairly effectively most of the time. A condition that has repeatedly been found to aid effective coping is that of available support from others in one's life.

Being redundant

Historically, long-term unemployment (over 12 months) has represented, in most developing countries, a small proportion of the total number of unemployed people. However, recent statistics from the Organization for Economic Cooperation and Development (OECD) indicate that this may be changing, particularly in Europe. Recent figures show that from the early 1970s to 1982 Belgium, France, The Netherlands, the UK and Germany experienced a large increase in the number of long-term unemployed, whereas in North America this figure is still fairly low. For example, the average duration of unemployment is 16.1 months in Belgium, 10.9 months in France, 9.1 months in The Netherlands and 8.9 months in the UK. In contrast, the figure for the USA is 3.2 months, for Canada it is 3.5 months, and for Sweden and Norway it is 3.8 months.

In an OECD report entitled 'Employment review and outlook', the figures for the UK are extremely disheartening. Nearly a third of all those unemployed in the UK have been in this situation for 12 months or more. Nearly 50 per cent have been unemployed for over six months. By comparison, in the USA, the proportion of those who have been out of a job for six months or more is less than 15 per cent, and the proportion of those unemployed for over 12 months is less than 10 per cent. The Manpower Services Commission quarterly report of November 1982 showed that by late 1982,

450,000 of the 1.1 million long-term unemployed had been registered for 2 years or more and 185,000 of these had not had a job for over 3 years. Numbers in these very long-term categories are increasing at an even faster rate than the over one year category . . . (Manpower Services Commission, 1982, p. 35).

An even more disturbing trend in these findings is that the major increase in the long-term unemployed (12 months or over) in the UK is in young people under 25 years old. In 1973, just over 6 per cent of the long-term unemployed were under 25, but by 1981 nearly 25 per cent were 'out of work' in this age group. The proportions of the long-term unemployed have also shifted. In 1973, 91 per cent of the long-term unemployed were men. That figure had declined to just over 78 per cent in 1981. For women, however, there was an increase from 9 per cent in 1973 to 22 per cent in 1981 (as a percentage share of the total of those unemployed for 12 months or longer). These trends are also prevalent in several other European countries such as Belgium and The Netherlands.

Since more and more people are taking early retirement in the UK, the number of older workers unemployed for over 12 months dropped from 70 per cent in 1973 to just over 40 per cent in 1981. The increase for those 'prime age' adults (25–44) was from just over 24 per cent to nearly 35 per cent during the same time period. At these two times, 1973 and 1981, the proportion of young people who were unemployed for over six months also changed dramatically. In 1973 only 10 per cent were under 25, whereas in 1981 30 per cent of them had been on the dole for over 6 months.

Another concern expressed in the OECD report is the impact on individual and community health of this increase in long-term unemployment. Preliminary research in the UK indicates that people who endure long periods of unemployment face potential problems in maintaining their self-respect, retaining a high level of job expectation and sustaining the self-confidence and energy necessary to find another job. In a US government report entitled 'Estimating the social costs of national economic policy: implications for mental and physical ill health and criminal aggression', research was reported that related the number of symptoms of physical and mental ill health to length of unemployment.

A number of research studies suggest that job loss can have significant consequences on the health and wellbeing of the unemployed and his/her family. Kahn (1956) looked at redundancy in the car industry in Birmingham, UK where 6000 men were suddenly left without jobs. Ten per cent of the men, mainly unskilled and semiskilled workers, were interviewed two years later. A great deal of data were collected concerning attitudes towards their unemployment, their age, length of time out of work, methods of job seeking and the individual's subjective impression of the new job compared with the old. The interview data revealed that, even after two years, some individuals were not only still recovering financially but also were still suffering from the loss of self-esteem and other partially debilitating psychological difficulties.

In addition, Daniel (1972) investigated the effects of several plant closures in a particular area of the UK over a four-year period. He used structured interviews to look at a wide range of factors, including demographics, type of job and skill level, and related these to variables such as length of time unemployed. He also compared the new job with the old. He found that older workers and men whose skills were important in a particular job or firm (such as supervisors and semiskilled workers) had the greatest difficulty in finding new work and expressed the least satisfaction with their new employment. Daniel also compared methods of job search and found distinct differences between occupational groups, which may reflect the different ways in which jobs come on the market for blue collar and white collar workers.

Warr and Lovatt (1975) examined the job status of those left unemployed by the complete closure of Irlam Steel Works, and related this to psychological wellbeing and pre-closure training. They found that psychological wellbeing was lower for people who were still unemployed at the time of the interview than for those who found alternative employment, and that this influenced a person's outlook beyond that of his work. For example, the unemployed tended to have more anxieties about their own health and even about the world political situation. Pre-closure training had no impact on wellbeing. They also looked at a person's job-seeking behaviour in terms of his 'orientation to work', using a simple measure of motivation for employment. For those individuals who scored high on this work-orientation measure, having a job was associated with psychological wellbeing, but there was no relation for those with low motivation for employment. It is clear that, for most people, work is very important both psychologically and financially. Involuntary unemployment can be extremely stressful, producing significant strains for the individual, family and society.

Managing stress at work

Although our ability to help the unemployed is limited, work organizations have within their power the opportunity for providing cognitive, emotional and behavioural support systems for their employees. But what is the reality? In many organizations only advice is offered, usually on issues that are directly related to work, such as safety. Some firms, although they are in the minority, encourage healthy lifestyles more actively by providing full fitness and health facilities for their employees. For example, Pepsico Incorporated has provided a comprehensive physical fitness programme at their world headquarters in Purchase, NY. They have a fully outfitted gymnasium that includes a sauna, a treadmill, a striking bag, stationary bicycles, a whirlpool, baths, showers and massage facilities. In addition, they have a 1.15 mile running track which circles the headquarters complex. This programme is under the supervision of a full-time physical therapist and medical physician. Tailor-made exercise programmes are planned for any interested employee by the physical therapist and doctor. Although this facility was originally planned for senior executives, it is now used by all interested employees. Specialized programmes such as aerobic dancing, weekly yoga sessions and diet training are also offered to meet the needs of individual employees. The corporate headquarters are located in an attractive park-like setting that encourages a positive quality of life. Increasingly, major corporations are developing premier facilities with similar characteristics. The majority of workplaces, however, do not provide such possibilities for health maintenance.

There is often a failure on the part of work organizations to provide 'emotional support'. Until recently, very few private or public sector institutions actively addressed employees' needs for emotional support systems. When this type of support is available it is provided by the informal network at work. Although the view is changing, for a long time top management maintained that it was outside their scope of responsibility to provide counsellors or other sources of human support for their employees, particularly if the problems stemmed from the home environment, even when the problems at home were affecting the work. Increasingly it has been recognized that it is difficult to draw a clear line between sources of stress that originate in the home and those that come from the workplace; the distinction is not easily defensible. There are several other factors forcing organizations to take an interest in providing social support systems at work. One is the increasing litigation against companies for the stress that is alleged to exist in the workplace (Cooper, 1981a). Another is the increasing incidence of stress-like epidemics in factories and offices in many companies which adversely affects absenteeism (Colligan & Murphy, 1979).

The first development is known as *cumulative trauma* and is a type of workers' compensation claim in which an employee contends that a major illness or disability is the cumulative result of job stresses and strains extending back over a period of years of employment. Any employed person, from a shopfloor worker to a corporate executive, if forced to give up work as a result of any illness (coronary heart disease, mental breakdown, nervous disability etc.) can claim that the illness was caused in part by work over the years. Since it is relatively easy to show that just about any job has a certain element of stress in it, and since the law in various states of the USA (in particular California and Michigan) allows a very liberal interpretation of stress-induced illness, the courts and appeal boards are accepting many of these claims. In addition, and more importantly, personnel executives and company medical directors have, in many cases, been unable to provide evidence that they are trying to minimize the stresses and strains within the work environment.

In addition to recent court decisions regarding cumulative trauma cases, another aspect of stress at work is worrying employers and health authorities. It is what the National Institute for Occupational Safety and Health terms 'mass psychogenic illness'. They define it as 'the collective occurrence of physical symptoms and related beliefs among two or more persons in the absence of an identifiable pathogen'. In other words, it is a situation in which a number of workers at a particular worksite develop similar symptoms although no noxious substance or micro-organism can be found. The specific symptoms vary from one industrial situation to another, but they usually consist of subjective somatic complaints such as headaches, nausea, sleepiness, chills etc. In all the reported cases of mass psychogenic illness, extensive biochemical and environmental tests (to check for harmful chemicals in the air) have been carried out. No causative agent can be found. What has been found, however, are moderate to severe psychosocial, work-related stressors in the absence of discernible social support systems.

Organizational attempts at improving emotional support

As a result of these developments and a generally more humanistic approach to people at work, there are an increasing number of stress-prevention programmes orientated towards providing emotional support. The efforts of a large US copper corporation provide a good example. Management has focused on the psychological health of their employees, providing extensive counselling facilities for all work- and home-related problems (Marshall and Cooper, 1981). Indeed, they have even helped to organize Alcoholics Anonymous groups for employees and their families. In another example, Converse Corporation of Wilmington, MA, provided a voluntary relaxation programme for their employees (Peters and Benson, 1979) and had its effectiveness evaluated. Over 140 employees volunteered and were compared with 63 non-volunteers who were selected randomly. The volunteers agreed to keep daily records for 12 weeks and to have their blood pressure measured. In addition, their general health and job performance were assessed during the experimental period. The results indicated that not only were relaxation breaks feasible within a normal work week but also that they led to improvements in general health, job performance and wellbeing, as well as significantly decreasing the blood pressure of employees from the beginning to the end of training.

Another even more adventurous emotional support programme was carried out in the UK by a large chemical company. They set up a stress-counselling programme, or what they termed an 'employee counselling service', with a full-time counsellor (with a psychiatric social work background). The goals of this facility were 'to provide a confidential counselling service to all employees and their families, to work with outside helping professions for the welfare of the employee and to develop other activities that enhance the quality of working life.' After four years of operation, the counsellor had been consulted by nearly 10 per cent of the employees per annum. About half the employees who sought the service came for advice on education, family matters, work-related housing problems, divorce, separation, children, aged parents and consumer affairs. The other half developed a longer-term case-work or counselling relationship with the counsellor on more fundamental individual or interpersonal problems. This is the kind of programme that needs to be encouraged in industry and other types of organizations if we are to provide the emotional social support people need in the kind of modern society we have all created.

Informal social support at work

One of the most important sources of social support is the informal work group. La Rocco and Jones (1978) performed a large-scale study of 3725 US Navy personnel (enlisted men spanning the range of enlisted pay grades) on leader and co-worker support and the stress–strain relationship. They concluded that the effect of support from one's boss and co-workers on coping was both positive and reinforcing, i.e. the more support one obtained from one's leader and co-workers, the less likely one was to exhibit signs of strain. This result may explain the desire people have to seek the support of others in situations of danger or stress. Wilson (1975) has suggested that man is genetically programmed to obtain security from the proximity of others because this supports survival. The complicated nature of relationships at work and their potential for conflict and ambiguity make it necessary for individuals to seek support from their peers. While the organization can have an impact on the support available, there are a number of different approaches that employees can take themselves. Taking responsibility for identifying others who can provide emotional support is an important first step. Acknowledging to others that their support is needed and appreciated, and that support will be offered in return, helps ensure a strong network.

Conclusion

A number of things can be done to help people at work, apart from health promotion and stress counselling. They can be as adventurous as encouraging greater worker participation in all the decisions in the workplace from profit-sharing schemes to job redesign experiments.

What we must begin to do is to create working environments which provide individuals with dignity, meaning, personal value and worth. Work is not simply about money; it is about more significant and important goals. As Studs Terkel claims:

It is about a search, too, for daily meaning as well as daily bread, for recognition as well as cash, for astonishment rather than torpor; in short, for a sort of life rather than a Monday through Friday sort of dying.

Research questions for the future

In the field of occupational stress, there are a number of fruitful areas of research over the next decade. First, although a great deal of work has been done on occupation-specific sources of stress, little research has attempted to generalize across occupations or to provide an empirically based conceptual framework. Over the last few years, the development of structural equation modelling (e.g. LISRL) and meta-analysis have meant that we are now able to undertake this task more easily. Research work should be able to help us to identify the key occupational stressors across a variety of organizational functions and jobs in different industries, which will make the task of stress prevention and management more feasible and effective. This will also have implications for the way in which we structure organizations and train managers to manage and facilitate employees' needs, talents and aspirations in the workplace, more effectively and humanely.

Second, we must begin to assess the various strategies for the management of stress at work more systematically. With increasing concern over employee health, lower productivity, absenteeism, alcoholism and a number of other negative manifestations of stress at work, more and more stress-management training programmes, stress counselling and job re-design experiments are being introduced. Little if any systematic research has been undertaken to assess the effectiveness of these approaches. The research that does exist suffers from major methodological problems, i.e. few pre- and post-measures, few controls or not using individuals as their own control, inappropriate measures or measures which are less than robust, subjective rather than objective measures etc.

Third, although we think we understand the mechanisms of stress in the workplace, only tertiary attention has been paid to the dynamics of the 'stress process'. Does one's personality mediate stress or does it act as a precursor to events? Does 'social support' at work or home moderate individual stress outcomes or have little impact on the stressors? These and other questions about the dynamics of occupational/organizational stress remain, and will be focal points of research attention over the next decade.

Fourth, the vast majority of stress research focuses on the deleterious impact of stressors on health. This bias is reflected in the measures of mental and physical health used in most studies, which primarily focus on illness and dysfunction. By focusing specifically on mental and physical illness, we ignore the possibility that certain aspects of stress may actually *improve* health and performance. The prospect that the appraisal of situations or events as positive, or that successfully coping with stress may *improve* health, is an intriguing possibility, and future research should include measures which allow for the detection of these positive health outcomes.

In the end, we hope that research and practice will provide the data for change, so that in the future we can redefine Studs Terkel's view of the nature of work.

References

Beehr, T.R., Walsh, J.T. and Taber, T.D. (1976). 'Relationship of stress to individually and organisationally valued states: higher order needs as a moderator'. *Journal of Applied Psychology*, **61**, 41–7.

Cobb, S. and Rose, R.H. (1973). 'Hypertension, peptic ulcer and diabetes in air traffic controllers'. *Journal of the Australian Medical Association*, **224**, 489–92.

Colligan, M.J. and Murphy, L.R. (1974). 'Mass psychogenic illness in organisations'. *Journal of Occupational Psychology*, **1**, 512–32.

Cooper, C.L. (1981a). *The Stress Check*. Englewood Cliffs, NJ: Prentice-Hall.

—— (1981b). 'Stress and small groups'. In *Small Group Behavior* (ed. C.L. Cooper), pp. 251–375.

—— and Davidson, M.J. (1982). *High Pressure: Working Lives of Women Managers*. London: Fontana.

—— and Marshall, J. (1976). 'Occupational sources of stress: A review of the literature relating to coronary heart disease and mental ill health'. *Journal of Occupational Psychology*, **49**, 11–28.

—— and Smith, M.J. (1985). *Job Stress and Blue Collar Work*. Chichester: Wiley.

——, Davidson, M.J. and Robinson, P. (1982). 'Stress in the police service'. *Journal of Occupational Medicine*, **24**, 30–6.

——, Mallinger, M. and Kahn, R. (1978). 'Identifying sources of occupational stress among dentists'. *Journal of Occupational Psychology*, **51**, 227–34.

Cox, T. (1980). 'Repetitive work'. In *Current Concerns in Occupational Stress* (eds C.L. Cooper and R. Payne). Chichester: Wiley.

Daniel, W.W. (1972). Whatever happened to the workers in Woolwich? *PEP Broadsheets*, **38**, 537.

Davidson, M.J. and Cooper, C.L. (1984). *Stress and the Woman Manager*. Oxford: Blackwell.

—— and Veno, A. (1980). 'Stress and the policeman'. In *White Collar and Professional Stress* (eds C.L. Cooper and J. Marshall). Chichester: Wiley.

French J. and Caplan, R. (1972). 'Organisational stress and individual strain'. In *The Failure of Success* (ed. A.J. Marrow). New York: Amacon.

—— and Van Harrison, R. (1982). *The Mechanisms of Job Stress and Strains*. New York: Wiley.

Kahn, H. (1956). *Repercussions of Redundancy*. London: Allen and Unwin.

Kasl, S.V. (1973). 'Mental health and the work environment'. *Journal of Occupational Medicine*, 15(6), 509–18.

Kelly, M. and Cooper, C.L. (1981). 'Stress among blue collar workers'. *Employee Relations*, 3, 6–9.

La Rocco, J.M. and Jones, A.P. (1978). 'Co-worker and leader support as moderators of stress–strain relationships in work situations'. *Journal of Applied Psychology*, 63(5), 629–34.

Manpower Services Commission (1982). *Quarterly Economic Report 1092*, London: Manpower Services Commission.

Margolis, B.L., Kroes, W.H. and Quinn, R.P. (1974). 'Job stress: an unlisted occupational hazard'. *Journal of Occupational Medicine*, 16, 654–61.

Marshall, J. and Cooper, C.L. (1981). *Coping with Stress at Work*. Aldershot, Hampshire: Gower Press.

Otway, H.J. and Misenta, R. (1980). 'The determinants of operator preparedness for emergency situations in nuclear power plants'. Paper presented at Workshop on Procedural and Organisational Measures for Accident Management: Nuclear Reactors International Institute for Applied Systems Analysis, Laxenberg, Austria, 28–31 January 1980.

Payne, R. (1980). 'Organisational stress and social support'. In *Current Concerns in Occupational Stress* (eds C.L. Cooper and R. Payne). Chichester: Wiley.

Peters, R.K. and Benson, H. (1979). 'Time out from tension'. *Harvard Business Review*, January–February, 120–4.

Shirom, A., Eden, D., Silberwasser, L. and Kellerman, J. (1972). 'Job stresses and risk factors in coronary heart disease among occupational categories in kibbutzim'. *Social Science and Medicine*, 7, 875–92.

Warr, P.B. and Lovatt, J. (1975). 'Well-being and orientation to work'. Unpublished paper.

Wilson, E.O. (1975). *Sociobiology*. Cambridge, MA: Harvard University Press.

2
Sharpbenders: the process of marked and sustained performance in selected UK companies

Peter H. Grinyer, David Mayes and Peter McKiernan

Introduction

This paper reports the salient results of a project undertaken under the auspices of the National Economic Development Office over recent years. The objective of the exercise was to explore the process by which companies which had been in relative decline, when measured against others within their industry, reversed this process and achieved sustained superior performance. These companies were called 'sharpbenders', the point at which their performance turned upward dramatically was called the 'sharpbend' and the process followed 'sharpbending'. Sharpbenders are to be distinguished from companies in a turnaround situation in that their decline is relative but not necessarily absolute. Consequently the sharpbender is rarely subject to the same external pressures from sources of finance and creditors that the company needing to turnaround faces. Our interest was in how geese can be turned into swans, and not in how they can be stopped from drowning.

Figure 2.1 shows the conceptual model underlying the research. Causes of relative decline were of interest in themselves, but can also be expected to affect both the sequence of events which triggers the change and the nature of the actions taken. Clearly we would expect actions, in part, to address themselves to correcting problems and mistakes which were undermining performance. Triggers for sharpbenders were defined as events which led immediately to actions taken to put the company on an upward path. Our idea in using the concept of the trigger, in the first instance, was that clearly some event must have occurred within the complacent company to lead to a fundamental change in its behavioural pattern. Our analysis subsequently led us to the view that market forces and internal pressures were often creating an accumulated pressure for change over a period preceding the sharpbend. Hence the observed

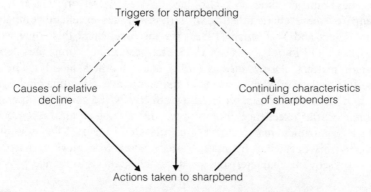

Figure 2.1 The broad conceptual model underlying the sharpbender project. The arrows show the assumed direction of causal relationships: the full arrows depict main relationships and the broken arrows depict those expected to be less strong.

'trigger' was frequently significant in that it tipped the balance or harnessed forces for change which were already present. Hence in these companies the trigger could not be regarded as either a necessary or sufficient condition for change, since had not the particular trigger occurred, some other might well have done. Perhaps the major exception to this general perception is where change occurred because of the introduction of a new chief executive or chairman on the retirement or death of his predecessor. A fuller theoretical analysis of the concept of triggering, involving the concept of aspiration levels, will appear elsewhere (Grinyer et al., 1988).

Actions taken to achieve a sharpbend are clearly a central focus of the study. It is these which might possibly be replicated in other companies. Naturally we would expect the nature of the triggering events, such as the introduction of a new chief executive, to influence to some degree the steps taken. As indicated above, the causal relationship with reasons for relative decline is again clear. During our research we sought to capture qualitative aspects of these actions as well as information as to whether or not specific steps had been taken. We found such information of considerable importance although difficult to handle quantitatively in subsequent analyses. Finally, we were interested in the continuing characteristics of companies with sustained superior performance. Much has been written on such characteristics in the recently burgeoning literaure on corporate excellence. On the whole, however, the companies classed as excellent are large and have been foremost in their industries for many years. Moreover, the methodology adopted in the literature on excellence involves purely taking a snapshot of characteristics at a specific point in time and also has its weaknesses in that it rarely compares these characteristics with those of non-excellent companies. Had Peters and Waterman (1982), for instance, done this, they would have certainly found that even the worst-performing companies control certain matters closely although they control others loosely. The key questions relate to which aspects of the company's operations fall within each of these two categories and how effectively the control is operated. Moreover, the 'excellence' literature tells us nothing about the process by which companies may achieve this elevated quality. We sought to address this deficiency by relating steps taken to achieve a sharpbend with subsequent characteristics of sustained high performance.

Stages of the project and methodology

Stages of the project are illustrated in figure 2.2. Given that our interest was focused on the phenomenon of sharpbending, a broadly interdisciplinary approach was taken to the literature research, with hypotheses being drawn from the literature on corporate excellence, corporate strategy, industrial economics and organizational behaviour. Additional hypotheses were generated on the basis of the experience of the researchers involved and from discussion with businessmen on the steering group overseeing the project. These hypotheses were classified as first, second and third order. The first-order hypotheses were those relating to the existence or otherwise of causes of decline, triggers for sharpbending, actions taken and sustained characteristics among the sharpbenders. Second-order hypotheses relate to interconnections between these four

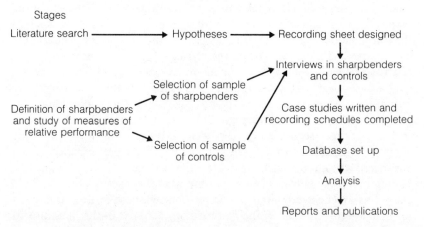

Figure 2.2   Phases of the sharpbender project.

categories of items and third-order hypotheses relate to intercorrelations between items within single categories (for instance between causes of relative decline). Given constraints of time and space, first-order hypotheses will be treated in the main in this paper, and fuller treatment of the second- and third-order hypotheses will be found elsewhere (Grinyer et al., 1988). A list of these first-order hypotheses and their principal sources is given in appendix 2.1.

The principal design of the study involved informal but semistructured interviews within a sample of sharpbenders and a sample of comparable control companies. The latter were drawn from the same industries as the sharpbenders to permit appropriate comparison. Table 2.1 provides information on the composition of our sample of sharpbenders. Because of lack of completeness of data, or for reasons of confidentiality, several further sharpbenders in which interviews were conducted are excluded from this list. Similarly, it would be invidious to list those companies which were taken as controls. In all, companies were drawn from 13 different industries, in most of which there was more than one company by design, to permit fuller comparison between sharpbenders.[1]

Difficulties in determining our sample of sharpbenders were substantial. The measures of performance by which we wished to judge the sharpbenders ranged from conventional financial ratios to sales growth, employment growth and growth of exports to measures of stability of employment. In the event, we were forced to place heavier emphasis on some than on others, in view of the fact that within the UK economy there was a negative correlation between, for instance, growth of employment and growth of return on capital employed. Hence we ultimately placed greater weight on measures of financial performance, growth of sales, financial stability (Z ratios) and growth of exports. Potential sharpbenders were identified by analysis of a computer database and by suggestions from contacts in industry and the city, and then subsequently screened rigorously against our somewhat restrictive criteria. Very few successfully passed this sieve. All the sharpbenders we identified agreed to participate in the study. Hence, although the size of the sample may be low by comparison with studies using publicly available information, we believe that we have captured a high proportion of the population of sharpbenders in the UK in 1984–5.

To aid subsequent analysis, a recording sheet was designed to ensure that information was collected to permit the hypotheses to be tested. This was broadly organized under the headings of causes of relative decline, triggers for sharpbending, actions taken and characteristics of sustained high performance. These broad categories were then used to structure loosely informal interviews with, where possible, the chairman, the chief executive, the executive directors and shop-floor representatives

Table 2.1 The sample of sharpbenders

Industry	Companies
1 Building materials and fittings	1 Rotaflex
2 Pharmaceutical–agrochemicals	2 Fisons 3 Glaxo
3 Offshore oil installations	4 John Wood 5 UDI Group
4 Building	6 McCarthy and Stone 7 Countryside Properties
5 Electronics	8 Ferranti 9 *
6 Plant and engineering	10 * 11 *
7 Distilling	12 Arthur Bell and Sons 13 Macallan–Glenlivet
8 Publishing	14 Collins Manufacturing Group 15 Associated Book Publishers
9 Papermaking and converting	16 Associated Paper Industries 17 Whatman Reeve Angel
10 Clothing	18 Ellis and Goldstein 19 Dawson International 20 Pringle
11 Knitting wool	21 Sirdar
12 Jute spinning and weaving	22 Low and Bonar 23 Sidlaw Industries 24 Don Brothers Buist
13 Footwear	25 Ward White

* The names of these companies are to remain confidential.

within each of the sharpbenders and the control companies. These interviews tended to extend over one day in each company. To ensure that the interviewer was reasonably well informed, annual financial reports were analysed for each company before it was visited and a scan of press statements relating to it over the previous three years was undertaken. Two interviewers attended most interviews, and certainly all early ones, to ensure that a homogenous and unbiased approach was taken as far as possible. Each interview was tape-recorded. Following the visit, the principal interviewer completed the recording sheet and also wrote a case study to capture qualitative and other aspects such as sequences of events not covered by the recording schedule.

Data recorded on the schedule were subsequently placed in a computer file, scales were developed and tested, and statistical analysis was undertaken. Descriptive statistics and some of the results of the analysis to test the hypotheses appear in subsequent sections.

Causes of relative decline

Table 2.2 shows the incidence of different types of cause of relative decline cited by the 25 sharpbenders. Detailed frequencies of the specific items in each type are to be found in the fuller account of the project available elsewhere (Grinyer et al., 1988).

For our purposes here, the interesting thing to note is the importance of external market forces as causes of relative decline, namely adverse changes in total market demand and falling revenues due to more intense competition. During our statistical analysis we found that the number of items quoted in each of these categories were positively significantly correlated. Clearly, where there are adverse longer-term changes in the total market, frequently including a cyclical downturn, competitive pressures mount strongly as rivals compete for a greater share of the smaller total market. The more intense is the cyclical downturn and the more closely suppliers approach their break-even points, the more intense this competition will tend to be. It is significant that companies

Table 2.2 Causes of relative decline

		Percentage of sharpbenders citing this cause
1	Adverse changes in total market demand	75
2	Falling revenues due to more intense competition	60
3	Lack of marketing/sales effort	30
4	Poor management	45
5	Inadequate financial control	45
6	High cost structure	65
7	Poor quality	10
8	Acquisitions	30
9	Large projects that fail	40

All figures rounded to nearest 5 per cent.

frequently quoted lack of product market focus, removal of trade (in the case of jute) or other barriers to entry and high exit costs as factors which resulted in falling revenues in such circumstances. Clearly, all of these would tend to remove a degree of shelter from the winds of severe competition.

Among the remaining causes the most frequently occurring was a high cost structure. Several reasons were cited. These clustered into five main categories. First, high costs were frequently attributed to financial factors, including excessive operational gearing, excessive capital gearing and poor financial policy. Second, in a large number it was also thought that competitors had 'absolute cost advantage', those being mentioned embracing cheap raw materials, cheap or higher-quality labour, more favourable locations and tied superior distribution channels. The third category related to the cost and quality of labour, including poor morale, inflexible job demarcation, opposition to new practices and excessive wage levels. The fourth category, including poor plant layout and poor production control, clearly reflected the design and planning capability of the company. Finally, there were frequent complaints of excess plant capacity; 30 per cent of the sharpbenders indicated this to be a source of high cost structure, and a number of other companies said that their market shares were too low to permit them to exploit economies of learning or scale.

As may be expected, a high cost structure was found to be associated with poor financial control, which was a cause of relative decline in 45 per cent of the sharpbenders. A variety of specific deficiencies were found to contribute to this inadequacy. The most frequently cited was that management accounting information was placed before top management too infrequently or late (25 per cent) or alternatively was too voluminous, complex, irrelevant or just wrong (10 per cent). Other companies quoted lack of cash flow forecasts (15 per cent), failure to control working capital (15 per cent), lack of budgetary control (10 per cent) and lack of a costing system (5 per cent).

A cause of decline for half the companies, as shown in table 2.2, was failure of large projects. A variety of reasons were adduced for such failures, with almost equal frequency; these were poor cost estimating, poor project control, changes in design, start-up difficulties, high market entry cost and overestimates of capacity needs. These problems in turn were found to be associated with high cost structures for the company in general.

Acquisitions, another frequent cause of decline, are a rather special kind of large project. The very fact that as many as 30 per cent of the companies indicated that poor aquisitions had been a major source of decline in itself suggests that acquisitions need to be approached with a degree of caution. The most common cause of failure among companies acquired was that they had a weak competitive position (20 per cent). In 10 per cent it was thought that the problem lay in post-acquisition management, the parent not having properly integrated the subsidiary or not having made appropriate changes to its senior management or control systems. Perhaps for this reason, we found that failure of acquisitions was associated significantly with poor financial control, as indeed was the failure of large projects in general. However, equally interesting was the association between failure of acquisitions and each of sustained drops in market demand and competitive pressure. Clearly, the latter relates to the frequency with which sharpbenders suggest that the acquired company had too weak a competitive position. This position would clearly be both more apparent and more damaging in a hostile market environment.

Another frequently cited cause of decline was lack of effective direction, control or use of the sales force (20 per cent), advertising (10 per cent) and market research (15 per cent). As can be seen from table 2.2, poor product quality was indicated in 10 per cent of the companies.

It can be argued that the decline of a company must ultimately be put at the door of top management. Poor acquisitions, large projects that fail, high cost structures, poor quality and inadequate financial control or marketing are all directly the responsibility of management. Equally, top management above all has the responsibility to monitor its environment to perceive changing trends within it and hence to make appropriate and timely responses to adverse changes in total market demand or the effect of more intense competition. It is perhaps not surprising, therefore, that during our statistical analysis we found associations between aspects of poor management and failure of large projects, poor acquisitions, high cost structures, poor quality and service, poor productivity and morale and poor financial control, this being the most pervasive of all the influences. Given its importance, it is clearly instructive to ask which particular items in the list of poor characteristics of management enter most frequently and consequently have most impact on the decline. In 30 per cent there had been a failure to communicate effectively with lower echelons of management and within 15 per cent to communicate effectively with the workforce. Related to such failures was the failure to create a shared vision and values in 30 per cent of the companies. Senior management was regarded as having been excessively cautious and conservative in 20 per cent of the companies but over-optimistic and incautious in 10 per cent. In 10 per cent of the companies problems were thought to stem from an inflexible chief executive and in 15 per cent from the fact that the roles of chairman and managing director were combined. In a number of cases, as at Bell's where the opening up of share ownership was blocked prior to 1971 by the then chairman and managing director, the combined roles gave such considerable influence to one individual that he was able to prevent changes that subsequently proved to be critical to the development of the company.

As indicated above, we were cautious about placing too much emphasis upon differences between the six control companies and the sharpbenders, even although this was allowed for by degrees of freedom within the statistical analysis. None the less, some of the differences appeared with such a high level of significance that it is unlikely that they occur from chance alone, and we would feel that differences significant at the 5 per cent level might reasonably be taken to be highly suggestive. With this qualification, it is worth noting that there were some significant differences between sharpbenders and controls with respect to causes of relative decline that were cited during the interviews. In general, a higher proportion of sharpbenders than controls made reference to specific causes of lack-lustre performance or relative decline.[2] When these differences were tested using the χ^2 test and also Fisher's exact probability test we found that they were significant at least at the 1 per cent level for sustained drops in market demand and high cost structures, whilst at the 5 per cent level they were at least highly suggestive of more intense competition, poor management and large projects which failed. These differences between the sharpbenders and controls might be explained by different circumstances for each. It is quite possible that the sharpbenders did indeed encounter much more hostile market conditions, for instance, together with factors like failure of large projects, whereas the control companies did not. Indeed it may be argued that it is the very coincidence of such difficulties which creates mounting accumulative pressure for change within an organization, and that leads to external intervention as a trigger for action. Such pressure also permits a further event such as the introduction of a new chief executive on retirement of the old to produce fundamental changes in the direction of the company. In contrast, we might be observing a substantial difference in diagnostic and analytical power between the sharpbenders and controls. The fact that the sharpbenders were mentioning a wider range of factors may reflect more upon their own current or retrospective diagnostic abilities than upon the situation confronted. This in itself is important, for only by analysing fully the problems of the company in decline and properly identifying the problems underlying it can management adequately proceed to appropriate corrective actions. Our own judgement is that the second of these explanations is the dominant one. After all, sustained drops in market demand were encountered by the sharpbenders and control companies alike, since the latter were chosen as being within the same industries. Yet it is exactly in these specific categories of cause that the differences between the sharpbenders' and controls' perception was most marked and significant.

Triggers for sharpbending

As mentioned above, there are reasons for believing that pressure for change was mounting in quite a number of the sharpbenders, as a result of external market-related difficulties as well as internal problems. However, unlike a turnaround situation, the financial difficulties engendered by the causes of decline had not reached a pitch which made fundamental change necessary. Indeed in many companies, such as Sirdar, there was absolutely no reason why the company should not jog along with its comfortable existence. This is precisely why we sought to determine if there was a specific event that was thought by the interviewees within the sharpbenders to have led to fundamental change. The broad results are shown in table 2.3.

One such event was recognition by management of major problems. In 35 per cent of the sharpbenders this amounted to realization that either actual performance or anticipated future performance fell below an acceptable level and that substantial changes were necessary to correct the situation. Equally, in a number of sharpbenders (30 per cent) there was intervention from an external body, such as the addition of a new non-executive director or chairman at the instigation of a merchant bank or institutional shareholder. Similarly, a threatened change of ownership, such as a failed contested take-over bid, also alerted management to the dangers inherent in its lack-lustre performance (25 per cent), which created dissatisfaction with what was being achieved and so jerked the company into action. Consistent with the literature, the injection of a new chief executive was quoted in a large number of the 25 companies

Table 2.3 Triggers for sharpbending

Trigger	Percentage of companies citing this factor
1 Intervention from external bodies	30
2 Change of ownership or threat of such	25
3 New chief executive on death or retirement of his predecessor	55
4 Recognition by management of problems	35
5 Perception by management of new opportunities	10

(55 per cent) as the trigger for change, this being in nearly all cases on the retirement or death of his predecessor.

From the figures quoted above it is clear that in a number of the sharpbenders there were multiple triggers, with dramatic change being attributed to the combination rather than to one singly, and we found that in 22 of the 25 companies at least one of these above-mentioned triggers was present. Moreover, as one would expect, the sharpbenders were significantly different from the sample of six control companies in that only one of the latter cited one of these events as leading to major external changes. None the less, an interesting question remains as to why no trigger was found in the remaining three sharpbending companies. Careful scrutiny of the case studies revealed the same answer for each. Perception of new opportunities made existing senior management aware of potentially considerably superior performance which in turn led to fundamental changes in direction for the company. This can be interpreted as perceived opportunities leading to a heightened aspiration level which in turn created dissatisfaction with the existing situation and generated change. Examples here include the John Wood Group at Aberdeen where a visit by the young managing director and his brother-in-law to Texas made them aware of the scale of the opportunities that North Sea oil was bringing to Aberdeen. Once this particular category was added to those mentioned above, it was found that there was at least one trigger present in each of the sharpbenders.

This very fact suggests the value of the simple concept of the trigger. Clearly those within the sharpbenders with whom we spoke perceived certain events as being pivotal. Since these perceptions were shared by a number of different individuals, in virtually all cases including a workforce representative, the events had clearly been notable within the context of the company and might well have become the subject of a corporate myth. It would be a mistake, however, to conclude that these events were necessary or sufficient conditions for change. As already observed, we recognized in many of the sharpbenders that there had been growing pressures for change over the period preceding the sharpbend as a result of an increase in the adverse market conditions, failure of major projects and other difficulties. In such cases the trigger might be seen as the last source of pressure which tipped the balance in favour of fundamental change rather than a single factor which by itself galvanized the company into action. In others, however, it is clear that in the period preceding the sharpbend the company remained relatively complacent. Frequently in these cases the trigger proved to be a change of chief executive, who generated a new vision of what was possible and created a dissatisfaction with the *status quo*. This amounted to change following the intervention of a new leader who raised the aspiration levels of his executive team. From detailed studies of the sequences of events surrounding the sharpbending within the 25 companies in our sample, it is clear that the process of sharpbending is complex and warrants a fuller exploration.

Actions taken to produce sharpbends

Major categories of actions

In many ways the central focus of the study was upon the action taken to secure sustained superior performance in the hope that other companies pursuing a similar course of action might stand a greater chance of successfully sharpbending themselves. As can be seen from table 2.4, the actions taken in many ways mirrored the causes of relative decline, as expected. Clearly, effective management would take action to correct earlier mistakes or to overcome major perceived problems. Several aspects of the table are of major interest.

First, there were certain categories of change which occurred in the great majority of the sharpbenders. There were major changes in management in 85 per cent, stronger financial controls in 80 per cent, a new product market focus in 80 per cent, more intensive effort to reduce production costs in 80 per cent and improved marketing in 75 per cent. However, these actions were also taken frequently in control companies, as can again be seen from table 2.4, the fourth column of which shows the difference in percentages between sharpbenders and controls. Indeed, as many as 80 per cent of the control companies introduced a

Table 2.4 Steps taken by the sharpbenders and controls to improve performance

Step		Percentage of firms citing the factor		
		Sharpbenders (a)	Controls (b)	Difference (a−b)
1	Major changes in management	85	(30)	55
2	Stronger financial controls	80	(70)	10
3	New product market posture	80	(80)	0
4	Diversified	30	(70)	−40
5	Entered export market vigorously	50	(30)	20
6	Improved quality and service	55	(50)	5
7	Improved marketing	75	(30)	45
8	Intensive effort to reduce production costs	80	(30)	50
9	Acquisitions	50	(80)	−30
10	Steps to reduce debt	50	(80)	−30
11	Windfalls	85	(70)	15
12	Other	25	(20)	5

new product market focus, exactly the same proportion as the sharpbenders, while 70 per cent also developed stronger financial controls. Hence these actions alone are clearly not sufficient, although they may well be necessary, conditions for a major improvement in performance. The major differences between sharpbenders and control companies in the most frequently occurring actions lie with major changes in management, more intensive efforts to reduce production costs and steps to improve marketing. In all these cases the differences between the sharpbenders and controls were statistically significant.

Second, there was a range of desirable actions taken by many of the sharpbenders and controls alike, which clearly again contributed to improved performance. Thus, 55 per cent of the sharpbenders improved quality and service, as did 50 per cent of the controls. Similarly, 50 per cent of the sharpbenders entered export markets more vigorously whilst 30 per cent of the controls did so. Third, there was a range of actions taken more frequently by controls than by sharpbenders, which may in part explain their failure to match the performance of the latter. Thus 70 per cent, 80 percent and 80 per cent respectively of the control companies diversified, undertook acquisitions and sought to reduce debt by disposal of assets or rights issues, compared with 30 per cent, 50 per cent and 50 per cent respectively of the sharpbenders. From both the data and the case studies produced as a result of interviews, it was evident that acquisitions and diversification were related – companies having taken over others as a means of diversifying – and in some cases at least both were associated with disposal of other companies to reduce debt as part of a portfolio approach to corporate strategy. What these differences between sharpbenders and controls seem to be suggesting, therefore, is that sharpbenders tended to focus more heavily upon making significant improvements in operational aspects of their businesses, such as marketing and production, and less on seeking grass that was greener. This is clearly consistent with the perception that diversification can lead to an erosion of profitability in so far as the specific experience-based skills and assets which give a company its competitive edge, and therefore on which it can earn higher margins or 'economic rent', may not be readily transferable into quite different businesses. However, it would be equally wrong to assume that diversification is not a sensible and indeed critical element in the strategy of some of the sharpbenders. For instance, each of the sharpbenders in the declining jute industry developed major alternative businesses – Low and Bonar by wide diversification involving extensive acquisitions, Sidlaw Industries by diversifying into the oil support business and Don Brothers Buist (now Don and Low Limited) by applying their textile technology to the weaving of polyprothene carpet backing. However, what is particularly interesting in the case of Don Brothers Buist is that, unlike the others, it stayed primarily within the textile business, and indeed bought up productive capacity as its rivals closed down. Theirs is an example of heavy focus upon cost effectiveness, quality and closeness to their customers within a specific business. However, what is also clear from the sharpbenders is that, even where they diversified by means of such acquisitions, they subsequently took steps to integrate their new subsidiaries and to ensure effective operational management.

Eighty-five per cent of the sharpbenders and 70 per cent of the controls also benefited from 'windfalls' such as depreciation of the pound which increased international competitiveness, exit of rivals from the industry or rationalization schemes within their industries. It is scarcely surprising that such chance factors impinge more or less equally on sharpbenders and controls. Good luck comes to both the effective and the less effective. From our scrutiny of our case studies, however, we found a qualitative difference between the two categories of companies. Sharpbenders seemed to perceive the full implications of such windfalls more rapidly, and to seize and exploit the opportunities they offered, whilst the control companies tended to do so less fully. We also formed the impression that the sharpbending companies tended to perceive more opportunities and experience more good luck in part because they were more actively and aggressively searching for them. In sharpbender after sharpbender we noted that senior executives tended to travel abroad more frequently, visiting equipment manufacturers and trade fairs, and learning what competitors overseas were doing in order to put and keep themselves ahead of the pack. This was much less evident in the control companies. Success tends to come more to the action orientated, success hungry and opportunity searching. Such companies tend, also, to take more action more energetically across a wider range of aspects of the business. Indeed, one of the statistically significant differences between our sharpbenders and controls was that the former undertook more actions than the latter when summed across the different categories.

Actions within key categories

Each of the broad categories of action listed in table 2.4 itself captures a range of different measures. Constraints of space prohibit us from a full treatment in this paper, and allow us to address only those categories in which the sharpbenders and controls differed most substantially. A full treatment, making heavy use of illustrative material from the sharp-benders, is given by Grinyer et al. (1988). Hence we address below major changes in management, intensive efforts to reduce production costs and improvements in marketing in particular.

Much of the recent literature (Peters and Waterman, 1982; Peters and Austin, 1986; Goldsmith and Clutterbuck, 1984; Inkson et al., 1986) sees the top manager, called the key-holder by Inkson et al., as a critical element in success. Such authors would not be surprised, therefore, to find that a new chairman or chief executive was introduced in 55 per cent of the sharpbenders as one of the steps taken to bend the performance of the company upwards. In 30 per cent there were also changes in executive directors, most frequently in marketing and sales (20 per cent), but also in finance (15 per cent), research and development or technical (15 per cent), production (5 per cent) and other areas such as personnel (10 per cent). In 10 per cent of companies there was an injection of non-executive directors with a view to creating a more balanced board. However, such changes were also common among the control companies. Indeed, there was no statistically significant difference between the sharpbenders and the controls in this respect. This is scarcely surprising if we allow for the probability of a new chief executive within a five- to eight-year period. The key difference between the sharpbenders and controls seems to have lain particularly in the qualities that the new chief executive brought to the former and not to the latter. Thus 60 per cent of the sharpbenders perceived that the new management had brought a more committed positive approach to management with a strong bias for action. In 40 per cent it was thought that a new top management had injected new values, a new vision, which drove the company and strongly motivated its members. In 40 per cent, also, the new top management was thought to believe in stimulating innovative entrepreneurial behaviour throughout management and in 35 per cent to have created a climate of productivity through people, communicating strongly with both the lower echelons of management and the workforce more generally. These qualitative aspects of management, promoted strongly by the more recent literature on excellence, were clearly seen to have substantial importance within the sharpbenders but were less evident in the control companies (see the next section). Time and again we found that one of the things which differentiated our sharpbenders so conspicuously from most other companies visited was the sense of involvement, strong motivation, shared vision and indeed excitement. In many of the companies we were told that this had been generated by the new chairman or chief executive, but this was not always the case. Indeed we were aware of the fact that winning tends to motivate positively and to energize in itself. Winning is personally rewarding!

This sense of new vision, and of Peters and Waterman's characteristics of excellence, also had a bearing on improved marketing as a step to sharpbending. Within 45 per cent of the sharpbenders there was mention of a greater stress on 'getting closer to the customer' within the company value system. This no doubt had a bearing on operational steps taken such as the provision of improved and more frequent marketing information to the board (20 per cent) and improved distribution channels (20 per cent). Other steps taken were raising of prices where demand was inelastic, rationalization of product range within existing markets, focusing on more profitable customers, more cost-effective advertising, more cost-effective marketing, optimized after-sales service, and rationalization of sales staff and delivery journeys (each 15 per cent). Better finished good stock control was thought to contribute to improvement of marketing in 10 per cent of the companies.

Similarly, a wide range of steps were taken to reduce costs. Among the sharpbenders labour productivity was improved by better training (25 per cent), steps to improve morale (40 per cent), removal of job demarcation (16 per cent), work study (30 per cent), wage incentive schemes (30 per cent) and consultation with the workforce on cost reduction (20 per cent). In addition, better quality control reduced wastage in 20 per cent of the companies, better production control was introduced in 35 per cent and better stock control in 30 per cent. These no doubt in part contributed to improved utilization of capacity in 35 per cent. Perhaps the most remarkable aspect of the cost-reduction programme within these companies was that in a high 65 per cent of the companies there was significant investment in new plant to reduce costs. In this respect the sharpbenders differed very significantly indeed from the control companies. They also differed significantly in terms of the number of steps taken, with the sharpbenders taking more steps to reduce their costs of production. These steps to reduce production costs were associated with somewhat less frequent but none the less wide-ranging steps to reduce costs in general. In a high 49 per cent of the companies steps were taken to cut head office staff, in 30 per cent cost-reduction targets were introduced and in 20 per cent profit or cost centres were adopted. The remaining steps taken in this respect were, however, less frequent, with only 10 per cent of the sharpbenders introducing zero-based budgeting, moving head offices to cheaper premises and cutting working capital by reducing finished good stocks, work in progress or debtors. When a comparison was made with the control companies with respect to general steps to reduce costs, it was found that they too took very similar action. The significant differences between the sharpbenders and controls lie in the area of reduction of production costs rather than general overheads.

Interrelationships among steps taken

Among the actions taken, our analysis of the data suggested that some were primary and others secondary, with the former tending to influence the latter. In the primary category we found three groups, namely new functional executives, introduction of profit incentives and analysis of the product market posture. Each of these was significantly correlated with subsets of secondary causes. That with least pervasive influence was profit incentives. These were found to be correlated significantly with improved quality and service by means of better control and reduced delivery delays. Such incentives were also associated with benefiting from more windfalls; it would appear that the prospect of higher financial benefits to executives may promote the search for and exploitation of random opportunities. The introduction of more new functional executives seems to have been more pervasive. They were significantly associated with more steps to reduce debt, introduction of a focused strategy, product differentiation, more vigorous export marketing, improved quality and service via better quality control and reduced delivery delays, all of which could clearly result from the introduction of more energetic operational executives. The exception to this list which is most surprising is that the introduction of new functional executives was not significantly associated with efforts to reduce production costs. One explanation for this is that the executives most frequently replaced during the sharpbend were marketing and financial directors. This does not mean, of course, that efforts were not taken to reduce production costs among sharpbenders, for as we have seen above one of the characteristics which marked them was multiple and wide-ranging steps to gain cost leadership by reduction of manufacturing costs. The third primary step taken was analysis of product market posture. This was significantly associated with a very wide range of further actions. Perhaps most obviously it was linked with the introduction of a focused strategy, product differentiation, raising entry barriers, diversification, acquisitions and exits from business that the company did not know well, each of which steps might be seen to stem directly from the effect of analysis of the existing product market posture and the options open to the company. What intrigued us more was that analysis of product market posture was also significantly associated with steps to gain cost leadership, including those to reduce production costs, and improvement of quality and service by means of better design and reduced delivery delay. Again there is a very clear explanation, namely that an adequate analysis of existing product market posture should highlight any deficiencies in terms of design and delivery delays relative to competitors and should also indicate weaknesses with respect to cost structure.

Moreover, the chosen strategy could well have gain of cost leadership as one of its key components. All in all the statistical analysis demonstrated clearly the major importance of this kind of strategic analysis in generating the sharpbend.

Characteristics of sustained improvements in performance

As indicated in the first section, the interviewers also recorded observed continuing characteristics of the sharpbending companies in order both to test some of the hypotheses in the literature on corporate excellence and to indicate how these were related to steps taken to achieve a marked improvement. Table 2.5 shows a summary of what we found among the sharpbenders. The most prevalent characteristic is what we have called 'good management', which captures four or more characteristics suggested in the literature to be associated with excellence. The most widely recurring characteristics among the sharpbenders were action-orientated management (85 per cent), management valuing people (80 per cent), good communications with employees and good industrial relations (80 per cent), management close to the customer (50 per cent) and top management projecting strong company values (55 per cent). In addition, in 70 per cent of companies the board members and chief executives had ownership or other profit incentives and in 55 per cent the board did not interfere with day-to-day operations. In contrast, only a third of control companies exhibited four or more such characteristics of good management. This difference between the sharpbenders and controls was highly significant at the 1 per cent level.

Given the difficulty of finding associations between organizational structure and performance, it is interesting to note that 75 per cent of the

Table 2.5 Characteristics of sustained improvement in performance

		Number of characteristics cited	Percentage of firms
1	Good management	4 or more	90
2	Appropriate organizational structure	4 or more	75
3	Effective financial and other controls	4 or more	50
4	Sound product market posture	5 or more	45
5	Good marketing management	2 or more	55
6	High quality maintained	2 or more	35
7	Tightly controlled costs	3 or more	40

sharpbenders displayed four or more characteristics of what we defined as appropriate organizational structures compared with none of the controls. Our approach to determining what was an appropriate organizational structure was, however, somewhat eclectic. Drawing on contingency theories we sought to determine whether structure was appropriate to the size and product market posture, assuming that larger and diversified companies were more appropriately divisional in structure as well as more bureaucratic. In all, 80 per cent of the sharpbenders were found to have an appropriate structure in this respect. Peters and Waterman (1982) also proved to be a useful source of widely recurring characteristics. Seventy per cent of the sharpbenders had a 'lean' head office, 75 per cent a simple structure and 50 per cent simultaneous loose–tight properties. Detailed scrutiny of controls as well as sharpbenders, however, taught us that virtually all companies have simultaneous loose–tight properties, the significant differences lying in those aspects of operations which are tightly as opposed to loosely controlled. Within the category of organizational structure we also included the approach of the company to strategic planning. In all, 95 per cent of the sharpbenders had what we regarded as an appropriate approach, in that strategic planning systems were used in large organizations (40 per cent), whilst regular but relatively informal reviews of strategy were adopted in smaller companies (55 per cent). Hypotheses relating mechanistic as opposed to organic decision-making systems to the maturity and stability of the product market proved less helpful, with only 30 per cent of the companies in all adopting the type of structure which would be suggested by contingency theory.

The third most frequently recurring characteristic of sharpbenders was that they had at least two of the characteristics of good marketing management. Again, these characteristics require further explanation. Thus management continuously monitored the market for signals of threats, opportunities and competitive intentions within 55 per cent of the sharpbenders, regularly consulted with key customers and sought to meet their needs in 50 per cent, regularly analysed sales and concentrated marketing effort on high contribution markets and customers in 45 per cent, consciously maintained high margins where the company is dominant and prices inelastic in 35 per cent, and sought to motivate strongly and coordinate the sales force in 30 per cent. Clearly, among the sharpbenders, a higher score on characteristics of good marketing management is reflecting particularly a strong focus on monitoring the market, consulting with key customers and regularly analysing sales as a basis for both strategic and practical decisions. These characteristics were less evident in the control companies, and indeed the difference between them and the sharpbenders was significant at the 5 per cent level in this respect.

It can be seen from table 2.5 that the other characteristics of sharpbenders were, in declining order, effective financial and other controls (50 per cent), sound product market posture (45 per cent), tightly controlled costs (40 per cent) and maintenance of high quality (35 per cent). However it would be a mistake to assume from these figures that these factors were not important. If we were to take the case, for instance, of effective financial and other controls we would find that in 85 per cent of the sharpbenders there were effective budgetary control systems, which also extended to effective capital budgeting systems. Moreover, in 70 per cent there were cash flow forecasts and liquidity was controlled frequently, whilst in 65 per cent there was timely monthly production of key ratios for the managing director and the board. Hence we find that financial controls were indeed of importance within the sharpbenders. However, they were equally prevalent among the control companies. Clearly, good financial control is a 'hygiene' factor, without which performance would tend to deteriorate (see the section above on causes of relative decline) but which in itself is not a sufficient cause of outstanding performance. The same is broadly true of the contribution of sound product market postures for it should be noted that in table 2.5 the 45 per cent relates to five or more characteristics of a sound market posture, but we should appreciate that this number was chosen largely on the grounds that it distinguished more fully between a sharpbending and a control company. Many of the sharpbending companies had an extremely sound product market posture whilst exhibiting less than four of the characteristics we were measuring. In this respect it would be useful to add a little detail. Thus in 70 per cent of the sharpbending companies there was a concentration on businesses that were known well, in 65 per cent the company had a relatively high market share in its major business, in 60 per cent it invested in growing markets where it was competitively strong, in 55 per cent it had a focused strategy, in 50 per cent it had differentiated products and in 30 per cent it had cost leadership. On the whole within the sharpbenders there was a heavier concentration on such positive aspects of product market strategy. Thus in only 30 per cent did the sharpbenders consciously harvest or divest competitively weak businesses, and in 30 per cent they were milking competitively strong but mature businesses. The very fact that there was no significant difference with respect to product market posture between our sharpbenders and our control companies indicates strongly the importance of effective action-orientated management who can properly exploit the market positions they hold.

It was disappointing to find that sharpbenders and controls are not differentiated by tighter control of cost and quality. The most frequently found approach to control of costs was a regular review of technology to seek cost reductions in 40 per cent of the sharpbenders, followed by production engineering or work study in 30 per cent and consultation with workforce about improvements in 30 per cent. The control companies were at least as active in this respect. Similarly, only 30 per cent of the sharpbenders operated a quality control system, 30 per cent analysed customer complaints and took appropriate action regularly, and in 30 per cent top management monitored product quality, delivery times and after-sales service and took appropriate actions. This raises the issue as to why the sharpbenders were found to be taking steps to improve quality but not operating systems to sustain it on a continuing basis. The answer lies in part in the fact that the steps primarily taken to improve quality and service were redesign of the products and reduction of delivery delays rather than the introduction of a quality control system. At Collins in Glasgow, the quality control system was actually removed as part of an approach to putting responsibility for quality back with the journeyman, a change which did indeed lead to improvements in quality and reduction in the level of wastage.

In this respect it is interesting to note, however, that steps taken to improve the quality of service of a company were statistically significantly associated with maintenance of higher quality, as well as with a number of other continuing characteristics. Also as expected, other principal associations, for instance between changes in management and the characteristics of excellent management and between a new product market posture and a sound product market position, were found. However, these were part of a richer more complex pattern of relations which will be explored more fully in a subsequent publication.

Concluding comments

In concluding let us first supplement the detailed analysis of earlier sections by strong impressions formed during our interviews, secondly make some general observations about the implications of the study and thirdly conclude with some qualifications relating to methodology.

The detailed statistics presented in earlier sections fail to capture certain critical qualitative differences between the sharpbenders and controls. In sharpbender after sharpbender we were impressed by the sense of commitment, excitement, shared vision and hungry search for improvements in all aspects of the business. The chief executive, or in some cases a small group of senior executives operating together, seem to us to be the key ingredient in producing this heady potion. This appears perhaps most strongly in the case studies of the sharpbenders to be found in Grinyer et al. (1988). This energetic, positive, action-oriented approach to management permeated virtually all aspects of the business, leading not only to new approaches to product market posture and better marketing but to wide-ranging and sustained action to reduce costs of production in order to give greater competitiveness. It is particularly interesting, for instance, that investments in new technology, which are particularly forward-looking, were used widely as a means of reducing production costs. For instance, at Collins in Glasgow, commitment was made to major investments in new production technology, with the full support of the trade union officials, at the very time at which redundancy schemes were being launched to slash the labour costs of production. An abiding impression with which we were left after visiting so many sharpbenders was that ultimately creative entrepreneurial courageous people are what really makes a company successful. Moreover, such people are in many respects quite ordinary. Although there are most certainly charismatic leaders among our sharpbenders, many of them were led by men and women without personalities that riveted attention and with apparent personality traits of all kinds. However, we cannot recollect one who was not seen by colleagues to be fully committed, to possess the strength to grasp nettles, and to have created by word and example a shared set of objectives, that in some cases could be called a vision, among senior colleagues and often among lower levels of the organizational hierarchy.

Second, turning to more general aspects, we would reiterate that this paper is addressing mainly the primary rather than secondary hypotheses, namely those relating to what was to be found in the sharpbenders and how these differed from control companies. In addition, a simple conceptual model relating causes of decline, triggers, steps for actions taken and sustained characteristics was advanced. A number of very general conclusions can be drawn from the work presented in this paper relating to these. First, although we found considerable difficulty in locating companies that could properly be called sharpbenders, they do indeed exist within the UK economy. Moreover, they are both qualitatively and, in terms of characteristics that we were able to measure, quantitatively different from the controls in key aspects. Further, within these sharpbending companies there was indeed a process which we were able to capture by means of the informal semi-structured interviews conducted with senior management and workforce representatives. This process was captured surprisingly well by the simple model advanced earlier, although it is clear that certain aspects such as the process of triggering fundamental change require more refined treatment. Moreover, this process, which produces not only higher immediate performance but the qualities which sustain success, is clearly replicable and involves few steps which are not available to virtually all companies. Obviously the appropriate steps taken are related to the causes of relative decline, but it is interesting that the sharpbenders were marked in part by the very range of actions taken. In other words, one of the sources of success is not only a critical, questioning, analytical approach to the problems being confronted and the options open but, above all, a sustained, wide-ranging pursuit of improvement in all aspects of the business. Finally, whilst we provide clear support for a number of the prescriptions of the recent literature on corporate excellence, such as lean head offices, action-orientated management and closeness to the customer, our findings suggest strongly that it is not good enough just to describe qualities. Clearly, the important questions are the processes by which excellence is achieved. Qualities of excellence then follow from this process.

Third, in closing we would underline again some of our qualifications about the research methodology adopted. In concept, the research design still strikes us as appropriate, overcoming the major limitations inherent in virtually all the literature on corporate excellence. The focus on process, rather than on qualities alone, and indeed upon the diagnosis of causes of earlier relative decline should make a substantial and useful contribution. Moreover, we are reinforced in our belief that comparison of sharpbending, or excellent, companies with control companies is essential, for the work we have done to date suggests clearly that certain aspects of good management, such as tight financial control systems, are shared equally between the outstanding and the less successful. Our reservations relating to our work turn principally on the size of the sample of control companies we were able to visit. All in all, the process of selecting, preparing for visits, interviewing, producing the reporting schedule, and writing a case study took at least one man-week for each visit, and often more like two. This was particularly so in view of the use of two interviewers for most of the companies. The sheer expenditure of time and the cost involved in visits meant that both time and money ran out before we were able to visit more than six control companies.[3] This sample is in many ways too small. Although it can be argued that the statistical methods adopted take into account the size of samples within the degrees of freedom used, none the less with a sample as small as six even one highly untypical company could distort the results. In view of this, we have been cautious about using the statistical results to date, making reference to them only where the level of statistical significance is so high that it is unlikely that it could be thrown by an exceptional control company. Even when this precaution is taken, a large number of interesting results still emerge and will be the subject of more detailed papers in the future. In addition, we would like to find resources to extend our sample of control companies so that we can place greater reliance upon comparisons between controls and sharpbenders. This we intend to do. In addition, by providing relative financial performance data for sharpbenders and control companies alike, it would be possible for us to analyse relationships between financial performance and growth of sales across a combined sample of sharpbenders and controls.

Acknowledgements

The authors would like to thank the National Economic Development Office for financial and other support in undertaking the research on which this paper is based.

Notes

1 Owing to restrictions on resources, we were unable to interview at this stage as many companies as controls as we had initially wished, which has both influenced the kind of statistical analysis subsequently undertaken and has also led us to be very cautious in interpreting the significance of differences between sharpbenders and controls.
2 It must be borne in mind that a number of sharpbenders like the John Wood Group, were *not* in relative decline. Others, like Sirdar before its bend and some of the control companies, were jogging along comfortably but unimpressively.
3 A seventh has since been added.

Appendix 2.1 Hypotheses

A Structure

First order

1 Causes of relative decline or stagnation before the sharpbend
2 Stimulus for sharpbending
3 Steps taken in achieving sharpbending
4 Resulting continuing characteristics of sharpbenders
   (NB   These can be seen to be an aspect of effective implementation of 3)

B First-order hypotheses

1 Causes of decline with which the company dealt relatively badly

Category of hypothesis	Number of hypothesis	Hypothesis: contingencies hypothesized to be associated with stagnation or decline rather than sustained success	Source
1.1 Adverse changes in total market demand	1.1.1	Changing technology, economic, social or political conditions which lead to a sustained drop in demand in market served (NB Under certain conditions this is likely to heighten price competition)	Schendel et al., 1976; Argenti, 1976; Sigoloff, 1981; Slatter, 1984
	1.1.2	Cyclical decline for which the firm is ill prepared	Slatter, 1984
1.2 Falling revenues due to more intense competition (NB Connection with 1.5 in strategic groups in which the company operates)	1.2.1	Falling revenues, increased competitive pressure, lack of responsive to competitive changes	Argenti, 1976; Schendel et al., 1976; Slatter, 1984
	1.2.2	Lack of 'product market focus', differentiation of product or strong cost advantages (see 1.6) to constrain competition (price)	Porter, 1980; Slatter, 1984; Hofer, 1977, 1980 (on differentiation)
	1.2.3	Failure to develop new products	Slatter, 1984
	1.2.4	Low 'switching' costs for customer	Porter, 1980

		1.2.5	High exit costs which increase price competition in face of decline of sales	Porter, 1980; Sigoloff, 1981; Harrigan, 1980, 1982
		1.2.6	Technological change which lowers costs of rival(s)	Sigoloff, 1981
		1.2.7	High threat of potential entry	Bain, 1956; industrial economics generally; Porter, 1980
		1.2.8	Threat from substitutes prevents higher prices	Porter, 1980
		1.2.9	Removal of protection or other barriers to entry	Porter, 1980; industrial economics generally
1.3	Lack of marketing effort	1.3.1	Lack of effective direction, use and control of sales force, advertising and after-sales and/or market research	Slatter, 1984
1.4	Poor management	1.4.1	Inflexible autocrat associated with stagnation or decline	Slatter, 1984; Handy, 1976
		1.4.2	Combined chairman and managing director associated with stagnation or decline	Slatter, 1984
		1.4.3	Ineffective board (unbalanced boards, non-active non-executives, no consensus, directors not major shareholders)	Slatter, 1984; Grinyer and Norburn, 1975
		1.4.4	Management neglect of core business as they (start to) diversify	Slatter, 1984; Argenti, 1976; Schendel et al., 1976; Grinyer and McKiernan, to be published
		1.4.5	Autocratic management style (and centralization of decision-taking)	Smart et al., 1978; Dunbar and Goldberg, 1978
		1.4.6	Overly optimistic, expansionary and incautious top management	
		1.4.7	Failure of communication from middle to senior management leading to lack of top management realism on market situation	Smart et al., 1978; Dunbar and Goldberg, 1978
		1.4.8	Management fails to communicate effectively with the workforce and unions: bad industrial relations	NEDO

(continued)

Category of hypothesis		Number of hypothesis	Hypothesis: contingencies hypothesized to be associated with stagnation or decline rather than sustained success	Source
1.5	Inadequate financial control	1.5.1	Absence or inadequacy of cash flow forecasts, costing systems or budgetary control	Slatter, 1984; Argenti, 1976; Sigoloff, 1981; Grinyer et al., to be published.
		1.5.2	Management accounting information before top management too infrequently or too late	Slatter, 1984
		1.5.3	Management accounting information too voluminous, complex, wrong or not that required	Slatter, 1984
		1.5.4	Top management not numbers orientated	Slatter, 1984
		1.5.5	Centralized organization structure hinders effective allocation of financial responsibility to operating management	Slatter, 1984
		1.5.6	Distortion of costs by arbitrary allocation of overheads	Slatter, 1984
		1.5.7	Failure to control working capital effectively, in particular stocks and creditors	
1.6	High cost structure	1.6.1	Relatively high costs of production owing to inability to exploit economies of scale	Slatter, 1984; Porter, 1980; general industrial economics
		1.6.2	Relatively high costs of production owing to inability to gain experience curve effects	Boston Consulting Group, 1970; Slatter, 1984
		1.6.3	Relatively high costs because of absolute cost disadvantages (competitors have tied up supplies of raw materials or best channels of distribution, access to cheap immobile labour, proprietary production know-how, favourable site locations etc.)	Bain, 1956; industrial economics generally; Porter, 1980; Slatter, 1984; Sigoloff, 1981
		1.6.4	Centralized organization structure with resultant head office overheads	Slatter, 1984
		1.6.5	Poor production control, plant layout and labour productivity	Slatter, 1984

		1.6.6	Working practices, e.g. involving job demarcation, that inhibit effective deployment of labour or adoption of improved methods	
		1.6.7	Poor sales control and marketing, excessive marketing costs, high number of low-volume expensive orders etc.	Slatter, 1984
		1.6.8	Increased wage levels, strikes	Schendel et al., 1976
		1.6.9	Excess plant capacity and hence high fixed costs	Schendel et al., 1976
		1.6.10	High bargaining power of supplier(s) has inflated costs	Porter, 1980
		1.6.11	Costs or difficulty with raw material supplies	Schendel et al., 1976
1.7	Poor quality	1.7.1	Poor quality and reliability of product relative to competitive products	
		1.7.2	Poor after-sales service relative to competitive products	
1.8	Acquisitions	1.8.1	Acquisition of companies with weak competitive positions	Slatter, 1984
		1.8.2	Acquisition at unjustifiably high price	Slatter, 1984
		1.8.3	Poor post-acquisition management of acquisition(s)	Slatter, 1984; Kitching, 1967, 1974
1.9	Large projects that fail	1.9.1	Underestimating capital requirements (poor cost estimates and project control, or design changes or external factors inflate costs)	Slatter, 1984
		1.9.2	Start-up difficulties	Slatter, 1984
		1.9.3	Market entry costs high	Slatter, 1984
		1.9.4	Overestimation of need for extra capacity (see 1.6.9)	Slatter, 1984
1.10	Financial policy leads to excessive interest charges	1.10.1	Overgearing	Slatter, 1984; Argenti, 1976; Altman, 1968; Taffler and Tisslaw, 1977

NEDO, National Economic Development Office; BCG, Boston Consulting Group.

(continued)

2 Hypothesized triggers of sharpbending

Category of hypothesis		Number of hypothesis	Hypothesis: contingencies hypothesized to be associated with stagnation or decline rather than sustained success	Source
2.1	Intervention from external bodies	2.1.1	Bank, other sources of finance	Slatter, 1984; Hedberg et al., 1976
		2.1.2	Institutional investors	Slatter, 1984
		2.1.3	Non-executive directors	
		2.1.4	Group (if subsidiary)	

2.2	Change of ownership, e.g. acquisition	2.2.1	Acquisition
			  Contested
			  Uncontested
				Slatter, 1984; Grinyer and Spender, 1979; Hedberg et al., 1976

		2.2.2	Inheritance by newcomer	

		2.2.3	Divestment by old owners
			  Management buyout
			  Purchase by another company	

2.3	Injection of new chief executive	2.3.1	Owing to above reasons (2.2)	Grinyer and Spender, 1979a,b
		2.3.2	Owing to death or retirement of old chief executive	
		2.3.3	Chief executive voluntarily moves to another job	

2.4	Recognition by management of problems and of impending or actual organizational collapse	2.4.1	This is rare owing to commitment to existing recipes	Grinyer and Spender, 1979a,b; Slatter, 1984
		2.4.2	New director(s) recruited who persuade board	
		2.4.3	NEDO publications, conferences etc. trigger recognition	
		2.4.4	Publications, conferences or advisory services of DTI trigger recognition	
2.5	Intervention by non-executive directors to replace chairman and/or managing director	2.5.1	Often more directly observable form of 2.1 where non-executives are representing interests of institutional shareholders	Slatter, 1984

NEDO, National Economic Development Office; DTI, Department of Trade and Industry.

(*continued*)

3 Hypothesized steps taken in sharpbending (assumed to be positively associated with improved performance) (NB The general question or risk; some sharpbenders may have taken high-risk actions which turned out well)

Category of hypothesis		Number of hypothesis	Hypothesis: contingencies hypothesized to be associated with stagnation or decline rather than sustained success	Source
3.1	Changes in management	3.1.1a	Changes in chairman and/or managing director	Schendel et al., 1976; Hofer, 1977, 1980; Grinyer and Spender, 1979; Slatter, 1984; Hedberg et al., 1976
		3.1.1b	New leader injects new philosophy, or vision, and values which drive the company	Peters and Waterman, 1982; Grinyer and Spender, 1979a,b
		3.1.2	Change in key executive directors (a) Market or sales (b) Finance (c) Production or technical (more rarely)	Grinyer and Spender, 1979a,b; Slatter, 1984
		3.1.3	Change in non-executive directors (normally following 3.1.1a)	
		3.1.4	Introduction of committed, positive management that encourages individual action and with 'bias for action'	Kenaghan, 1983; Peters and Waterman, 1982
		3.1.5	Key executives have ownership interests or other strong profit incentive	
3.2	Organizational change	3.2.1	Decentralization (normally associated with the creation of divisional structure and profit centres)	Slatter, 1984
		3.2.2	Reduction in size of head office (associated with 3.2.1): 'simple form, lean (corporate) staff'	Slatter, 1984; Peters and Waterman, 1982
		3.2.3	Centralization to tighten central controls; normally of cash and capital expenditure only but sometimes of recruitment decisions	Slatter (1984) refers to centralizaon of financial decisions

		3.2.4	Simultaneous 'loose-tight' properties, i.e. decentralization of innovative and operating decisions whilst strong centralization of issues involving key values	Peters and Waterman, 1982
		3.2.5	Introduction of corporate (strategic) planning	
3.3	Strong central financial control	3.3.1	Introduction of (1) cash flow forecasts, (2) budgets, (3) management accounting data on production, (4) overhead costs and (5) control over capital budget	Slatter, 1984; Pearson, 1977; Taylor, 1982/83
		3.3.2	Frequent use by managing director and board of a limited number of key financial ratios for control	
3.4	New product market focus	3.4.1	Evaluation of existing strategy and of available alternatives and determination of a corporate plan (see 3.2.5)	Slatter, 1984
		3.4.2a	Cut back to profitable core by closure or divestment of businesses, markets or products in which competitively weak	Boston Consulting Group, 1970; Slatter, 1984; Taylor, 1982/3; Hambrick and Schecter, 1983
		3.4.2b	Divest businesses company does not know well	Peters and Waterman, 1982
		3.4.3	Increase prices and 'harvest' businesses in which competitively weak prior to closure	BCG; Slatter, 1984
		3.4.4	Seek 'focused strategy' by differential prices or emphasis to permit domination of market segments	Slatter, 1984; Porter, 1980
		3.4.5	Seek to differentiate products or move into markets where strong product differentiation	Porter, 1980; Slatter, 1984
		3.4.6	Seek to enhance switching costs and other barriers to entry to the main markets in which the company operates	Porter, 1980; Slatter, 1984
		3.4.7	Seek to achieve costs leadership by (a) gaining economies of scale (b) gaining economies of learning (c) tight control of marketing costs and discouraging high-cost customers	Porter, 1980; Slatter, 1984

(continued)

Category of hypothesis	Number of hypothesis	Hypothesis: contingencies hypothesized to be associated with stagnation or decline rather than sustained success	Source
		(d) tight control of production and marketing expenses	
		(e) control of materials and energy costs	
	3.4.8	Invest in new plant to enter new product market or give cost leadership in existing market	Slatter, 1984
	3.4.9	License new products from others	Kenaghan, 1983
	3.4.10	Plan mergers and cooperative supply agreements to reduce capacity	Taylor, 1982/3
	3.4.11	Sell existing technology in LDCs in form of turnkey factories and systems	Taylor, 1982/3
	3.4.12	Create idle capacity to signal to potential entrants that growth in demand will be met by existing producers and that new entry will trigger a price war	Porter, 1980; Harrigan, 1980, 1982
	3.4.13	Vertical integration to secure supplies or distribution channels	Schendel et al., 1976; Harrigan, 1980, 1982
3.5 Improved product quality and service	3.5.1	Introduction or improvement of quality control	
	3.5.2	Tighter planning of production and delivery to reduce delivery delays	
	3.5.3	Introduction or improvement of after-sales services	Pearson, 1977
3.6 Improved marketing	3.6.1	Raising prices where products have price-inelastic demand	Eisenberg, 1972; Pearson, 1977; Slatter, 1984
	3.6.2	Provide more competitive discounts	Eisenberg, 1972; Pearson, 1977; Slatter, 1984
	3.6.3	Analyse and rationalize the product range within the existing businesses and markets	Eisenberg, 1972; Pearson, 1977

3.6.4	Analyse and revise distribution channels within the existing businesses and markets	Eisenberg, 1972; Slatter, 1984
3.6.5	Analyse profitability due to different categories of customers and focus on the more profitable within existing businesses and markets	Slatter, 1984
3.6.6	Analyse and revise post-sale services (either slimming, pricing to cover costs or expanding as a marketing device)	
3.6.7	Analyse and revise advertising and promotion	
3.6.8	Change the systems for controlling salesmen, communicating with them and motivating them	
3.6.9	Improve marketing information to management	
3.6.10	Better control of finished stock levels and distribution	
3.6.11	'Get close to customer'	Peters and Waterman, 1982
3.7 Cost-reduction strategies (NB Some are also mentioned under other headings but are also collected here for convenience)		
3.7.1	Introduce zero-based budgeting or set targets for cost reduction	Slatter, 1984
3.7.2	Introduce profit or cost centres	
3.7.3	Cut overheads: (a) head office staff; (b) buildings occupied etc.; (c) work in progress, materials stocks, finished goods stocks	Pearson, 1977; Schendel et al., 1976; Slatter, 1984; Hofer, 1977, 1980; Taylor, 1982/3; Hambrick and Schecter, 1983
3.7.4	Cut marketing and distribution costs by (a) concentrating on customers who give greatest contribution (b) concentrating on products which make greatest contribution to profits (c) rationalizing sales staff and delivery journeys (d) rationalizing advertising and promotional activities	
3.7.5	Reduce costs of production by (a) seeking improved productivity via better training and higher morale (b) introducing work study or other means of reducing costs (c) tighter production and stock control to reduce working capital	Pearson, 1977; Slatter, 1984; Schendel et al., 1976; Taylor, 1982/3; Hofer, 1977, 1980; Hambrick and Schecter, 1983

(continued)

Category of hypothesis	Number of hypothesis	Hypothesis: contingencies hypothesized to be associated with stagnation or decline rather than sustained success	Source
		(d) tighter security to reduce pilferage	
		(e) improved utilization of capacity	
		(f) investment in new plant to reduce production costs	
	3.7.6	Consult workers on methods of cost reduction	
3.8 Acquisitions	3.8.1	To facilitate new product market orientation	Eisenberg, 1972; Slatter, 1984
		(a) In related businesses	
		(b) By diversification	
	3.8.2	Acquisition of competitors to increase competitive advantage in existing business	
	3.8.3	Acquisition of suppliers or distributive channels to secure or improve competitive position of existing business	
	3.8.4	In each of the above cases managerial action taken to integrate the acquisition effectively into the company	Kitching, 1967, 1974
3.9 Debt restructuring/new financial strategy	3.9.1	Dispose of saleable assets (including subsidiaries) to reduce debt	Slatter, 1984
	3.9.2	Sell assets and lease back	Slatter, 1984
	3.9.3	Float subsidiaries as public companies and so reduce debt	
	3.9.4	Rights issues to replace debt by equity	
	3.9.5	If private company, go public to raise new capital for expansion	Vaughan et al., 1977
3.10 Changes in the environment which remove	3.10.1	Recovery in demand in major specific markets or segments in which the market is relatively strong generally owing to	
		(a) cyclical upturn	

		(b) secular upturn including changes in taste etc.	
		(c) government policies or operation of its agencies	
causes of decline or benefit the firm without action by it	3.10.2	Reduce costs relative to competitors owing to (a) falling prices of raw materials relative to competitors (b) falling interest rates where more capital intensive than competitors (c) falling real wages of labour relative to competitors (d) improved technology from equipment suppliers and/or lower equipment costs relative to competitors	
	3.10.3	Competitive position in the major specific market segments served improving owing to (a) competitors going out of business (either through failure or a rationalization scheme, e.g. foundries) (b) competitors erecting barriers to entry that reduce potential competition (c) changes in exchange rate or other factors that make products more competitive internationally	Caves & Porter, 1977; Porter, 1980
	3.10.4	Government agencies acting to break power of suppliers to or buyers from the company	
3.11	Others		
	3.11.1	Switch from specialist to flexible plant ⎫	
	3.11.2	Lease rather than buy plant ⎬ in declining market	Harrigan, 1980, 1982
	3.11.3	Strong public relations efforts ⎭	Taylor, 1982/3; Slatter, 1984 Kanaghan report
	3.11.4	Development of financial incentives to motivate management to innovate which *this* company responds to more than others	
	3.11.5	Use of consultants to pinpoint weaknesses and help refocus strategic thinking	
	3.11.6	Injection of 'respect for people' or 'productivity through people' perspective	Peters and Waterman, 1982

(*continued*)

4 Resulting characteristics of sharpbenders

Category of hypothesis	Number of hypothesis	Hypothesis: contingencies hypothesized to be associated with stagnation or decline rather than sustained success	Source
4.1 Management	4.1.1	Energetic top management strongly orientated to achieve good results	Grinyer et al., to be published
	4.1.2	Top management develops and implements strategic plans	Grinyer et al., to be published
	4.1.3	Less conservative top management	
	4.1.4	Management operates using adequate management control information	Slatter (1984) implies
	4.1.5	Communications to employees good and industrial relations healthy; company philosophy stresses 'respect for individuals'	Slatter (1984) implies; Peters and Waterman, 1982
	4.1.6	Chairman exercises controlling role over separate managing director	Slatter (1984) implies
	4.1.7	'Active' non-executive directors	
	4.1.8	Board does not interfere in day-to-day operations	
	4.1.9	Management at all levels has bias for action	Peters and Waterman, 1982
	4.1.10	Management at all levels keeps 'close to customer'	Peters and Waterman, 1982
	4.1.11	Top management projects strong company philosophy or values to all levels in organization	Peters and Waterman, 1982
	4.1.12	Management fosters leaders and innovators throughout company and encourages practical risk-taking	Peters and Waterman, 1982
4.2 Organizational structure	4.2.1	If company large and diversified is divisional. If company smaller and more narrow in product range is functional	Chandler, 1962; Rumelt, 1974; Grinyer et al., 1980
	4.2.2	Where market environment is dynamically changing the organization is less formal than would be expected for it size	Burns and Stalker, 1961; Child, 1974, 1975
	4.2.3	Close links between marketing, R & D and design	

		Description	Reference
	4.2.4	Where the environment is stable and the product is at the mature stage of the product life cycle, the organization is formal and mechanistic for its size (especially where cost leadership sought)	linked with concepts of Hofer (1977, 1980) and Porter (1980)
	4.2.5	Profit (or, where inappropriate, cost) centres operated and decision-making delegated to them	
	4.2.6	Centralized large head office staff avoided/minimized and organizational structure kept simple	Peters and Waterman, 1982
	4.2.7	Firm has different types of managers and systems in businesses at different strategic stages	
	4.2.8	'Simultaneous loose–tight properties', i.e. decentralized innovative and operating decisions, tight control and control of key values	Peters and Waterman, 1982
4.3 Effective financial and other control systems are operated	4.3.1	Timely and relevant management accounting information which is not excessive produced monthly for managing director and board	
	4.3.2	Cash forecasts made and liquidity controlled	
	4.3.3	Effective capital budgeting system operated	
	4.3.4	Effective budgetary control operated	
4.4 Sound product market posture	4.4.1	Company is making investments in growing markets in which it has a strong competitive position	
	4.4.2	Company is 'harvesting' businesses (or divesting) where it has a weak competitive position and the market is not growing	Boston Consulting Group and other portfolio models
	4.4.3	Company is maintaining but not investing in growth, i.e. 'milking' businesses in static markets where is competitively strong	

(continued)

Category of hypothesis	Number of hypothesis	Hypothesis: contingencies hypothesized to be associated with stagnation or decline rather than sustained success	Source
	4.4.4	Company has successfully established one of the following with major businesses: (a) focused strategy (i.e. concentrating on specific market segments which the company can dominate) (b) differentiated product strategy (c) cost leadership strategy which protects it from competitive pressures	Porter, 1980
	4.4.5	Company has a higher bargaining power in its major businesses relative to its suppliers	Porter, 1980
	4.4.6	Company has a higher bargaining power in its major businesses relative to its customers	Porter, 1980
	4.4.7	Company 'sticks to the knitting', i.e. it stays close to business it knows	Peters and Waterman, 1982
4.5 Good marketing management both at home and overseas	4.5.1	Marketing effort focused on high-contribution customers, products and countries	
	4.5.2	Sales force properly motivated and work well coordinated	
	4.5.3	Competitive discount structures	
	4.5.4	High margins maintained in markets where company is dominant and demand is price inelastic	Slatter, 1984

	4.5.5	Marketing management conscious of need to monitor market continuously for signals as to	After Porter, 1980
		(a) competitive moves	
		(b) new products which could be substitutes	
		(c) changing needs which could provide threats or opportunities	
		(d) technological changes which could create threats or opportunities	
	4.5.6	Marketing management ensures good delivery times and rapid and effective after-sales services	
	4.5.7	Effective marketing information systems operated	
4.6	Appropriately high product quality maintained		
	4.6.1	From time to time top management monitors deliveries, product quality and after-sales service, e.g. analyses customer complaints	
	4.6.2	Quality control systems operated	
4.7	Cost controlled tightly		
	4.7.1	Cost control over raw material costs, production costs and productivity maintained; top management regularly reviews cost components; shop floor consulted as well	
	4.7.2	Marketing and distribution costs for products and customers maintained and efforts made to minimize them	
	4.7.3	Controls over pilferage maintained	
	4.7.4	Technology regularly reviewed to ensure that production costs are minimized	
	4.7.5	Production engineering, work study and other approaches to cost reduction used regularly	
	4.7.6	Productivity measured and reviewed regularly with shop floor (NB Above likely to be particularly important when products are mature and non-differentiated)	

(continued)

Category of hypothesis	Number of hypothesis	Hypothesis: contingencies hypothesized to be associated with stagnation or decline rather than sustained success	Source
	4.7.7	Firm makes good use of computers, office automation, O&M, operational research, consultants, management training, NEDO advice etc.	

NEDO, National Economic Development Office.

Bibliography

Beaver, W.W. (1967). 'Financial ratios as predictors of failure'. *Journal of Accounting Research*, 5, 71–111.

Dunbar, R.L. Dutton, J.M. and Torbert, W.R. (1982). 'Crossing mother: ideological constraints on organisational improvements'. *Journal of Management Studies*, 19(1), 29 et seq.

Grinyer, P.H. and Spender, J.C. (1979). 'Recipes, crises and adaptation in mature businesses'. *International Studies of Management and Organisation*, 9(3), 113–33.

Hambrick, D.C., MacMillan, I.C., Day, D.L. (1982). 'Strategic attributes and performance in the BCG matrix – a PIMS-based analysis of industrial product businesses'. *Academy of Management Journal*, 25(3), 510–31.

Hay, D.A. and Morris, D.J. (1980). *Industrial Economics: Theory and Evidence*. Oxford: Oxford University Press.

Khandwalla, P. (1978). 'Crisis responses of competing versus noncompeting organizations'. *Journal of Business Administration*, 9(2).

MacMillan, I.C., Hambrick, D.C. and Day, D.L. (1982). 'The product portfolio and profitability – a PIMS-based analysis of industrial-product businesses'. *Academy of Management Journal*, 25(4), 733–55.

Mair, A. (1978). *Corporate Turnaround*, M.Sc. Dissertation, City University Business School.

Miller, D. (1982). 'Evolution and revolution: a quantum view of structural change in organizations'. *Journal of Management Studies*, 19(2), 131–51.

Mintzberg, H. (1978). 'Patterns in strategy formulation'. *Management Science*, 24(9), 934–48.

Schendel, D. and Patton, G.R. (1976). 'Corporate stagnation and turnaround'. *Journal of Economics and Business*, 28, 236–41.

Scherer, F.M. (1980). *Industrial Market Structure and Economic Performance*. Chicago, IL: Rand McNally.

Starbuck, W.H. (1982). 'Congealing oil: inventing ideologies to justify acting ideologies out'. *Journal of Management Studies*, 19(1), 3–27.

Starbuck, W.H. (1978). 'Responding to crisis'. *Journal of Business Administration*, 9(2), 107–37.

References

Altman, E. (1968). 'Financial ratios, discriminant analysis, and prediction of corporate bankruptcy'. *Journal of Finance*, 23(4), 589–609.

Argenti, J. (1976). *Corporate Collapse: The Causes and Symptoms*. New York: McGraw-Hill.

Bain, J.S. (1956). *Barriers and New Competition*. Cambridge, MA: Harvard University Press.

Burns, T. and Stalker, G.M. (1961). *The Management of Innovation*. London: Tavistock.

Caves, R.E. and Porter, M.E. (1977). 'From entry barriers to mobility barriers: conjectural decisions and contrived deterrence to new competition'. *Quarterly Journal of Economics*, 41, 241–61.

Chandler, A. (1962). *Strategy and Structure*. Cambridge, MA: MIT Press.

Child, J. (1974). 'Managerial and organisational factors associated with company performance'. *Journal of Management Studies*, October.

Dunbar, R.L. and Goldberg, W.H. (1978). 'Crisis development and strategic response in European corporations'. *Journal of Business Administration*, 9(2).

Eisenberg, J. (1972). *Turnaround Management: A Manual for Profit Improvement and Growth*. New York: McGraw-Hill.

Goldsmith, W. and Clutterbuck, D. (1984). *The Winning Streak*. Harmondsworth: Penguin.

Grinyer, P.H. and McKiernan, P. 'A simultaneous equation model for growth in the UK electrical engineering industry'. Submitted to *Journal of Industrial Economics*.

Grinyer, P.H. and Norburn, D. (1975). 'An empirical investigation of some aspects of strategic planning: perceptions of executives and financial performance'. *Journal of the Royal Statistical Society*, Series A, 138(1), 70–97.

Grinyer, P.H. and Spender, J.C. (1979). *Turnaround: The Fall and Rise of the Newton Chambers Group*. London: Associated Business Press.

Grinyer, P.H., McKiernan, P. and Yasai-Ardekani, M. 'Market structure, control of overheads, and profitability in the UK electrical engineering industry'. Submitted to *Journal of Industrial Economics*.

Grinyer, P.H., Mayes, D.G. and McKiernan, P. (1988). *Sharpbenders*. Oxford: Blackwell.

Hambrick, D.C. and Schecter, T. (1983). 'Turnaround strategies for mature industrial-product SM business units'. *Academic of Management Journal*, 26(2), 231–48.

Handy, C. (1976). *Understanding Organisations*. Harmondsworth: Penguin.

Harrigan, K.R. (1980). *Strategies for Declining Businesses*, Lexington, CT: D.C. Heath.

Harrigan, K.R. (1982). 'Strategic planning for the endgame'. *Long Range Planning*, 15(6), 45–8.

Hedberg, B.L. Nystrom, P.C. and Starbuck, W.H. (1976). 'Company on seesaws: prescriptions for a self-designing organisation'. *Administration Science Quarterly*, 21, 46–65.

Hofer, C. (1977). *Conceptual Constructs for Formulating Corporate and Business Strategies*. Report No. 9–378–754, Intercollegiate Case Clearing House, Boston, MA.

Hofer, C. (1980). 'Turnaround strategies'. *Journal of Business Strategy*, 1(1), 19–31.

Inkson, K., Henshall, B., Marsh, N. and Ellis, G. (1986). *Theory K – The Key to Excellence in New Zealand Management*. Auckland: Bateman.

Kenaghan, F. (Chairman) (1983). *Encouraging New Business Activity*. Report by the New Business Panel of the BIM Economic and Social Affairs Committee.

Kitching, J. (1967). 'Why mergers miscarry'. *Harvard Business Review*, November–December. 47(6), 84–101.

Kitching, J. (1974). 'Winning and losing in European acquisitions'. *Harvard Business Review*, March–April. 54(2), 124–36.

Pearson, B. (1977). 'How to manage turnarounds'. *Management Today*, April, 74–77, 134, 136.

Peters, T. and Austin, N. (1986). *A Passion for Excellence: The Leadership Difference*. London: Fontana.

Peters, T.J. and Waterman, R.H. (1982). *In Search of Excellence*. New York: Harper and Row.

Porter, M.E. (1980). *Competitive Strategy*. New York: Free Press.

Rumelt, R.P. (1974). *Strategy, Structure and Economic Performance*. Boston: Harvard Business School.

Schendel, D., Patton, G.R. and Riggs, J. (1976). 'Corporate turnaround strategies: a study of profit decline and recovery'. *Journal of General Management*, **3**.

Sigloff, S. (1981). Lecture given to the Graduate School of Management, UCLA, 27 May 1981. Reported in Slatter, 1984.

Slatter, S. (1984). *Corporate Recovery: Successful Turnaround Strategic and their Implementation*. Harmondsworth: Penguin.

Smart, C.F., Thompson, W.A. and Vertinsky, I. (1978). 'Diagnosing corporate effectiveness and suspectibility to crises'. *Journal of Business Administration*, **9**(2).

Taffler, R.T. and Tisslaw, H.J. (1977). 'Going, going, gone: four factors which predict'. *Accountancy*, **88**(1003), 50–2, 54.

Taylor, B. (1982/3). 'Turnaround, recovery, and growth: the way through crisis'. *Journal of General Management*, 8(2), 5–13.

Vaughan, D., Grinyer, P.H. and Birley, S. (1977). *From Private to Public: An Analysis of the Choices, Problems and Performance of Newly Floated Public Companies, 1966–74*. Cambridge: Woodhead-Faulkner.

3
Diversity and profitability: evidence and future research directions

Robert M. Grant and Howard Thomas

Introduction

Academic research into the relationship between diversification and firm performance has contributed to a substantial shift in business opinion concerning the merits of diversification. In the decade 1962–72 a stream of research emanating from the Harvard Business School identified a consistent trend in corporate development in the USA and Western Europe that pointed towards the diversified divisionalized corporation as the highest evolutionary form of business enterprise (Caves, 1980). These findings, which occurred at a time when both large established corporations and the newly emerging conglomerate enterprises were embarking upon ambitious diversification strategies, reinforced the prevailing view that diversification offered the primary route for large firms to secure higher, more stable earnings.

However, one of the Harvard studies sounded a discordant note. Richard Rumelt's research confirmed the trend towards diversification among the *Fortune 500*, but found first that diversified firms did not in general outperform more specialized firms and second that firms pursuing unrelated diversification were less profitable than firms which diversified into closely related fields. Further study, in both the USA (Palepu, 1985) and other countries produced similar findings, particularly regarding the superiority of related over unrelated diversification. These results have been summarized by Peters and Waterman as follows:

. . . virtually *every* academic study has concluded that unchannelled diversification is a losing proposition . . . it seems worthwhile to illustrate rather exhaustively the almost total absence of any rigorous support for very diversified business combinations. (Peters and Waterman, 1982, pp. 294, 296)

Another management consultant, Milton Lauenstein of Lauenstein and Associates, has summarized the evidence even more succinctly:

. . . we know that, on the whole, diversified companies have not done so well. (Lauenstein, 1985, p. 49)

On the basis of their own observations and their reading of other people's research, Peters and Waterman have carried one of their golden rules – 'stick to the knitting':

Organizations that do branch out but stick very close to their knitting outperform the others. The most successful are those diversified around a single skill. . . . The least successful, as a general rule, are those companies which diversify into a wide variety of fields. Acquisitions especially among this group tend to wither on the vine. (Peters and Waterman, 1982, p. 293)

Yet, despite the findings of Rumelt and others and the well-publicized failures of diversification initiatives among many leading companies, the case against broad-spectrum diversification is far from proved. It has been observed that the highly profitable 'constrained' diversifiers in Rumelt's sample tended to inhabit high-growth, high-profit industries (e.g. pharmaceuticals) (Bettis and Hall, 1982) There is also doubt over direction of causation: unrelated diversification may be a response to low profitability rather than a cause of it. Furthermore, recent studies are producing evidence of relatively strong profit performance by highly diversified companies – particularly among the 'new conglomerates'.[1]

The study reported in this paper is an analysis of the relationship between diversification and profitability based upon a large sample of British manufacturing firms. The main findings are first that diversification can be measured better using diversification indices, second that there are diminishing returns to diversity associated with increasing administrative and monitoring costs, third that international diversification is more profitable than product diversification.

The research

We used a database containing details of both product and multinational diversification for 304 large British manufacturing companies which had been meticulously compiled by Jammine (1984) for the years 1968–84.

We started with three principal propositions concerning the relationship between diversification and profitability.

Competitive advantage   Diversification builds competitive advantage for the firm either when it exploits *economies of scope* or where it permits the transfer of a key skill from one business area to another. If the success of diversification is dependent upon these conditions then it follows that

1 diversification into related businesses is more profitable than diversification into unrelated businesses
2 multinational diversification is more profitable than product diversification since it is usually easier to transfer skills and resources between countries than between industries.

Complexity Diversification increases the complexity of corporate management and causes problems in communication, coordination, accountability and control. This implies that there may be a limit to the degree of diversity that can be effectively managed (Rumelt, 1982).

Profit-led diversification The usual assumption is that diversification strategy influences profitability. However, it is also likely that firms can use their profit earnings to finance diversifying investments. Indeed, in the latter case managers may be tempted to use internal funds to build corporate empires or protect employment rather than to pursue stockholders' objectives.

Measuring diversification

Three measures of diversification were employed.

Rumelt's (1974) classification of diversification strategies Rumelt's classification is based upon two criteria: first the *specialization ratio* of the company (the proportion of sales which the major activity accounts for) and second the relationship between the activities. Rumelt identified three types of relationship: vertical integration (the output of one activity is an input of another), 'constrained' diversification (activities are related to one other by a common core skill) and 'linked' diversification (each business activity is related to at least one other but the businesses are not all related to one another). Rumelt's eight-cell classification of strategies is shown in table 3.1. Firms are thus judgementally allocated to different categories of corporate strategy depending upon the extent of product diversity and the relationships between different businesses.

Product diversification index This is measured as $1/\Sigma_i s_i^2$ where s_i is the share of a company's total sales in industry i. This is a very common measure of diversity in industrial organization research. Hence a company specialized within a single industry has a product diversification index (PDI) of 1, and a company with sales equally distributed among four industries has PDI of 4.

Table 3.1   The Rumelt classification of firms according to their diversification strategy

(i) Single business
   A corporation with SR ≥ 0.95
(ii) Dominant business
   A corporation with 0.95 > SR ≥ 0.70
   (a) Dominant vertical
      A vertically integrated corporation
   (b) Dominant constrained
      A corporation, the major portion of whose (minor) diversified activities is closely
         related to its basic (dominant) business
   (c) Dominant linked
      A corporation, the major portion of whose (minor) diversified activities is only
         vaguely related to its basic (dominant) business
   (d) Dominant unrelated
      A corporation, the major portion of whose (minor) diversified activities is unrelated
         to its basic (dominant) business, i.e. RR < ½ (SR+1)
(iii) Related business
   A corporation with SR < 0.70 and RR ≥ 0.70
   (a) Related constrained
      A corporation, at least 70 per cent of whose businesses are closely related to one
         another through a specific core skill common to each
   (b) Related linked
      A corporation, the majority of whose businesses are only vaguely related to one
         another via a string of linkages between them
   (c) Unrelated business

Firms are classified in different strategy types according to their *specialization ratio* (SR)
(the sales of the major business activity as a proportion of the firm's total sales) and *related
ratio* (RR) (the proportion of the firm's total sales that are in businesses that are related).

The overseas ratio   This is an index of multinational diversity. A
company's multinationality is measured by the proportion of its sales
accounted for by overseas subsidiaries.

It should be noted that the chief merit of the product and
multinational diversity measures is that they are continuous quantitative
measures which measure differences in diversity across firms and time.
The merit of the Rumelt classification is that it measures relatedness as
well as breadth of diversity.

The findings

Because firm profitability is influenced by a very large number of factors,
it is necessary to use multiple regression analysis to separate the influence
of diversification from that of industry variables, firm size and leverage.
A summary of the equations used is given in table 3.2. Our first general
finding was that diversification accounted for only a small proportion of

Table 3.2   Summary of regression equations

A   Relationship between return and diversity: examination of relative value of product and
     multinational diversity
     Return = f (product diversity, multinational diversity, size, leverage, industry,
              membership)[a,b]
B   Direction of causation
     (i) Changes in return regressed on changes in PDI and MDI
          Δ RETURN = F(ΔPDI, ΔMDI, industry membership)[c]
     (ii) Changes in diversity regressed on cash flow and other factors
          ΔPDI (or ΔMDI) = f (cashflow, size, leverage, industry membership, initial levels
          of diversity)

[a] Product diversity varied between regressions. One set used the Rumelt classification and
another set used the PDI in both linear and quadratic form (to reflect diminishing returns
to PDI).
[b] The multinational diversity index (MDI) in both linear and quadratic form was also
included.
[c] ΔRETURN denotes change in return etc.

interfirm differences in return on investment (ROI). Differences in
diversity between firms explained between 5 and 9 per cent of total
interfirm variance in ROI, while industry effects explained around 12 per
cent. However, although diversification did not appear to be a major
factor in explaining differences in performance between companies, its
relationship with profitability was both significant and interesting. The
key findings were as follows.

The impact of diversification strategies

In contrast with a number of previous studies, we found that the Rumelt
strategic categories were of little value in explaining why some firms were
more profitable than others. Table 3.3 shows the profitability differences
associated with each category relative to the profitability of the single
business strategy.

   Over the period as a whole (1972–84) the differences in percentage
ROI between the strategic categories (after excluding the effects of firm
size, industry membership and other variables) were small and all were
statistically insignificant from zero. The only notable finding was that
more diversified categories tended to perform better than the more
specialized categories. Also, the relative profitability of the different
categories changed *substantially* over time; in particular, the profitability
of the single-business firms declined by an average of 74 per cent over
the period, while the related-business categories improved their relative

Table 3.3 Average differences in return on investment between the Rumelt strategic categories (1972–84)

	ROI relative to the single business category (%)	
	Before adjusting for other variables	After adjusting for other variables
Single business	0	0
Dominant vertical	+1.3	−0.5
Dominant constrained	+0.3	−0.7
Dominant related and unrelated	−0.8	−1.0
Related constrained	+1.6	+2.5
Related linked	+2.2	−0.2
Unrelated	+1.4	+1.2

'Other variables' include multinational diversity, firm size, leverage and industry effects. None of the above category differences are significantly different from zero at the 90 per cent level of probability.

profitability even after taking account of other variables.

Our finding that there were no significant performance differences between related and unrelated diversification strategies contradicts the findings of several earlier studies. However, this finding does not necessarily mean that relatedness between businesses is irrelevant in affecting the success of diversification. It is more likely that the empirical measure of relatedness incorporated into our classification was too narrow to encompass the full range of relationships between a company's business units. The Rumelt categorization is based largely upon technological and market linkages, but firms may create competitive advantage through the exploitation of 'distinctive competencies' which may involve other dimensions of relatedness such as financial synergy. We shall return to the issue of relatedness in our conclusions.

Product diversification and return on investment

Our dissatisfaction with the strategic categories approach was confirmed by the regression analysis which showed that the simple PDI explained a higher proportion of interfirm differences in ROI than did the Rumelt classification. Hence we utilized the PDI in our subsequent analysis of product diversification.

The key finding was that the relationship between product diversity and ROI was *quadratic* in form. In essence, the costs of managing a complex diversified firm overwhelm the benefits of diversity beyond a certain level of diversification. Once the influences of multinational diversity, industry membership, firm size and leverage were taken into

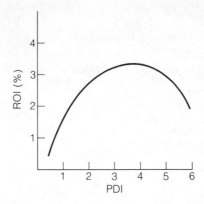

Figure 3.1   The incremental impact of product diversity on return on interest.

account, ROI increased with product diversity up to a PDI of 3.7, after which further increases in PDI reduced ROI. The relationship is shown graphically in figure 3.1. Thus, at high levels of diversity, the dominant influence on profitability was the increased costs of managerial complexity associated with very diverse companies. However, the positive association between diversity and profitability over most of the range of our observations could not be unambiguously interpreted. The positive relationship could be due to either efficiency benefits from diversification through economies of scope or transfer of skills or the use of profitability to finance diversification.

To shed light on the issue of causation we examined changes in product diversity and ROI over the period. By switching dependent and independent variables and examining which changes occurred first, the predominant direction of causation could be established. If diversification was driving profitability, then changes in PDI would be positively associated with future changes in ROI, with a lag of around five years. If profitability was driving diversification, then changes in PDI would be positively associated with the rate of cash flow generation by the company (where cash flow was defined as past tax earnings plus depreciation).

We found that changes in product diversity had an insignificant relationship with future changes in ROI. Cash flow, however, had a positive, if weak, association with product diversity. The implication, therefore, is that our positive relationship between profitability and product diversity is due primarily to the use of retained earnings to finance diversification.

Multinational diversification and return on investment

In contrast with product diversity, multinationality showed no quadratic relationship with ROI once product diversity, firm size, leverage and industry effects were taken into account. The best fit between overseas ratio and ROI was a simple straight-line relationship (see figure 3.2). As with product diversity, this relationship was consistent with either the generation of increased profitability by multinational expansion or with the use of retained earnings to finance overseas direct investment. Hence, we followed the previous procedure in investigating causation. We found the following results:

1 changes in the overseas ratio were positively and significantly related to future changes in ROI (with a five-year lag);
2 changes in the overseas ratio were even more strongly related to future changes in sales;
3 cash flow was positively and significantly related to changes in overseas ratio.

Unlike product diversification, therefore, we observe a strong two-way relationship between multinational expansion and profitability. The firms in our sample which were responsible for most of the overseas expansion over the period displayed the following characteristics:

–they were large;
–they were largely UK based at the beginning of the period;
–they were earning above-average ROI on their UK operations.

At the same time, overseas expansion appeared to be successful in

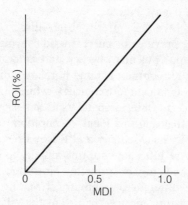

Figure 3.2 The incremental impact of multinational diversity on return on interest.

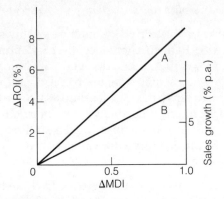

Figure 3.3   The impact of changes in multinational diversity on changes in return on investment (A) and sales growth (B).

generating increases in both ROI and sales. The relationships which we estimated are shown in figure 3.3.

Implications for the management of diversification

On its own, our study offers little guidance to managers on whether or how to undertake diversification. The relationships which our study identifies are for British companies over the period 1972–84. These relationships cannot be assumed to hold in other countries and in other time periods. In order to make recommendations for the management of diversification we must fit our findings into the overall framework of knowledge concerning diversification and firm performance to see what general relationships, if any, emerge.

The key problem here has already been discussed: no consensus emerges either among previous or current studies which permits any set of rules to be drawn up. Thus many earlier studies found strong evidence of related diversification outperforming unrelated diversification – yet our study found no significant differences – while other recent studies have shown unrelated diversification to yield superior returns. Several studies have shown that multinational corporations perform less well than domestic corporations (Melicher and Rush, 1973; Montgomery and Singh, 1984), but our results show multinationality to be associated with higher profitability and higher growth. However, it is in seeking explanations of these differences in empirical findings that deeper and more valuable insights into the true nature of the relationships between corporate behaviour and performance can be gained.

On the basis of our own and other researchers' findings we identify four major lessons for practising managers.

There is no strong evidence of product diversification leading to superior profitability While there is a weak positive relationship between product diversity and profitability, up to fairly high levels of diversity, there is no tendency for diversification to increase the rate of profitability and the primary direction of causation appears to be from profitability to diversification. Although other studies have not specifically addressed the causation issue, there is broad agreement that diversification does not generally lead to higher profitability. Why then does diversification take place? Two explanations are feasible.

The first is that diversification is directed towards reducing risk rather than increasing return. However, most studies show that, in terms of returns to stockholders, corporate diversified companies have neither lower overall risk nor lower systematic risk than undiversified companies (Melicher and Rush, 1973; Montgomery and Singh, 1984). Our study also supports this finding. Moreover, modern financial theory suggests that in efficient securities markets, corporate diversification yields no benefits to stockholders who are able to diversify their own portfolio holdings.

The second is that diversification is promoted largely by managers promoting their own rather than stockholder interests. Thus diversification may offer managers the benefits of larger corporate size and greater security from hostile take-overs. Our finding that profit earnings tend to promote diversification together with the accumulating evidence on the poor returns from mergers to the stockholders of acquiring firms (Firth, 1979) suggests that the underlying motives for diversification may be top executives' drive for self- and corporate aggrandizement.

There are limits to the degree of organizational complexity that firms can successfully manage Our study showed the following:

beyond fairly high levels of product diversity, diversity was *negatively* associated with profitability;
the most diverse firms (both product and multinational) tended to *reduce* their degree of diversity from the late 1970s onwards.

These findings, together with others that report generally poor performance from highly diversified companies, support the notion that, for most companies, there is some limit to the number and range of activities that can comfortably be managed within a single enterprise. However, it is also true that, both in our UK sample and in some US studies, some of the most profitable companies have been highly diversified conglomerate companies.

Multinational diversification in general offers greater profit potential than product diversification We found that multinational diversification is conducive to both increased profitability and growth. This confirms a number of theoretical arguments supporting the competitive advantages of multinationals. What is interesting, however, is that few other studies have found similar evidence (Michel and Shaked, 1986). Hence the suspicion remains that the relationship between multinational diversification and increased profitability that we identify may reflect the particular circumstances of the British economy over the period – notably the low ROI earnings in British manufacturing industry as compared with those in other countries.

On related and unrelated diversification strategies Probably the most interesting issues for the management of diversification concern the differential success of different diversification strategies. The principal finding of earlier research was the superior performance of related diversification over unrelated diversification. However, our study found no significant performance differences between related and unrelated strategies.[2] Other recent studies have found similar results, while two have found unrelated diversifiers earning higher ROI than related diversifiers. The inconsistencies of these findings are not easily explicable. Our prior hypotheses argued strongly for the advantages of related diversification in terms of exploiting economies of scope and transferring distinctive competencies. However, these arguments concern the potential benefits from diversification and ignore the organizational and administrative costs incurred in exploiting these gains. The main finding arising from organizational studies of diversification is that the costs of managing related businesses exceed those of managing unrelated businesses.

To understand why, consider the multidivisional corporation. The primary benefit of the multidivisional structure in the management of diversity is that it economizes on coordination costs by separating operational management from strategic management. However, the benefits of the multidivisional structure in permitting differentiation of functions and management systems between the corporate head office and the operating divisions and in allowing divisional autonomy in operating policy are severely compromised where there are important interdependences between the divisions. Lorsch and Allen (1973), in their study of managing diversity and interdependence in six multidivisional firms, found that the problems of coordination encountered in managing

Table 3.4 Types of relatedness between the business units of a diversified corporation

Type of relatedness	Examples	Performance implications
Operational relatedness	Inputs and activities common to several business units	Exploits economies of scope in joint activities but imposes costs of coordination on corporate management, lowers divisional autonomy and flexibility
Transfer of core skills	Transfer from one business unit to another of R&D capabilities, marketing skills, manufacturing expertise etc.	Permits transfer of competitive advantage between businesses at low additional cost but also requires some corporate-level coordination which may conflict with the benefits from decentralization
Corporate	Application of common systems of resource allocation, performance monitoring and strategy formulation to different business units	Permits increased effectiveness in the conduct of corporate-level management processes, while maintaining business units as autonomous profit centres

diversity depended upon the degree and the type of interdependence between divisions. The existence of 'operating synergies' necessitated lateral coordination between divisions, a corporate headquarters that exercised important functional responsibilities and modifications to the concept of an autonomous division profit centre.

The implication, therefore, is that in analysing the potential for diversification to create competitive advantage we need to consider different types of relatedness between businesses. Table 3.4 proposes three types of relatedness that may occur between businesses. The main prediction from table 3.4 is that, while operational relatedness offers the most tangible benefits in the form of cost reductions from economies of scope, these benefits are likely to be offset by the costs of managing the necessary coordination. In contrast, the benefits of skill relatedness and corporate management relatedness may be less observable, but may pose significant coordination problems. Thus Lorsch and Allen report:

. . . the conglomerate firms we studied seemed to be achieving appreciable degrees of financial and managerial synergy but little or no operating synergy; others had met with little success in trying to achieve it. (Lorsch and Allen, 1973, p. 168)

The role of corporate management relatedness has been largely overlooked in the literature. Many of the firms that we (and others) have classified as 'unrelated' show little or no operating or skill relatedness (e.g. techological, marketing etc.) but can be effectively managed because the operating subsidiaries face similar strategic issues and respond to similar control, incentive and resource allocation systems. Thus the diverse activities of the Hanson Trust in the UK are linked by their being mature businesses with a high market share and limited exposure to international competition which are fitted to Hanson's particular type of financially based corporate management style.

Other companies have perceived certain synergies arising from operating and skill relatedness, but have ignored the issue of whether these areas of relatedness can be effectively harnessed by corporate management. A classic example here is EMI in the UK whose diversification from phonograph records and consumer electronics into medical electronics offered elements of technological relatedness but was a total mismatch in terms of corporate management systems and style. The ability of management to handle the medical electronics area was very poor. The consequent disastrous performance of the medical electronics divisions eventually led to EMI's demise.[3]

Thus it appears likcly that the key aspects of relatedness that determine success in diversification may be compatible corporate-level management style and systems, or what Prahalad and Bettis (1986, pp. 485–502) have termed the 'dominant general management logic'. Or, to put it simply, diversifications may offer certain potential areas of relatedness and synergy. But they can only be made to work by knowledgeable and effective management.

Conclusions

The empirical findings presented in this paper indicate that corporate diversification is neither generally successful nor generally unsuccessful. The variation in the experiences of individual companies is considerable, and it is clear from other evidence (including case studies such as EMI) that the profitability of diversification is crucially dependent upon factors which are specific to the industries which the firm is spanning, the firm's resource base and the characteristics of its organization and management systems. The only findings which emerge from our research which are consistent with other studies are first that very high levels of product diversity are associated with relatively poor profitability and second that the tendency for a strong cash flow to drive diversification is consistent with diversification's being directed towards non-profit goals.

The most important issue arising from our research and that of others concerns the vital role of business relatedness in influencing the success of diversification. The central problem in managing diversification is how to exploit the benefits of relatedness through economies of scope and transferable distinctive competencies while minimizing the organizational and managerial costs of coordination. We argue that the balance between the costs and benefits of diversity differs between different types of relatedness. While operational relatedness is likely to impose managerial difficulties that outweigh the potential economies, corporate-level relatedness through strategically similar businesses is likely to offer a much more favourable ratio of potential benefit to managerial cost.

Future research directions: a postscript

In the spirit of constructive debate about research issues we offer the following suggestions for appropriate directions for future research work.

The coarse-grained research[4] presented here adds some needed clarification to previous research, particularly with regard to work on UK-based rather than US-based databases. This research, like many US-based studies shows that performance is more strongly influenced by such factors as industries, markets and size than by the diversification strategy chosen. However, there are certain interesting issues raised by the current research which merit increased attention.

1 While diversification is preferable to specialization, the research suggests that beyond a certain diversification level there are limits to managing diversity, i.e. the costs of managing a complex diversified firm overwhelm the benefits of diversification.
2 While related diversification is superior to unrelated diversification, there are concerns about both the measurement of relatedness and the practical realization of the benefits of relatedness and synergy.
3 In the UK context multinational diversification is better than product diversification. Indeed, multinational related diversification is far superior to domestic unrelated diversification.
4 Profitability tends to drive diversification, implying that diversification is supply led as firms seek profitable opportunities for retained earnings.

The principal problem in drawing concrete conclusions from such coarse-grained analyses is that the total impact of diversification upon performance depends upon the interactions between diversification and industry membership, firm resources, organization and managerial capabilities. Consequently, in the paragraphs which follow, we argue that future research should focus primarily on implementation issues, theory building and the concept of relatedness.

Therefore, given the finding (i) above that diversification is affected by the ability to manage complexity, it is necessary to take account of implementaiton effects in diversification strategy. For example, within any given diversification category (related, unrelated etc.) the effect of diversification strategy on performance could be influenced by reward systems designed to make business-unit managers in diversified firms act like their counterparts in more specialized firms. Similarly, within any given diversification strategy corporate managers may be motivated to maximize shareholder wealth, satisfy growth objectives or reduce risk at the expense of shareholder concerns. Because coarse-grained studies do not control for the influence of reward and control systems or managerial motivations, the empirical results are generally unenlightening and only 'partial' analyses of the problem. Future studies should clearly incorporate reward systems, managerial motivations, organization and managerial capabilities so that their moderating influences on the diversification–performance relationship can be properly examined and tested.

Theoretical frameworks can also guide future research. Williamson's (1979, 1981) work on transaction costs provides theoretical underpinnings for the assessment of the total impact of diversification strategy on performance. Williamson's analysis of the firm as a governance structure points to the internalization of transactions within the diversified firm as generating efficiences through economizing on transactions costs and correcting agency problems. Therefore diversified firms may be more profitable than specialized firms. Indeed, the economic theory of organization also gives grounds for predicting that, over time, the costs of internal organization (through, for example, improved planning, control and financial systems) may decline relative to the costs of market organization. However, it is also possible to argue for an alternative thesis which is consistent with the evidence of a trade-off between managing complexity and the level of diversity. This alternative thesis is that markets provide flexible and efficient means of resource allocation and that substituting corporate governance for market transactions increases cost and reduces efficiency. In an early paper, Williamson (1967) analysed how increasing firm size necessitates additional levels of management hierarchy with consequent information distortion, control loss and increased administrative costs. Diversification by creating an additional level of corporate management to control and coordinate operating costs not only imposes increased administrative cost but may cause inefficiencies arising from inflexibility to environmental change, politicization of strategic decision-making and increasing strain on top management as the corporate centre seeks to manage an increasing number and diversity of businesses.

A related theoretical issue concerns the concept of relatedness as an organizational strategy construct. In view of the complexity of, and time involved in, the application of Rumelt's categorization scheme it may be sensible to develop new tools for categorizing firms on the basis of interrelatedness among businesses. Possible approaches include the following.

1 Analysing the networks of linked pairs of businesses along a variety of strategic dimensions (Davis, 1987).
2 The use of continuous measures of diversification drawn from the literature on industrial organization:
   (a) the total diversification measure (Jacquemin and Berry, 1979), often referred to as the entropy measure;
   (b) the related diversification measure (Palepu, 1985);
   (c) the unrelated diversification measure (Amit and Livnat, 1987);
   (d) the synergy measure (which requires line-of-business data) which is a distance measure across SIC codes.

However, the key issue with relatedness (assuming satisfactory measurement) is the decision of how to exploit it in the competitive context and measure its value. Rumelt's relatedness construct is made up of two constructs: the specialization ratio and the related ratio. The specialization ratio indicates resource focus (i.e. a lower versus a higher number of businesses), whereas the relatedness ratio shows the degree to which firm revenues are dependent upon a set of related 'core' skills. However, the concept of relatedness is problematical in practice because it classifies firms in terms of potential (not actual) synergies. More importantly, it does not differentiate between firms which fall in the same relatedness category but which may differ widely with respect to resource focus (number of businesses) and pattern of revenue dispersion. Clearly, an implication is that a high degree of resource focus (i.e. fewer businesses) may provide greater managerial potential for exploiting synergies. In addition, unrelated diversification with a high resource focus may, in fact, lead to improved performance. Consequently, in exploiting relatedness the overall conclusion is that the relationship between *relatedness* and *resource focus* may jointly influence *market power* which may, in turn, lead to improved profitability. To test this hypothesis, we would need (apart from continuous measures of relatedness previously suggested) measures of resource focus and market power (Shepherd, 1975; Montgomery, 1985).

Finally, these conjectures do not exhaust future research avenues. For example, in-depth field studies of diversification strategies in practice should provide rich inductive insights about effective implementation. This, in turn, may lead to theoretical generalizations which should stimulate more comprehensive deductively orientated coarse-grained analyses. Either way, it would be worthwhile to see multiple research methods adopted in future studies in this field.

Acknowledgements

We acknowledge the contribution of Azar Jammine to this paper and the support provided by the Centre for Business Strategy, London Business School.

Notes

1 In the US Dolan (1985) found that conglomerate firms earned a higher ROI than any other group once industry differences in profitability had been taken into account, while Michel and Shaked (1984) found that risk-adjusted returns to shareholders were higher for unrelated than for related diversifiers.
2 See footnote 1.
3 See *EMI and the CT Scanner (B)*, HBS Case Services No. 9-383-195, Cambridge, MA, 1983.
4 Harrigan (1983) draws the distinction between coarse-grained research (often data-driven, quantitative) and fine-grained research (more contextual, qualitative) and argues for hybrid mixes of the two approaches in strategy research.

References

Amit, R. and J. Livnat (1987). 'Diversification and risk–return trade off: accounting and market analyses'. Working Paper, Kellogg School, Northwestern University, Evanston, IL.
Bettis, R.A. and Hall, W.K. (1982). 'Diversification strategy, accounting risk and accounting determined return'. *Academy of Management Journal*, 254–64.
Caves, R.E. (1980). 'Industrial organization corporate strategy and structure'. *Journal of Economic Literature*, 18, 64–92.
Davis, G.M. (1987). 'On an inconsistency in Rumelt's (1974) methodology'. Working Paper, University of New Brunswick, Canada.
Dolan, M. (1985). *The Case for the New Conglomerate*. Booz, Allen and Hamilton, unpublished paper.
Firth, M. (1979). 'The profitability of takeovers and mergers'. *Economic Journal*, 89, 121–36.
Harrigan, K.R. (1983). 'Research methodologies for contingency approaches to business strategy'. *Academy of Management Review*, 8(3), 398–405.
Jacquemin, A.P. and Berry, C.H. (1979). 'Entropy measure of diversification

and corporate growth'. *Journal of Industrial Economics*, **27**, 359–69.

Jammine, A.P. (1984). *Product diversification, interactional expansion and performance: a study of strategic risk management in UK manufacturing*. Unpublished Ph.D. London University.

Lauenstein, M. (1985). 'Diversification: the hidden explanation of success'. *Sloan Management Review*, **17**, Fall, 49–55.

Lorsch, J. and Allen, S.A. (1973). *Managing Diversity and Independence: An Organizational Study of Multidivisioinal Firms*. Boston, MA: Harvard Business School.

Melicher, R. and Rush, D. (1973). 'The performance of conglomerate firms: recent risk and return experience'. *Journal of Finance*, **28**, 381–8.

Michel, A. and Shaked, I. (1984). 'Does business diversification affect performance?' *Financial Management*, Winter, 13(4), 18–24.

— and — (1986). 'Multinational corporations versus domestic corporations'. *Journal of International Business Studies*, Fall, 89–106.

Montgomery, C.A. (1985). 'Product-market diversification and market power'. *Academy of Management Journal*, **27**, 789–98.

Montgomery, C. and Singh, H. (1984). 'Diversification strategy and systematic risk.' *Strategic Management Journal*, 5(2), 181–91.

Palepu, K. (1985). 'Diversification strategy, profit performance and the entropy measures.' *Strategic Management Journal*, **6**, 239–55.

Peters, T.J. and Waterman, R.H. (1982). *In Search of Excellence*. New York: Harper and Row.

Prahalad, C.K. and Bettis, R. (1986). 'The dominant logic: a new linkage between diversity and performance.' *Strategic Management Journal*, 7, 485–502.

Rumelt, R. (1974). *Strategy, Structure and Economic Performance*. Cambridge, MA: Harvard University Press.

— (1982). 'Diversification strategy and profitability'. *Strategic Management Journal*, 3, 359–70.

Shepherd, W.G. (1975). *A Treatment of Market-Power*. New York: Columbia University Press.

Williamson, O.E. (1967). 'Hierarchical control and optimal firm size'. *Journal of Political Economy*, **75**, 123–38.

— 'Transactions cost economics: the governance of contractual relations.' *Journal of Law and Economics*, **22**, 232–61.

— (1981). 'The modern corporation: origins, evolution, attributes.' *Journal of Economic Literature*, **19**, 1537–68.

4
Managing strategic investment decisions

Paul Marsh, Patrick Barwise, Kathryn Thomas and Robin Wensley

Background

If we look at any organization today, most of what we see is the result of past strategic investment decisions (SIDs). The firm's assets, be they tangible (plant and equipment, retail outlets etc.) or intangible (know-how, people, brands, reputation etc.) can all be traced back to past investment decisions, years or even decades ago. We label these decisions 'strategic' in so far as – at least after the event – they have a significant impact on the firm as a whole and on its long-term performance.

Management teachers in most disciplines address SID-making, especially in finance, business policy, strategic marketing, decision science and operations management. Organizational behaviour and economics also have much to say about SIDs and their organizational and market context. Therefore research on SID-making is particularly relevant to an interdisciplinary forum like the British Academy of Management. Some of the interdisciplinary aspects of SIDs have been discussed elsewhere (Wensley et al., 1983; Barwise et al., 1987a).

We report here some initial results from a London Business School study which has tracked three SIDs 'in the making' over a period of more than two years. The SIDs, in three different large diversified UK firms, were monitored in real time using document analysis, interviews and direct observation of meetings. In analysing these data, we use four perspectives:

1 the evolution and development of the project through time, and the process of *learning and innovation*;
2 the forms of financial, strategic and operational *analysis* used;
3 the SID as a 'political' process, with *negotiation* between the project team and others inside and outside the firm;
4 the impact of *formal systems* and the *senior management hierarchy*.

In this paper we focus on the last of these perspectives. Large diversified firms are hierarchically structured, and final authority for major investments is vested in top management. This poses a dilemma since most strategic development in such firms comes from the divisions, rather than being top-down. (The main exception is major acquisitions.) This is because effective product-market strategies grow from a detailed understanding of the market and the firm's competitive capabilities, and most of this knowledge resides in the divisions (Barwise et al., 1987a). Thus most of the process and analysis of SIDs occurs at divisional level, especially among the small project team of managers directly involved in developing – and probably also later implementing – the project. In practice, perspectives 1–3 above focus mainly on this divisional project team. However, ultimate formal responsibility for SIDs lies with senior group (i.e. corporate) management and not the divisions. Top management thus faces the classic dilemma of decentralized firms, namely how to delegate effectively while still retaining responsibility and control. To achieve this, in the context of SID-making, management sets up formal structures and systems based (ultimately) on formal authority as well as intervening directly.

Our perspective in this paper is thus concerned with the direct and indirect means by which senior managers 'manage' SID-making. We specifically discuss the role of formal planning, capital budgeting, top management's direct role as 'players', and their wider role in setting the organizational context. Finally, we outline the key research questions which our paper raises for the 1990s.

As background, we first review the previous research which our study aims to replicate and extend, and we then describe the study itself.

Research in finance and strategic planning

SIDs are so central to the firm's development that a great deal of what is said and written by business academics and consultants is relevant to SID-making. In particular, modern finance theory says how capital investment decisions should be made, assuming that the aim is to maximize the value of the firm to its shareholders. Similarly, strategic planning techniques aim to give guidelines for allocating resources – including capital – to different parts of a diversified firm. Unfortunately, both approaches have evolved in almost total isolation, and neither aims to reflect closely the actual process of SID-making (Barwise et al., 1987a).

Although financial economics is centrally concerned with real invest-ment decisions, it concentrates on analysis and valuation techniques and the criteria to use in project selection. To parody somewhat, SIDs are characterized as being a single act of top management deliberation.

Furthermore, the main focus is theoretical and normative. While finance can boast a wealth of empirical studies, these relate to the behaviour of firms in markets, and not to managers in firms. The handful of empirical studies on capital budgeting which have been conducted by financial economists consist of surveys into the formal criteria and techniques used (Klammer, 1972; Carsberg and Hope, 1976; Scapens et al., 1982; Pike, 1983; McIntyre and Coulthurst, 1985).

This bias is revealed in most finance textbooks and journals. For example, Copeland and Weston (1983), a respected and widely used post-graduate textbook with an empirical bias, devotes only eight out of some 32,000 lines to studies of capital budgeting. Out of nearly a thousand empirical studies which it cites, only two relate to real investment decisions. Copeland and Weston are quite clear about how they see the boundaries of their subject:

(The) first major problem facing managers when they make investment decisions is that they have to search out new opportunities in the market place or new technologies, and estimate expected cash flows from these projects. Unfortunately, the Theory of Finance cannot help them with this problem.

Similar criticisms can be levelled at much of the business strategy literature, particularly in the 1970s. Much writing in this area has come close to equating strategy and planning simply with resource allocation and product-market choices. This bias can be seen in many of the major strands in thinking, including those derived from observed market regularities (e.g. market share/return on investment (ROI) (Buzzell et al., 1975)), portfolio models (e.g. policy matrices and box diagrams (Hedley, 1977)) or industrial organization economics (such as strategic groups (Porter, 1980)).

In most of this work, the link between strategy and specific decisions to invest is unclear. It is assumed that investment projects can somehow be subordinated to prior definitions of strategy, and that this is primarily the domain of top management. In common with financial economics, normative prescriptions predominate, with little detailed supporting empirical work.

Previous research on strategic investment decisions

The orthodox finance and the mainstream strategy literature has therefore shed only a very partial light on SID-making. However, a few researchers, principally from the general management and organizational behaviour fields, have specifically studied investment decision-making in practice. The most widely cited study is that by Bower (1970), who tracked four decisions in a large diversified US company. This research had itself followed on from a number of previous Harvard studies of SID-making (Berg, 1963; Sihler, 1964; Aharoni, 1966; Ackerman, 1968). The best-known UK study is that by King (1975a,b), who tracked three decisions in two large firms, although this too had its UK antecedent in Williams and Scott (1965). Other studies include those by Carter (1971), Pettigrew (1973), Berry (1984) and Butler et al. (1987), and also the Granada Television 'Decision' films (1975). Outside the specific context of SID-making, we find a much larger number of empirical studies which have looked at decision-making processes in general. These include those of Mintzberg et al. (1976) in the USA, Hickson et al. (1986) in the UK and Allison (1969) in the public policy area.

These studies highlight the importance of process, stressing that decision-making is an incremental activity taking place over an extended period of time and involving many people at different organizational levels. These observations have given rise to a number of descriptive models (Bower, 1970; King, 1975a; Mintzberg et al., 1976) which typically view the process as a sequence of stages, beginning with idea generation and extending (generally with some iteration) through to final approval. This chronological sequence tends to map on to the organizational hierarchy, but, although top management retains the formal responsibility for final approval, it is generally argued that the real 'decisions' are effectively taken much earlier, further down in the organization, by a complex socio-politico-economic process.

King's (1975a) research highlights the crucial nature of these earlier stages of SID-making. Investment ideas have to be generated and identified. In many cases this involves overcoming managers' natural resistance, since projects can mean considerable work and personal risk for their proposers with little tangible reward. King found that opportunities were often not recognized until the need became pressing. Once triggered, the technical and economic characteristics of the project have to be chosen and defined. King found that typically only one or two alternatives are seriously considered, and the choice of a favoured option is inevitably based on limited information and restricted criteria. As Aharoni (1966) has pointed out, the process of project definition and information gathering leads to implicit but strong commitments:

In order to collect information, it is necessary to communicate with people, to make certain decisions, and often to give tacit promises. In this process commitments are accumulated until a situation is created which leads inevitably to investment.

By the time the 'evaluation' stage is reached, the conclusion tends to be that 'everything we have found confirms our original choice' (King, 1975a). The proposal is likely to be approved 'not simply if the evaluation favoured it, but unless the evaluation was very much against it' (Williams and Scott, 1965). By now, alliances will have changed as the proposal has progressed upwards and those who were previously evaluators will become proposers and allies, until by the time it reaches senior management it has become a sales document from a united front. Few projects are ever rejected at this stage, since to do so would be a serious vote of no confidence in the judgement of those closest to the problem (Berg, 1963; Sihler, 1964; King 1975a).

However, Bower (1970) argues that projects progress upwards towards funding only if a higher-level manager sponsors the project and gives 'impetus'. This is a political process, and whether such sponsorship is forthcoming depends on the track records and the personal stakes of the managers involved. Bower and others (Berg, 1963; Williams and Scott, 1965; Aharoni, 1966; Ackerman, 1968; Carter, 1971) have observed that managers involved in SIDs inevitably consider the personal benefits of being 'right' and the risks and costs of being 'wrong'. Their perceptions are strongly influenced by the formal organizational systems and procedures, including the way that managers and businesses are monitored, evaluated and rewarded. These systems may also either aggravate or ameliorate the conflicts of interest which can exist between group and divisions, for example in terms of attitudes towards growth and risk (Berg, 1963). Bower pointed out, however, that these formal systems are themselves subject to management control. He argued that top managers should manage the SID-making process, not by transmitting corporate standards downwards for ROI but instead by control of the organizational context.

Those who have looked in detail at the process of SID-making have thus reached three broad conclusions. First, it is a complex lengthy process, which can be characterized as a series of stages through time, in which the earlier activities and choices can be crucial. The traditional emphasis on the 'decision' or final-approval stage is therefore seen as misplaced (King 1975a; Pinches 1982). Second, the whole activity must be seen as part of a wider 'political' context, embracing potential differences of interest between groups and divisions and the personal stakes of managers. Estimates and forecasts cannot be isolated from the individuals and groups that provide them (Bower, 1970). Third, all stages of the process are interrelated and will to some extent be influenced by the structural context, including the formal organization, and the systems of information, control, performance measurement and rewards. For example, the post-auditing procedures, and the way managers are evaluated and rewarded, can markedly influence project initiation (Carter, 1971; King, 1975a), forecasts (Sihler, 1964) and implementation (Berg, 1963).

These studies thus paint a radically different picture from the orthodox finance and strategy literatures. To be fair, mainstream financial economics does not claim to be describing the forms of analysis and specific behaviour of individual managers and firms. However, from a managerial perspective, it can be criticized on grounds of usefulness and relevance. Somewhat provocatively, we might argue that orthodox finance is technically correct, but of limited practical relevance to SIDs, while much of the strategy literature from the 1970s is potentially useful except for the fundamental flaw that it is either empirically wrong or untested.

In strategy, such concerns have recently led to a number of more research-based studies such as those of Kanter (1984), Pettigrew (1985) and Mintzberg (1987). Although these studies have a wider focus than just resource allocation, specific investment decisions have inevitably featured. These studies provide a more compatible context in which to place the earlier studies on SID-making. Indeed, both sets of studies present a picture which is more consistent with the 'emergent' rather than the 'deliberate' concept of strategy development (Mintzberg and Waters, 1985; Mintzberg, 1987), at least in the context of organic growth of diversified companies.

However, the previous empirical studies of SID-making also have limitations. They have been few in number, they relate mainly to US firms and many were conducted 20 years or more ago. Furthermore, while they have much descriptive validity, they have more to say about process than analysis, and they play down the economic perspective. Yet all SIDs involve analysis and will at some stage be formulated and discussed in financial language; one ultimate aim of SIDs is to add value to the enterprise. It is hard to believe a priori that the decision outcome will be independent of the nature and form of the economic analysis. Yet very few studies have focused on both process and analysis in enough detail to link the financial, strategic and organizational perspectives on SID-making. Our own research is an attempt to start redressing this imbalance.

The SID research project

Our research explores the analysis and process of SID-making in large diversified UK companies. Since our interests embrace both analysis and process, we are concerned not only with how managers structure SIDs (in terms of options, assumptions and criteria), but also with the types of communication, negotiation and debate that take place and the ways in which an emergent project changes and develops over time. We are also interested in the impact of formal systems and structure, and the general influence of organizational context.

Give this wide range of issues, we clearly needed to track individual decisions 'in the making' and in detail. We therefore adopted a real-time clinical case-based methodology in the tradition of Bower (1970) and King (1975a). Because resources were limited – the main resource was one field researcher working somewhat less than half-time over three years – we estimated that three research sites were the maximum feasible.

Our sites were chosen from non-competing industries and to represent varied settings. We needed not only willing host organizations but also a suitable SID to track within each. This raised the question of exactly what we meant by 'strategic'. While *ex post* we can define a strategic decision as one with long-term consequences for the firm (Barwise et al., 1987a), it is hard to tell what will be strategic *ex ante*. In research terms we therefore simply sought projects which the managers concerned felt were of strategic importance. The projects typically suggested were large capital investments (relative to the company's 'norm'). We wanted projects which originated in one of the divisions, but which would still need board approval. We also wanted projects which were at an early stage, with many options and uncertainties (including market uncertainty) still to be resolved, and where the decision was still very much open. We stressed to the companies that our research was observational, descriptive and exploratory, and that we would not be evaluating nor offering advice.

We approached 11 different companies and eventually selected three SIDs to track (Barwise et al., 1986). The first involved backward integration via investment in manufacturing capacity by a producer of industrial consumables. The second was an investment in mechanical handling and packaging equipment by a capital-goods manufacturer–service group to implement a new product concept. The third involved the restructuring of the distribution network for a large manufacturer of fast-moving consumer goods.

Data

Once on site, we aimed to carry out as much direct observation as possible since this was our richest source of data. However, with only one part-time field researcher covering three partly parallel cases, the coverage had to be selective, aiming to observe the key meetings and events for each project. An obvious shortcoming was that this caused us to miss most of the informal processes, telephone calls, debates and negotiations between meetings. We therefore supplemented our monitoring of meetings by keeping up to date with the paper trail, and through contacting/interviewing key players to elicit information about recent informal contacts and events.

In principle, there was some danger of influencing the process we were observing. Here, we relied on two factors. First the participants were already highly involved, so that there was little danger of making them think about decisions which would otherwise be unconsidered. Second we relied on the judgement, sensitivity and skill of the field researcher. Thus, while the decision was still in progress, interviews were open-ended, non-directive and designed simply to elicit descriptions and clarifications about the latest state of play. Our experience suggested that participants soon became accustomed to the presence of the researcher.

The three projects we monitored were all eventually approved and implemented. After the formal approval point, we conducted more detailed interpretative interviews tailored to each key player. Here, we asked more searching and personal questions, checking out any inconsistencies or puzzles, probing the logic, suggesting various counter-arguments, testing alternative explanations and exploring each player's motivation. This process was clearly more obtrusive, which is why it took place only *after* the formal approval stage.

By the end of our research we had amassed an average of some 2000 pages of notes, documents, reports and minutes. Since nearly all meetings and interviews were audiotaped, we had also accumulated 40–70 hours of tape per project, plus the corresponding transcripts. In addition, we had collected background information on each company's systems for planning, capital budgeting, financial reporting and perform-ance appraisal.

Analysis and interpretation

The raw data were dispersed, sequential rather than simultaneous, unstructured and extremely bulky. Their analysis and interpretation therefore presented a formidable challenge. Initially, we planned to carry out data analysis, interpretation and validation in parallel with data collection. However, given the time demands and limited resources, this proved too difficult. The bulk of our analysis was therefore postponed until after the fieldwork.

We had, however, invested substantial effort prior to the fieldwork in spelling out the issues of interest (Barwise et al., 1986). In some cases we conjectured on what we might or might not find, but essentially we tried to adopt a neutral stance. As part of this, we avoided using any single over-arching analytical framework. Indeed, we concluded that, to make sense of the complex decision processes without excessive distortion and oversimplification, we would need multiple perspectives. An obvious exemplar here is Allison's (1969) multiperspective description of the Cuban missile crisis. Another is Morgan's (1986) use of eight metaphors to discuss organizations.

Although we experimented with a number of ways of analysing and interpreting our data (Barwise et al., 1986, 1987b), in the end we found no satisfactory alternative to the laborious process of careful reading, annotation and interpretation, subsequent debate and then returning to the data to check suggested interpretations. We proceeded by the fieldworker taking the lead role on all three cases, with the other team members acting more as 'consultants', mainly specializing on one case each. This teamwork ensured that at least two of the four researchers were familiar with the detailed source data on each case and were therefore in a position to challenge and question each other and reduce researcher bias. For the same reason, we retained the disaggregated data so that we (and, in principle, other researchers) could re-examine it to seek alternative explanations and interpretations.

The fieldworker, in conjunction with the relevant 'consultants', produced a detailed case write-up for each project, which chronicled the events from the beginning of the project until final approval. In addition, we developed four cross-case comparisons, using the four different perspectives outlined in the first section.

Formal systems and the hierarchy

This paper focuses on the fourth of these perspectives, namely the role of formal systems and the hierarchy. Like all large organizations, our host companies had clearly established formal systems for capital investment decisions, structured on hierarchical lines. All were divisionalized, with each division serving a different product market. All produced longer-term plans, both at group and divisional level. These plans contained objectives or strategy statements which had implications for the type of investments required and sought and for the overall level of investment. These longer-term plans (typically five years) contained estimates of future capital expenditure and listed any major projects envisaged. Planned projects also had to be included in the annual capital budget, but in none of the three companies did this confer authority to spend money. In all three companies spending approval had to be obtained for each project individually. This required a full analysis of the project, including its financial projections and likely profitability. Because of their size, projects needed group and main board, as well as divisional, approval.

The formal aspects of the process are helpful from a research perspective. As King (1975b) puts it:

The larger (and more diversified) the organisation and the more layered the hierarchy, the more formal will be the decision process; written rather than in the minds of men.

With a formal process, there is a clear paper trail, showing the proposals submitted at each stage, the minutes of committees and meetings, and a record of the point at which capital was officially committed. Our concern in this paper, however, is not simply to look at the formal written record; instead, it is to look at the totality of our data, and to try to assess what impact these formal systems and the hierarchy had on the particular SIDs we tracked.

Some previous writers in finance might be accused of implying that formal systems are the all-important factor in decision-making. At the other extreme, much of the empirical work on SID-making has come close to suggesting that formal systems are mere ritual, and that SID-making is a purely informal and political process. Our own data support neither of these polar views. Thus, while we find that formal systems and the hierarchy provide a very partial perspective on SID-making, we do not conclude that investment decision-making is a purely informal process or that the 'real decisions' are independent of the formal systems or that top management is simply a rubber stamp. Instead, our evidence suggests that systems, roles, procedures, structure and hierarchy do have an important influence on the decision-making process, although often in a subtle and indirect manner.

Our particular concern in the remainder of this paper is with how senior management actually 'manages' and controls the SID-making process both indirectly, through systems, structure and context, and directly, through their own roles as actors. In the next four sections we draw on our research findings to address four questions. First, did the investment decisions flow from a prior strategic plan and, if not, what was the role of planning and 'strategy'? Second, in what ways, if any, did the capital budgeting procedures adopted affect the ultimate decisions taken? Third, did senior management really 'make the decisions' and, if not, what direct role did they play as actors? Finally, in what ways did the formal organizational structure and the organizational context and climate impact on the decision-making process?

Formal planning

Which comes first, the strategy or the projects? Many writers assume that SIDs 'should flow from a sound strategic plan' (Rudden, 1982), or at least await a clear prior definition of objectives (Burton and Naylor, 1980; Wind and Robertson, 1983).

This is far from self-evident. As we have noted, SID-making is a long and complex process of learning and exploration, involving extensive concern with operational details. These details will determine how appropriate and implementable the strategy is – how much it builds and exploits real competitive advantage, rather than being a mere collection of slogans. In the extreme case 'strategy' can be seen as an *outcome* of particular SIDs and their implementation. Pascale (1982) has argued that Japanese firms evolve through this kind of 'strategic accommodation' and, indeed, that 'the Japanese don't use the phrase corporate strategy'.

An empirical question, then, is the extent to which explicit strategic planning preceded the three SIDs we monitored: how much was there 'deliberate' as opposed to 'emergent' strategy (Mintzberg and Waters, 1985; Mintzberg, 1987).

Group planning

We look first at the role of group, rather than divisional, planning. Group planners played no direct role in the identification and definition of the three projects. As one group planner put it:

Because of the way that things are delegated, it is very much in the division's court to come up with a project that meets our criteria. Now that may seem to be not very much contribution from the centre, but the centre has established a framework. The ideas, the entrepreneurial ideas – because of the fact that we are based so widely – must come up from the division.

Interestingly, group planning also played a minimal role in project evaluation. In one company, whenever the division put the project up for group approval/information, the project went to a policy committee of main board directors, who formed their own judgements without recourse to group planning. In a second case, projects were sent to group finance, prior to board submission, and, again, group planning played no role. In the third case, group planning became involved quite late on. The planner tried to feed in evaluative issues, but with limited success, and ultimately took on the role of clarifier and analytical assistant, helping the division prepare its case for the board.

Group planning therefore provided no inputs to the projects in two cases, and only a limited supporting contribution in the third. It may nevertheless have had an indirect influence, by helping specify and predefine the kinds of projects which came up, through encouraging the submission of projects consistent with group strategy. As a main board director in one company put it:

It's increasingly rare that preliminary project suggestions get a negative response [from group] because everybody now is well tuned-in to the strategy and nobody wants to put up things with a view to getting them knocked on the head. People put up things that they think are likely to be getting the nod.

One major difficulty in evaluating the influence of 'group strategy' lies in defining what is meant by this term in the context of large diversified firms. The three divisions in which the projects arose were themselves substantial potentially stand-alone companies. Corporate plans were developed at divisional level, in one case by divisional corporate planners (in conjunction with the divisional chief executive officer (CEO)), and in the other two, by the divisional CEOs. As one division put it:

Group corporate planning has no direct expertise or contribution to make. We are charged with developing the group's strategy in this business area.

In reality, therefore, group planning in all three companies had only a limited role to play in setting divisional strategy and was more concerned with *administering* planning than with developing plans. In one company the functions were formally 'to design and administer the planning system (between group and divisions), to provide some information input (especially environmental), to draft papers for the Chairman, to assist on project planning teams, and to provide advice on planning methods and techniques'. This staff orientation was also apparent in the other two organizations.

To the extent that 'group strategy' did impose guidelines for investment, in all three organizations these were largely articulated in 'macrolevel' terms, such as which countries/areas to invest/expand in, and broad-brush judgements about potential growth industries and businesses with a general eye towards acquisitions. Portfolio and matrix-planning type thinking, emphasizing the distinction between growth areas and cash generators, was in evidence in two of the companies. While the efficacy of such approaches is itself in some doubt (Barwise et al., 1987a), we in fact found only very tenuous links between such 'group strategies' and the three divisional projects we monitored.

In one case, the investment took place in a region identified some years earlier as a promising prospect by group, but this was largely coincidence. Nevertheless, perhaps group views had discouraged other projects in locations deemed to be undesirable. In one of the other companies the investment seemed largely inconsistent with group strategy. The project involved investing in two geographical regions, spanning two businesses. At a macrolevel, the initial group view of both locations and both businesses was negative. One of the businesses was seen as a poor prospect for investment because of lack of growth potential, while the other was seen as an area to be avoided because of its industrial relations history. Arguments could be made, however, that the project addressed a growth segment within the declining sector, and that the company had a competitive advantage in managing industrial relations, which would anyway act as a deterrent to competitive entry. The project was eventually undertaken and felt to represent a sensible investment.

The dominant planning concern at group level appeared, however, to be finance. The prime concern was with the fit between the division's financial projections and group's financial objectives/constraints. While we have evidence that the general financial climate can influence divisional investment (see below), these objectives were largely set by group finance, the CEO and the main board. Group planning's role was mainly to act as a conduit for these concerns and to aggregate divisional plans in order to compare the overall picture against group financial objectives.

Divisional strategic planning

These observations raise questions about the role of group planning, its heavy emphasis on finance and whether it can be anything but predominantly administrative. However, if we wish to assess whether formal planning helped shape the projects we monitored, we must look at *divisional* planning, since this is where most strategic planning actually took place. Yet, even with our wealth of detailed information, this question proved hard to answer, as the following example illustrates.

The division in question had historically pursued a niche strategy in high-margin, lower-volume speciality products. However, for some years, the formal annual 10-year review had been exploring ways of moving upstream through vertical integration, making the division the lowest-cost producer and allowing them to move into lower-value-added more commodity-like products. As a strategic mission, this thinking was mainly shared between the CEO and the divisional corporate planner, but the division's other senior managers were aware of the exploratory exercise. Various options were contemplated, and amongst many other possibilities the corporate planner identified the project which we eventually monitored. This was considered briefly, but was not pursued. Having failed to find a feasible route into the 'low cost strategy', the most recent strategy review had moved away from this idea and was focusing on quite different opportunities.

The project was then reintroduced to the division (quite coincidentally by a third party), was evaluated and subsequently went ahead. When the SID was later announced, the *Financial Times* described it as a 'marked change of strategy'. Compared with prior actions and with the conclusions of the most recent internal strategy review, the *Financial Times* was correct. However, both the divisional CEO and the corporate planner argued that this was not a change in terms of the ideal intended strategy as they had debated it. While the other senior divisional managers supported the project, there were differences of understanding in the strategy it represented (e.g. securing raw material supplies versus low-cost production through vertical integration). Subsequently, the company has pursued a follow-up investment, consolidating its new direction. Arguably, this, and the 'new' strategy generally, would not have been possible without the original project, and the latter would never have been recognized if it had not been for the discipline of the strategy reviews.

Cynics might argue that, since the strategy reviews were so wide ranging, almost any subsequent project could be related back to some prior option discussed. On this view, the project was simply a chance 'arrival' and history was later rewritten to conform to the new sense of direction. Seen this way, the role of strategic planning would be more that of scribe than priest. These dual interpretations were summed up well by the divisional director in charge of the project team:

It's quite interesting to understand how these strategic things come about . . . It's an opportunity that can't be planned. Of course there is a strategy at the back of it but we weren't looking for it. At the divisional board we discussed whether we should or shouldn't do it. [The third party's] role in this has been key. If they hadn't talked, we might not be here today . . . In a way, one could be forgiven for thinking that this was an apple that fell off a tree and that [we] suddenly produced a strategy that explained why we ought to catch it and not let it fall. A sort of instant strategy. In fact, it wasn't really like that.

The difficulty of judging whether strategies preceded projects or vice versa is equally apparent in the other two cases. In one, divisional strategic planning was the responsibility of the divisional managing director (MD). There was no divisional planning staff, and much of the division's strategy resided in the MD's mind rather than on paper. Since the divisional MD was also the project sponsor who headed the project team, it is almost impossible to determine whether the strategy came before the project or vice versa. It is clear, however, that the project did not flow out of any *formal* process of planning.

In the third case, the strategic plan for the division specified the desirability of certain types of cost reduction activities and even laid down relevant targets. However, this implied that the division recognized that projects could be introduced which would reduce costs in this way in order to meet these targets. While the precise shape of these projects would not have been clear, their general nature would have been. Thus although the project we monitored was entirely consistent with, and apparently flowed from, the division's strategic plan, it would be equally true to say that the strategic plan was itself shaped by the foreshadowed existence of the project.

Capital budgeting systems

Formal capital budgeting systems specify the procedures and criteria for (i) including projects in the annual capital budget and (ii) their subsequent analysis, presentation and approval. Numerous surveys provide information on corporate practices in this area (Klammer, 1972; Rockley, 1973; Carsberg and Hope, 1976; Scapens et al., 1982; Pike, 1983; McIntyre and Coulthurst, 1985; Kennedy and Sugden, 1986), although their main focus is on the selection criteria specified. They give the impression that formal procedures and criteria are the most important aspects of investment decision-making.

The surveys reach two broad conclusions. First, companies have become more systematic over time in their approach to capital budgeting. For example, most large firms now have formal, written investment procedures and manuals (Pike, 1983). Second, companies have also become more sophisticated, with most large firms now using the theoretically preferred Discounted Cash Flow (DCF) approach (Klammer, 1972; Klammer and Walker, 1984; Pike, 1983). Both findings are generally heralded as 'improvements'. The surveys do, however, sound a few cautionary notes. First, in addition to DCF, many companies also use other criteria, such as payback and accounting rate of return (return on investment (ROI)). Second, several surveys which have asked more detailed questions have noted errors in the way in which DCF is applied. Amongst UK companies, the most notable errors were in the treatment of tax (Rockley, 1973) and inflation (Carsberg and Hope, 1976). The more recent study by Pike (1983), however, suggests that there are now fewer errors in the use of DCF.

Our three companies all conformed to the large company stereotype described in these surveys. All had formal capital budgeting procedures and manuals, all operated annual, as well as longer, look-ahead capital budgets and individual projects of any size required formal approval at both divisional and group level. The approval process involved a formal presentation of a written capital appropriation request describing the rationale for the project and including a full financial analysis, incorporating cash flow forecasts plus summary measures of profitability. The main criterion of project profitability in all three companies was the DCF rate of return, although two companies also computed Net Present Value (NPV), two used payback and one used ROI.

The reality behind the formal systems

One of the benefits of detailed clinical case research is that it allows us to dig more deeply into the reality behind the formal systems and to see how the procedures are actually 'used'. Here we found an altogether different picture.

First, although all three firms had formal capital expenditure procedure manuals, these proved quite hard to locate! One company was embarrassed to give us a copy since it was so out of date. In a second company, we were told:

This kind of project [a partial acquisition of a start-up situation] probably wouldn't go through the capital appraisal system. You could call our approach cavalier, undisciplined or informal, depending on how you saw it, I suppose.

In the third company, the situation was summarized by the following interchange:

Group finance director I can give you a copy of our capital expenditure control manual.
Interviewer Did you have any hand in putting it together?
Group finance director Absolutely not. I think they're extremely boring. I have no idea of my way around it.
Interviewer Obviously a live document.

Second, although the formal systems stressed that inclusion of projects in the annual capital budget implied no authority to spend money, managers nevertheless saw this as an important 'foot in the door'. As one project team member commented:

We then were doing the budget for the new financial year . . . We put into that, agreed a [given] sum. To get the money earmarked – we'd still got to justify it, but the money was budgeted.

Similarly, the group finance director of another company commented:

So (the project) crept into . . . the budget and thus has a reasonable chance that it will carry on being in the budget, but that doesn't mean anything for that size of project. The budget is no indication of approval at all . . . er, although creeping commitments. All the same if it comes up and doesn't show a good enough return . . . it won't get approved.

Third, although all three SIDs formally required two levels of authorization, the project teams did not always perceive it that way. In one company, where group approval was seen as what 'really mattered', the presentation to the divisional board was described as 'a con job'. Conversely, in another company, where the group CEO sat on the divisional board, the division referred to group's approval as 'rubber stamping'.

Fourth, although all three companies 'used DCF', we noted many 'errors' in the way in which it was applied. We document these, not as criticisms of the companies involved, for we are not suggesting they led to wrong decisions, but to illustrate how the formal financial proposal can give a distorted view of the project. For example, one company used their average tax rate rather than their (much higher) marginal rate. Two companies handled inflation incorrectly in the context of tax. In one company initial one-off costs (e.g. redundancies) were regarded as somehow not part of the project. Equally, in all three projects the terminal values of both fixed assets and working capital were ignored, and this was aggravated by the arbitrary choice of project lives. In one company the layout of the appraisal form led them to evaluate the project over 10 years. No terminal value was included for a major asset with a very long physical life and which for accounting purposes was depreciated over 40 years. Neither the asset's nor the project's economic life was ever discussed. In another company a major plant was evaluated over 15 years, when its economic life was probably some 25 years. Finally, in one project, which involved a partial acquisition, there was a thorough DCF analysis of asset values, but the target company's extensive debts were not subjected to the same valuation process, instead being implicitly taken at book value.

The cut-off or discount rates also often seemed arbitrary. As one team member put it when discussing the Internal Rate of Return (IRR):

But the IRR becomes – yes, we've got an IRR – wow, we're over whichever the magic number is at that point in time.

Views also differed greatly about what was acceptable. In one company, a real IRR of 22 per cent was seen as inadequate, while in another case the project team was uneasy about showing an IRR as high as 22 per cent real as 'they'll never believe it's that good'. In the former company, there was anyway a lack of clarity between real and nominal terms. Cash flows were not inflated, but discount rates were thought of in nominal terms. On several occasions we noted confusion between IRR and ROI. In one project the company applied its normal thinking in terms of cut-off criteria for return on assets to a return-on-equity calculation when acquiring shares in a highly geared start-up situation.

Incremental to what?

Perhaps even more fundamentally, the input to a DCF analysis should be net *incremental* cash flows, where 'incremental' means the difference between the firm's cash flows with and without the project. In a competitive market the 'without' case is unlikely to be a continuation of the *status quo*, and, typically, there is no single or simple 'base' case 'without' the project, just as there is no single or simple 'with' case (Barwise et al., 1987a).

This said, we found that very little management effort went into evaluating the 'without' cases. Generally, projects were evaluated against the *status quo*. Sometimes, this meant that benefits were overstated, for example, when it was assumed that cost savings would lead to profit increases despite a continuing trend of competitive pressures on margins and although some of the savings might have been achieved through improved operating efficiency without the investment. In other cases benefits were understated because, without the project, business prospects looked worse than under the *status quo*. Such factors were generally recognized and were sometimes referred to as part of the 'strategic' rationale for the project. But they did not find their way into the financial analysis as incremental cash flows.

The lack of exploration of 'without' cases may have arisen partly because the formal financial procedures seemed geared to treating each project as a stand-alone investment with cash flows independent of the rest of the business. However, it may also reflect the fact that managers are likely to have a strong emotional preference for the 'with' option, since generally it will involve growth, or at least defence, of their business. Certainly, when one project team was asked, as part of their brief, to look at the extreme 'without' case option of ceasing internal operations, this alternative was not even explored.

Forecasting cash flows

Quite apart from these problems, there is the whole issue of cash flow forecasts. Forecasting is obviously difficult, and forecasts are hostages to fortune. Perhaps for this reason, we found that the extent of forecasting was quite limited, certainly in two of our companies. For example, no overall market forecasts were developed, and forecasts were frequently partial (for example, assuming current volume, what size facility do we need?). Typically, costs and benefits which were hard to quantify were excluded from the financial analysis. This was partly because of the extreme difficulty of turning intangible and strategic benefits into projected cash flows, and partly through wishing to include enough benefit to gain acceptance without promising more than necessary. The preference seemed to be to justify each project on the basis of enough quantifiable return to gain acceptance: 'and then there's cream afterwards', in the words of one project team member.

Forecasting also has a political dimension, and in all three projects the managers involved had a strong emotional bias towards going ahead with the project. This is not to suggest that they were making consciously biased forecasts, but those involved were conscious of the temptation. As one project team member commented:

> You have to be quite careful. I found it quite insidious, the ability to change the financial model to give you the answers you wanted. If you weren't careful, you started to say 'Well, of course, if we got this price in three years' time, that part would all look different'. Then you go to the economist and say 'Do you think we could get that?' and he says, 'We might, you know.' In the end you were almost saying 'Well, that's the answer we want, now make up the question', which isn't to say that that's the way it came out in the end, but there was a danger of it.

Project proposers also knew that it would be hard for those above them to check the detailed forecasts. There were occasional comments like 'Who's going to twig that up there?' in one case, and 'Nobody's going to be able to check out the figures' in another.

When 'forecasts' for the project as a whole were finally required as input to the financial analysis, they were not seen as complete best-guess estimates but as oversimplified and incomplete projections, giving a good enough financial return to justify the project. As one project team member reflected:

> We went through all sorts of processes which, at the end of the day, were to some extent in order to justify the decision it was a good thing. They always are. Because, the problem about an IRR is that it demands that you use one set of cash flows only . . . I don't actually believe any of the numbers, certainly not more than five years out and yet there is a sort of culture which says you must do them because that is the way it's done. It's not. I think you tend to make the IRRs come out right if you think that all the other things about the investment are right. The IRR then becomes the peg on which everything else is hung, but it's actually all the wrong way round.

The role of formal capital budgeting

These observations are based on only three cases, but they do throw light on the survey findings reported above on firms' formal budgeting systems and selection criteria. All three would have shown up in such a survey as 'using' DCF techniques, and all three would have been at the most sophisticated end of the spectrum. Yet, as we have seen, there were widespread differences between the formal systems and reality. Our observations raise fundamental questions about what 'using DCF' really means and about what surveys can really tell us. They also rechallenge the emphasis in the finance literature. Many of the 'distortions' that we observed could, in principle, lead to far more serious errors in project acceptance decisions than the much more frequently cited issue of whether companies use NPV, DCF, ROI or payback (Marsh and Brealey, 1974).

While we are arguing that the formal proposal can paint a very distorted picture of the project, we are certainly not suggesting that the companies concerned made the wrong decisions. All three projects appeared to us worthwhile on financial grounds, although we were obviously unable to second-guess detailed operating assumptions, nor could we judge whether even better options might have been available. Nor, however, are we implying that the methods of financial appraisal used have no effect whatsoever on which investments are made. This would be a gross exaggeration, but it contains more than a nugget of truth.

Certainly, the formal capital budgeting systems can be very time-consuming:

In the old days . . . we used to write the capital application, a page of justification, and that was it, and it all went through. That's now gone – you write a Bible of stuff.

If people basically propose projects they believe in, and the board usually says yes based as much on the proposers' track record as on the evaluators' analysis, then are the formal systems just an expensive ritual?

Our observations suggest that, while the formal systems are ritualistic, they are nevertheless necessary. In all three companies they forced the players to be more explicit about their key assumptions, both to themselves and in order to justify them to others. In at least two of our companies the financial analysis was carried out only in response to the formal systems – it was to some extent 'added on' afterwards. Yet it nevertheless helped, to some extent, to guide the decision and reveal new concerns. Again, in so far as alternative options were explored, this was largely in anticipation of questions at the formal approval stage.

The formal systems, through annual budget rounds and via the preset dates of the various committee and board meetings, also helped to set deadlines and thereby force the project pace. They facilitated the movement of information up, down and sideways within the organization, generating awareness of and commitment to the project. At the same time, they provided a scheduled set of occasions for face-to-face communication across multiple levels of the hierarchy. This gave a chance for the specific project and the strategic assumptions on which each business was being conducted to be debated. Finally, the procedures had a marked influence on later implementation. They forced the project team to think through and agree a plan, build their personal commitment to it and then make a formal public commitment to its success.

Senior management's direct role

In all three SIDs, the final decision rested with senior group management. In a formal sense, their job was to appraise and decide on the division's proposal. These proposals summarized the projects' strategic and financial rationales. An implicit assumption of the formal systems in all three companies was therefore that this kind of data would give the decision-makers (assumed to be top management) a rational basis for decisions between alternatives and about which projects to fund.

Constraints on SID-making at the top

There is a large gap here, however, between the form and the substance. Our findings, in line with those of previous researchers (Bower, 1970; King, 1975a), indicate that top management face a number of serious problems. First there is the span of knowledge required. Our three companies were large and diversified. They ranged in size from over 10,000 to over 100,000 employees, were each split into at least six operating divisions and had extensive overseas activities. Group management faced formidable problems in understanding the detail of this large variety of products and services, markets, businesses, managers and countries. In the three projects we monitored, only one of the key 'decision-makers' at group level had any direct operating experience of the business involved.

Second, this information asymmetry between group and division is accentuated by the amount of time that top management can devote to even a large SID. As the group deputy chairman of one company who sat on the key capital authorizations committee explained:

This project was sizeable . . . there aren't too many this size that we look at . . . it kept on coming back and being referred to at board meetings. So it must have amounted to at least a whole day of my time.

In contrast, the divisional board member in charge of the project estimated that he spent eight months (full time equivalent) on the project prior to approval. His project team members spent a further two man-years. The contrast with the time spent by group is dramatic. Similar comparisons can be made in terms of the volume of paperwork. In another company we accumulated over 200 documents, totalling more than 2000 pages, about the project. This was reduced to a 60-page document for group finance and the CEO. Finally this was boiled down to a two-page summary for the group board.

Third, the notion that top management 'weighs' projects and selects between alternatives depends on having alternatives to weigh (Schon, 1967). In practice, for all three projects, the proposals put to both division and group included just one option. In each case variants, and sometimes quite different options, had been considered by the project teams. Top management was thus shown only one real alternative. We saw strong evidence of 'selling' behaviour, born of a desire to put a strong case *for* the project. The word selling was often used explicitly, e.g.

You've fought it out, you've decided that's what you want to do, now you've got to sell it. You've got to justify it.

Given how hard it is to identify and evaluate non-proposed options, senior management can make only a go/no-go decision. But in any event, their ability to 'weigh' the project is limited. 'Weighing' requires specialist scales (knowledge and data), which are mainly available at divisional level. Thus while the project may have been weighed 'inaccurately' (perhaps deliberately), top management's own scales can detect only grossly overweight or underweight projects. But the latter would have been screened out earlier and would never reach top management. Therefore, in reality, top management may not even face a go/no-go decision. Instead, the choice may be between saying yes, or else 'we do not trust you to manage' (King, 1975a).

In all three companies it was regarded as rare for a project to be turned down by group. Divisional managers sometimes referred to board approval as 'rubber stamping'. In one case the division placed a key order for capital equipment prior to obtaining group approval for the project. In another, divisional management nearly applied for local government planning approval prior to seeking group's go-ahead. All this was seen as justifiable in the context of decentralized management – a philosophy embraced by all three companies. Even if senior group management did have the time and knowledge needed to 'second-guess', this would have been at some variance with decentralization. Second-guessing is not easy, and as researchers trying to make sense of our observations we empathized with top management's position.

All this might suggest that the role of top management was fairly trivial in these particular decisions. Indeed, previous researchers suggest that top management's main role should be indirect. Thus, King (1975a) argues that if top management wishes to improve investment decisions, it should develop a process of decision-making which allows it merely to rubber stamp most proposals. Similarly, Bower (1970) claims that top management can best manage the resource allocation process not directly, by trying to take the decision itself, but indirectly, by manipulating 'structural context' including the formal organization and the systems of information, control, performance measurement and rewards. However, our research suggests that top management often has a more critical and key role to play in SID-making, albeit in a more complex manner than the simple concept of ultimate authority at a single and identifiable decision point. Furthermore, this role includes direct intervention as well as indirect context-setting.

Not just a ritual

Even at the level of ultimate authority and the go/no-go decision, we should not dismiss the formal hierarchical model too readily. Group senior management saw its role very much as a 'resource allocator' on behalf of shareholders. As one main board director put it:

We do have the advantage of not being emotionally involved. But it isn't necessarily seen as that, it's seen as just a responsibility for resource allocation . . . It's just a question of exercising one's responsibility towards the shareholders. Is this a good deal for the shareholders or isn't it? Could it be improved? What other choices have we got?

Resource allocation was not seen as just a formal responsibility to be achieved through context-setting and delegation, but as a direct responsibility which might require direct intervention. Such intervention was seen as consistent with decentralization rather than as interference.

The most extreme case of direct intervention we encountered was when one of the three projects was actually turned down by the main board, at the behest of the group CEO. The CEO felt that, despite the project's high DCF rate of return, too few options had been considered and that the project included some capital costs which could be avoided. As the divisional MD put it, 'when the project got to the group CEO, he blew it all over the walls'. The project was referred back for a complete rethink, and subsequently a quite different and much cheaper alternative was proposed, giving most of the savings promised by the original proposal. Interestingly, the group CEO's intervention was not seen simply as 'second-guessing'; it was also viewed as a 'deliberate learning point' for those involved.

Similarly, in the other two companies, group was not regarded as a 'pushover'. Even in the division which jumped the gun with the order of equipment, there was a respect for the authority of group and the gun-jumping was recognized as a gamble. In the third company, the idea of group taking a cold rational look at the project and submitting it to analytical scrutiny was given considerable emphasis. No one at divisional level saw group as a mere formality. On more than one occasion, group's attitude was regarded as 'touch and go'. At one critical point, the divisional CEO had to go and argue the case with group. As one project team member described it:

The group CEO was on the point of scrapping the whole thing – had enough after one of the many delays . . . Tuesday was the group board meeting, and the CEO was going to bonk it – had enough. And the divisional MD went up especially and persuaded him not to do it. That I would regard in the whole exercise as the single most crucial point. The MD persuaded the CEO not to kick it in. Had he not gone and done that, it would have been gone.

Thus, although projects were rarely turned down by group, the threat of rejection was taken very seriously. Indeed, rejections were probably rare *because* group was taken seriously and because the divisions had a fairly clear idea of what would prove acceptable. Furthermore, quite apart from senior management's formal final decision-taking role, we noted a number of ways in which they intervened directly in the three projects prior to this point.

Direct intervention

In none of the cases we observed did senior management merely wait for the final presentation upon which they could make their decision. They intervened directly in various ways to influence the project as it evolved. These interventions included 'wearing two hats', questioning assumptions, testing for commitment, setting limits and deadlines, imposing project-specific criteria, appointing key personnel and protecting the interests of the group and other divisions.

Wearing two hats

In all three cases the problems of information asymmetry between group and division were reduced by having the same people wearing both a group and a divisional 'hat', e.g.

We have at least one main board director on each divisional board. And that enables us to get the information flow better because it's carried by people as well as paper. And that as far as we're concerned is a very, very important element of making sure we get decent communication.

In this company the CEO of the division in which the project originated sat on the group main board. At the same time, one of the key decision-makers at group level had previously sat on the board of the division for some years. Similar arrangements occurred in one of the other two cases. Dual-level hats were again common one level down the hierarchy. In one case the head of the project team was also the divisional CEO, and in the other two cases the project teams were headed by managers with their own operating-level responsibilities who also sat on the divisional board.

The wearing of dual-level hats seems closely related to Bower's (1970) concept of the integrating manager. Bower argued that projects originating within business units will move towards funding only if they gain 'impetus' from the decision of a higher-level ('integrating') manager to sponsor the project and act as its advocate to group. As one member of a project team described it:

He [the divisional MD] was the guy that we're going to have to convince that we're right . . . so we had to get him on board – educate him, brief him and point him in the right direction. And we were very nervous about that.

This divisional MD was a clear example of Bower's integrating manager. Similar integrating behaviour was observed in the other two companies, although here there was considerable overlap between the project and divisional levels of management anyway. This was because in both cases the projects either originated from or were headed by the divisional CEO, who in one case sat on the group board and thus again wore two hats.

Questioning assumptions

The group's role in questioning and policing project assumptions varied considerably. In one company, group maintained a questioning stance throughout. Besides informal discussions, we tracked 11 occasions when the project was formally discussed by senior group managers. A senior group board member described this process as follows:

We'd expect division to do most of the analysis, and that would be tested by interrogation and discussion . . . .In so far as the analysis may then not answer the questions group has, it will get referred back, and there's quite a lot of to-ing and fro-ing and referring back and so on, in an attempt properly to satisfy the questions being raised. So it really was fairly exacting and it took a long time until everything was right . . . And the closer the thing was to the margin of viability, the more precisely the questions had to be answered.

In the second company, where the project was initially rejected by group, project assumptions were effectively debated only within the project team, prior to the project reaching the group board. On its way up through the organization, questions had been raised at a presentation to the divisional MD and board, but the project had passed on unchanged to group finance who suggested only minor cosmetic alterations. However, when it reached the group board, the CEO referred it back for a complete rethink. Apart from one site visit, the CEO then subsequently took no further part in the project debate (although he was kept informally briefed) until the project came back to the group board in a quite different form, when it was then approved. However, his intervention made the divisional MD take a closer interest in the project and question its various assumptions. It also forced the project team to spend considerable time ensuring that they could justify their new position. Finally, although the CEO approved the revised project, he did request a post-audit mechanism to ensure that a key assumption was actually met in practice.

In the third company, group appeared to remain even more aloof from the project debate. Although the group CEO was chairman of the divisional board, he did not seem to adopt a very probing pro-active role. Although on one occasion he asked for a more detailed breakdown of figures, the general approach was to question various assumptions but then to accept the replies without following through with penetrating supplementaries. Similarly, the group finance director did not become involved except to ask questions when the formal systems brought the project to his notice.

A danger here is that questions raised only in the context of the formal systems and presentations can be pure ritual. By then, the project team's commitment has hardened and it may be difficult to follow questions through without challenging their credibility and legitimacy. Yet the right challenge at the right time might improve the project. As a project team member in the first company referred to above put it:

I would say we had as difficult a negotiation internally as we did externally. That's not a bad thing in the interests of better decision-making. You need challenge of that sort, otherwise you are far too comfortable as a result, and that could lead you I would guess down some wrong alleys.

Equally, questioning from group may help ensure 'external objectivity'. As one divisional manager summed it up:

I think to some extent [group] played the role of the cold objectivity if you like. None of them were from this industry . . . so no reason why they should get carried away with an investment of this kind, and therefore, I think they do play a role which helps to ensure that someone's personal wild enthusiasm gets looked at fairly coldly . . . They are fairly analytical and objective people.

However, too much questioning can lead to another very time-consuming ritual, wherein the project team spends much effort anticipating the thrust of the group's (or division's) interrogation and preparing contingency arguments to justify their position. This happened in two of the project teams. Similarly, the more group asks, paradoxically the more they may be told only what they have asked for and given only replies which are consistent with responses to prior questions. This is exemplified in the following conversation between project team members:

Team member 1:   Do we need to bring (those factors) into it. . . . You've never mentioned them up till now?

Team member 2:   And it wasn't in the minute from group.

Team member 3:   You're quite right. We are going to complicate life because we want to address specifically that minute from group . . . The basic thing that group asked for was for us to verify those assumptions . . . You see, I'm worried about starting down rabbit holes with group because we know what can happen when they get hold of a rag. I think this is absolutely right, because we ourselves have got to be sure, and have numbers we can have faith in – we ought to invest in the project. And when it comes to dealing with group, we've got to feed them numbers that they can understand, and link with what happened before.

A similar statement made at a project team meeting in another company echoed the same theme:

If we say that now, then we may get it held against us in the future, and we don't actually need to say it now, so let's not say it.

Equally, if group became over-involved, this could stifle independence of views amongst those closest to the project, and foster endless questioning about how those above them will view things. Similarly, too much questioning by senior management can make life very onerous for those involved, and could make them reluctant to pursue similar initiatives in the future.

Testing for commitment

In all three SIDs, divisional managers treated the process of arguing their case to group as at least a serious ritual. This is scarcely surprising, since they were dealing with 'their masters', their reputation for good analysis and presentation was on the line and they were making explicit promises about future delivery. Indeed, King (1975a) argued that the main function of formal project presentations to senior management is 'the development of commitment to the success of the project'. This theme was echoed in at least one of our companies, where group's 'toughness' was seen as a test for commitment on the part of the project proposers. As one divisional director put it:

They weren't basically against us, they were testing out whether we were basically for it . . . Let's put it this way. If someone within my division wants to invest £2 or £3 million, my reason for questioning him is not that I disbelieve him, but I want to believe that he has faith in the project, that he is going to argue it through. I want to see enthusiasm shining through the figures and the commitment to really making the thing work.

Interestingly, group management described their behaviour rather differently, as essentially testing the project rather than the proposers' commitment. They saw their actions as a process of detached evaluation through rational analysis, economic logic and strategy assessment. Here, and to some extent in the other two companies, they believed they could understand enough about the SID to judge it, but that getting any 'closer' to the detail could compromise their position as 'detached analysts'.

Setting limits and deadlines

Senior management intervened directly in all three projects by setting limits and deadlines. In two cases, limits were set when the division obtained group's approval to proceed with external negotiations. In one case the division anticipated receiving a particular package of government assistance and group gave the go-ahead, subject to this being forthcoming. In another case, which involved a partial acquisition, group gave the go-ahead, conditional on the price negotiated not exceeding the estimate in the project proposal.

In both cases it seems unlikely that group believed that the projects were so marginal that any slippage implied abandonment. Rather, these limits can be seen as control and motivational devices. As one project team member reflected:

They wanted to make sure that we negotiated as hard as we possibly could for the lowest amount and therefore they fixed a number and said, 'You're damn well going to do it for that, and not a penny more'. I think they wanted to make sure that we didn't get into a meat slicing situation where the amount just went slowly up and up. I don't think this was a result of saying 'We think that the project is not worth more than this much'. It was a management control mechanism if you like and a negotiating tactic.

Equally, such limits set from above were seen as useful when negotiating with outside parties:

Look, your hand is strengthened by having a board minute that specifies the conditions . . . and you need the strongest hand you can get.

All three SIDs took much longer than originally anticipated. When we began monitoring, all three companies expected to reach a decision within three to six months. In practice, final approval was not obtained until 7, 13 and 27 months later. In two companies, group intervened in the time-scale and deadlines to try to speed things up. The project teams, while equally anxious to proceed, had to pull together and check all the details, and conduct lengthy external negotiations. They also had other problems to address and activities to service. This led to some friction and impatience. In one company, the group CEO asked, 'How are you getting on with it? I don't want to wait a year'. However, as one of the project team members explained:

Our time-scale was different from his . . . and we were saying, hang on, we can't do everything that fast. We were committed, but we were realistic as well.

A second case involved protracted external negotiations. An initial deadline came and passed. Group then insisted on a second deadline 90 days later. When this was not met, the division broke off negotiations. After difficult discussions, negotiations were reopened and a new deadline was set up by group for 10 weeks later. Contracts were signed on the last possible day. Although two deadlines were missed, group managed, by imposing them, to communicate a sense of urgency to the project team and, presumably, to the outside party. Furthermore, everyone believed that this final deadline was 'the end of the road'.

Deadlines and limits imposed by an 'external' body in a position of authority within the hierarchy can be useful and effective focusing devices. The danger, however, is that those who are distant from the problem may not understand the pressures and realities involved. They may misinterpret inevitable delays as signs of bad faith, lack of commitment or incompetence. As one project team member commented:

When you've got a guy upstairs, and he says, 'Why the hell aren't you getting on with it? You go down there tomorrow morning'. And you say, 'But Chairman, I can't go down there tomorrow morning. All these guys (that we're negotiating with) are at a funeral for some colleague . . . If I went down and insisted it would be quite inappropriate'. 'I don't give a stuff', and so you go. Those are the trying things which become an irritation, which there has been a tendency for them to get over-involved from that point of view in things which actually they did not understand. It's very difficult to get over to them and really . . . a very trying and tiring exercise having to explain to the people up the line the totality of these complications and why it's taking so long . . . when one ought to be doing something more useful with your time.

Imposing project-specific criteria

As we have already seen, all three companies had established formal criteria for new projects. However, in two of our three cases, group also introduced supplementary project-specific criteria. First, in the company where group initially rejected the project the CEO indicated that he still wanted the cost savings while minimizing capital spending. From this point on, this became the dominant concern for the project team. In a second company the project involved a large initial investment plus an option to make a later major investment. This second phase was central to the company's strategy, and was also the prime concern of the local government which wanted a commitment on Phase Two and was prepared to offer incentives. Group intervened by insisting that Phase One had to be 'washing its face financially' (i.e. pay back most of the initial investment) before embarking on Phase Two. Henceforth, this quasi-payback period became a major criterion ahead of IRR.

In both cases, group's 'tailor-made' criteria shifted the focus away from the theoretically preferable DCF evaluation. This had its dangers. In the first situation, when comparing two options, the one with the higher savings-to-spending ratio could nevertheless have the lower NPV. In the second company, insisting on payback prior to Phase Two apparently ruled out earlier investment which, in a competitive environment, might have had a higher NPV. However, these criteria were not intended as 'static' measures for selecting between already existing alternatives. Instead, they can be seen as motivational devices to encourage specific behaviour in a particular setting – biased measures designed to counter-balance biased behaviour. They seem to have been intended to elicit new options, changes in project definition or changes in implementation.

In the first case the CEO felt that too few alternatives had been explored, and emphasized the savings-to-spending trade-off as a way of stimulating the search for a cheaper way of achieving the project benefits. Similarly, the 'payback prior to Phase Two' criterion can be seen as part of the negotiating strategy to maximize incentives (since these advanced the payback date), a signal to the local government that Phase Two was discretionary and depended on the business and fiscal climate during a 'probationary period', and a strong incentive to all parties to ensure that Phase One was successful as soon as possible.

Intervening by introducing project-specific criteria still has its drawbacks. First, the project team's creativity may be devoted to changing the project's paper representaton rather than its real configuration. We observed some of this. As one project team member put it:

It was becoming very tricky to find a projection that would actually meet the formula we'd established and agreed with group.

Second, criteria which may be helpful in a specific project setting can become ingrained in permanent thinking and can be applied in screening future projects for which they are inappropriate, e.g. a subsequent failure to suggest an earlier date for Phase Two.

Appointing senior management

One important way in which group can influence the direction of divisions is through senior management appointments. While the needs of individual SIDs are generally only a minor consideration here, such personnel changes can have important consequences for nascent projects.

In one company, a divisional director was replaced at group's request. Group had a candidate for his job, which they saw as a training position for people rising through the group hierarchy. However, the incumbent had been heavily involved in evaluating the project and was currently midway through crucial external negotiations. His early retirement could therefore have affected continuity and the perceptions of the third party. *Ex post*, group's intervention was seen to have had an important influence on the project, even if it was made for largely other reasons.

In a second company, group appointed a new divisional MD part-way through the project. Again the project team later saw this as having had an important influence on the SID. The group CEO in this company also endorsed the consultants who were brought in to validate the project strategy. In the third company, group promoted the business unit MD who headed the project team. His significant extra responsibilities had implications for the project in terms of the time he could put in. The group CEO also made several direct suggestions on project staffing. For example, he suggested that the division collaborate with the head of another related business unit and offered the assistance of group corporate planning to work on the project.

Moving one level down the hierarchy, senior divisional management also intervened in the SIDs via personnel decisions, mainly on the project team's composition. In one case, the divisional CEO chose a divisional director who normally covered a different area to head the project. Reflecting on why he was chosen, the board member speculated:

Maybe [the CEO] was looking for a guy who he thought was committed to this sort of project. I think you've got to be. It would have been difficult for a guy who's not convinced that this is the right thing to do, to put him in charge . . . You could find all sorts of reasons down the track why we shouldn't have done it.

Equally, senior management can influence projects by deciding who should *not* be involved. In another organization, the divisonal CEO himself headed the project and ran a tight two-man project team, deliberately excluding a business unit that would be critically involved in implementation. The divisional CEO argued that if he involved them 'they'll have all sorts of reasons' why the project will not work. They were eventually brought in much later, when the time was felt to be right.

Projecting the interests of group and other divisions

If SIDs impact on the interests of group or other divisions, we might expect top management to intervene to reconcile potential conflicts. However, we encountered only one example of this.

Here, the project involved a joint venture. The other shareholders wished to restrict future share transfers to avoid the sale of the holding to any hostile third party. The division agreed, but group overruled them since restrictions on share transfers would constrain them if they ever wished to divest the division, or even reorganize internally, transferring the shares to a different division or regional company. As the group CEO put it:

We are the trustees for our successors. We cannot allow these negotiations to put in any constraints for our successors in terms of commercial ability.

This seemed a natural role for group. Divisions cannot be expected to consider their own divestment or closure, nor even the transfer of a major business to another division. Equally, divisions might be somewhat biased in evaluating a project's implications for sister divisions. However, although the projects we monitored all had such implications, potential conflicts were handled by direct interdivisional and intradivisional discussions. Perhaps group would have arbitrated had these discussions not worked.

Controlling the organizational context

Apart from their direct role in SID-making, senior management can also influence investment choices indirectly through the design and management of organizational context (Bower, 1970; Barwise et al., 1987a). Clearly, tracking a single investment in each of three companies gives very limited data for investigating the general influence of context. Nevertheless, we encountered interesting suggestive evidence on the role played by three 'context' variables: organizational structure, measurement and reward systems, and corporate climate.

Organizational structure

In principle, organizational structure sets the context for SIDs and influences the kinds of opportunity the firm sees and exploits. Since most new investments originate within divisions, the way in which divisional boundaries are drawn, in terms of product/market focus and geography, is likely to be crucial.

All three SIDs fell clearly within the existing boundaries of the division in question. However, in one case the divisional planner also described some of the alternative investments that the division had considered:

But we *could* see a way to expand our activity in Country X. That's the other big area of . . . future potential . . . We at the time thought that (a specific acquisition) might have been a possibility . . . but subsequent to that, things have changed, a geographic line has been drawn [by group] . . . so had we succeeded with the acquisition at that time, we'd have lost it anyway, as far as [our division] is concerned, it would have gone into [another division] . . . if we had been planning then under the regime now, we would not have picked that up as an opportunity.

These and similar comments revealed a keen sense of internal organizational boundaries and a 'them-and-us' attitude towards other divisions and group, which set constraints on identifying opportunities outside their own boundaries. The reverse side of this coin was a strong desire by divisions and subunits to grow their own patch. For example, one project team member commented:

But you get to that stage, and then you're beginning to talk about this (business unit) as a division rather than a company . . . As I see it, you try and plot it in the future, where you want to be and that's how I'd like to see it go. . . . so how does it go back into group . . . They want to see it grow. I'm anxious that it will grow. I'm anxious that it should be an effective part of the group organisation.

In a similar vein, a divisional Board member in another company explained:

One should be perceived to be growing, and not . . . [as] people here think . . . getting smaller . . . a dissolution of an empire . . . Group is getting bigger . . . but it's less easy for people to relate to, because it's one stage removed. So that's a problem, it's the reason for the positive attitude to investment directly behind our own business.

This desire for growth has many positive aspects. One danger, however, is that business units may wish to expand almost irrespective of how this maps onto the opportunity cost of capital (Bower, 1970). Furthermore, 'tightly' defined organizational boundaries may exacerbate managers' identification with subunits rather than group. This may make the firm less effective at identifying and implementing investments which require extensive cooperation. Equally, it may make it harder to analyse cross-unit implications.

The natural desire for growth may explain why all three projects involved an element of vertical integration, i.e. bringing or maintaining certain activities within the internal domain of the division. In one case the project involved backward integration into raw material manufacture. In a second it involved a series of 'make or buy' decisions. Originally, it was assumed that various suppliers would invest in specific capital assets required for the project. Successively, however, arguments were made for the division itself purchasing these assets. The net result was to treble the division's capital investment. The third SID involved a major reorganization of a physical distribution network, while still maintaining this activity within the ambit of the firm. Although the project team was specifically asked to consider the option of contracting out, this was not looked at seriously.

Indeed, the argument that the activities in question might be better handled outside the firm (e.g. via normal contractual arrangements) was in no case fully explored. Furthermore, the analysis of the benefits of vertical integration was frequently confused. For example, in the case involving raw material manufacture the IRR indicated that this was a profitable project, based on the difference between the open-market price of the raw material (essentially a commodity) and the costs of its manufacture. However, it was claimed that the project also brought a strategic benefit through access to 'cheap' raw material. This was clear double-counting, since 'cheap' referred to its production costs, yet in the project appraisal the raw material had already been valued at its market price. We encountered several other arguments where the benefits of 'make' versus 'buy' seemed to involve double-counting.

We noted above that all three SIDs had implications for other business units within the group. In general, the project definitions tended to 'favour' the initiating division or business unit. One project involved the initiating division in purchasing a stake in company A which competed directly with another division's associate company, B. Furthermore, both A and B were suppliers to the initiating division, which was also involved in joint technical and research programmes with B. Company B was clearly concerned about loss of sales and technology transfer, yet it was not consulted until after the project go-ahead. In another case, the initiating division provided services for two sister divisions within the group. Although the SID impacted on these, the dominant concern was with optimizing the project with respect to the initiating division's own business. In the third SID a decision was taken to locate a major part of the investment on the site of an existing business. This was partly influenced by a desire to grow this business, which previously had been seen as peripheral by group.

To repeat, we are not suggesting that any of these decisions was inappropriate. We are simply noting three observations. First, the divisions tended to want to grow within their boundaries, although this also implied that they might miss opportunities perceived as outside their domain. Second, there seemed to be an inbuilt bias in favour of 'make versus buy', or vertical integration, in terms of bringing (or maintaining) activities within the internal domain of the division. Third, although all three projects impacted on other divisions within group, they were developed to 'favour' the initiating division. At least in these three ways, organizational structure clearly mattered.

Performance measurement and reward systems

We have argued elsewhere that the measures used to monitor business and project performance and the ways in which managers are evaluated and rewarded will influence which projects they put forward and what sorts of forecasts they commit themselves to (Barwise et al., 1987a). Our research evidence supported this conjecture.

In all three companies the link between business unit performance and managerial rewards was indirect. Even at senior level, managers' salaries were not linked directly to divisional profitability. All three parent companies ran employee and executive share option schemes, but these can be seen more as tax-efficient perks rather than performance-related incentive schemes, given the tenuous link between individual effort and the group's share price. However, despite the lack of direct links, divisional managers seemed to view their own interests as being quite closely associated with the performance of their business unit or division.

Business unit performance, as revealed in the regular performance reviews, therefore assumed considerable importance. Indeed, these performance reviews, and comparisons with other divisions, may have contributed to managers' desires to make their own businesses grow:

It's a difficult thing to accept that the long-term future of the business that you manage is declining because you know (that at every) quarterly review meeting, the chap from (division A) or the chap from (division B) is going to be talking about sort of onward upward growth.

While the desire for growth and performance can influence project initiation, managers' concern over business performance can also affect the project forecasts they commit to. In two of the companies the project teams came exclusively from the business unit in which the project fell, and the managers involved were to be directly responsible for project implementation. In both cases the project team was reluctant to 'promise too much'. This is typified in the following conversation:

Team member 1: The other question we need to decide in a wider context is how much we want to declare we want to save.

Team member 2: Yes, we'll decide on the politics . . . Don't want to be putting too much savings . . . we can come back with another little bit later on.

In another project the team also avoided 'unduly raising expectations'. As a team member explained:

I can be accused of being too foxy . . . But I don't seem to get any slaps on the back if you come and you fail . . . You know you've still got to achieve it (the project) and maybe there is something we haven't thought of.

In one SID, successful negotiations achieved a better price than projected in the initial project proposal. Instead of 'declaring' this by updating the financial proposal, it was kept private, and the comment was 'that's in the bank'.

In these two companies, managers' concern 'not to promise too much' from projects thus seemed mostly related to future business unit performance. Managers wanted to produce a continual year-on-year performance improvement, and projects helped them to achieve this and also gave some extra 'slack'. By promising 'enough' profit from the project to ensure that capital was forthcoming, any 'surplus' profit would show up as outperformance against the business target. In fact, at least one project team seemed to view capital expenditure as almost a 'free issue' from group. The project was seen as a way of achieving already agreed targets for future profit improvement. Although the project capital expenditure was approved on the basis of the increased profit it would bring, there was much ambiguity about how this fed back, if at all, to changes in the original profit targets. Whether the latter meant very much was anyway doubtful:

You have this corporate plan, this was the one we put in recently . . . this bears no relation to what will happen – none whatsoever! This is sufficient not to get criticized, and one can confidently achieve – whatever happens.

Managers' concern about their business units' performance relative to budget partly reflects the anticipated link with their own remuneration and promotion prospects. When 'managerial rewards' are defined more broadly to encompass personal challenge, status and individual development, we found that involvement in major projects was seen as a rewarding activity in its own right. As members of the three project teams put it:

I've never had as big a project to try to pull together like that . . . it's been good experience.

It was very satisfying for me . . . the best single thing I've done (for some years) as far as my own sense of achievement was concerned . . . quite important in my own formation also . . . I certainly learned a lot.

This particular project gave me an excellent opportunity to get involved. Without it we'd have been fairly flat really. I think as a management team, you've always got to be driving at something.

Project team members may also have seen the projects as a chance to catch the eyes of those above them. Certainly, senior management recognized the development aspects of working on major proposals and noticed those who did well:

The whole experience is important for individuals . . . there are six or seven people who got very deeply embroiled in this, and they're all better for it at the end of it . . . there is a plus in a personal sense. I don't mean that . . . suddenly everybody is ready for promotion, it just means that we've now got a much more convincing development core.

Corporate climate

The importance of an informal organizational climate or 'atmosphere' is stressed by recent writers in business policy (Peters and Waterman, 1982). Climate is notoriously difficult to define. In part, it reflects formal systems such as budget constraints. But as Pascale (1984) has argued, people are more sensitive to the priorities revealed by actions (such as which memos are put at the top of the action pile) than to those enshrined in formal procedures. More generally, organizational climate will be heavily influenced by informal actions, such as who talks to whom and the kinds of debate that take place.

In the SIDs we monitored, when managers used the word 'climate' they were invariably referring to financial climate. Sometimes the financial climate was set by the formal systems through explicit financial objectives defined by group:

They give us the guidelines for financial performance . . . we get two or three sheets of written guidelines. They'd say for example we want X per cent ROI . . . they'd spell out the absolute amount of dividends they want for the next five years and that they want us to [achieve a Y per cent] debt–equity ratio.

In this case, divisional managers argued that the financial climate had influenced strategy and investment behaviour. They had recognized that the growth objective set by group could not be met in the constraints of their pre-existing strategy. This had caused them to reject several investments and to explore a range of new options, including the project we monitored.

Similarly, in a second company, group took a view of what the level of company-wide aggregate capital spending should be. As the group finance director explained:

Divisions put forward what they want . . . we'd have set the climate prior to that, so . . . they were told the sort of capital expenditures we were looking for which were very tight . . . we want to generate more cash . . . to put the clamp on – battening down – because we have relatively mature businesses, some of them aren't going to produce very good room for growth, therefore what they can produce is cash.

The danger of this top-down approach is that group does not have detailed knowledge of the investment opportunities available at divisional and business unit level. Yet their signals and behaviour may prevent divisions from putting forward worthwhile ideas quite apart from being demotivating. Labelling divisions ex-growth may thereby become a self-fulfilling prophecy.

Besides being set through the formal systems, financial climate is also inferred from the words and deeds of group-level managers. Based on the group CEO's behaviour at a recent meeting, a divisional manager in one company reported:

The financial state of this business has changed dramatically. We have more cash and we're more profitable. And the attitude of group, considering their nervousness on spending large cash figures, has changed . . . (the group CEO) wasn't capital rationing, but he was certainly watching every penny he had . . . now it's not the capital that's his worry, it's profit growth. He's not slacker, but he's got different pressures.

Within the division, this was interpreted as signalling an important shift in financial climate.

Perhaps inevitably, in the context of SIDs, the financial climate can be the dominant feature of the wider corporate climate. Furthermore, the climate depends heavily on top management's actions and revealed concerns. Their response to investment proposals gives a good indication of their actual commitment to innovation and entrepreneurship (Kanter, 1984).

Each firm's top management also influenced the informal climate for investment by their style of intervention. Thus a tough questioning attitude by group set a very different climate than a more aloof style (see the section on the direct role of senior management). Indeed, an ever-present danger is that climate can become set too readily, in that all group's actions and views become 'tablets of stone'. As one project team member commented:

We tend to respond to a great degree to what we judge (group's) current view to all that, and sometimes we may be mistaken . . . I've come across certain instances of over-enthusiastic interpretation of (group's views) and it has been turned into a tablet of stone.

One final observation is that the very act of going ahead with new investment was seen as a very positive influence on divisional climate. In the words of divisional managers from two different companies:

Project team member: I think (the project) would be good for the people, and good for the company . . . I get it from the staff, I'm bound to, (they're concerned about) what's happening next . . . (but) if they now see group investing, it will be absolutely . . .

Interviewer: A very positive thing?

Project team member: Oh, yes.

Board member: And therefore (there's) a good deal of enthusiasm too . . . what better for (our) growth and prosperity to be investing in a new and directly relevant operation . . . and I think these things are important to a company, it's all part of the ethos.

Discussion

Ultimately, the board has formal responsibility for investing shareholders' capital. But in practice, most organic SIDs in large diversified firms are initiated and developed by the division that will have to implement them. The research reported here is about three such 'bottom-up' SIDs.

The issue that such SIDs pose for corporate top management is that their profitability depends strongly on product-market specifics which can best be judged by the divisional managers closest to the problem, who have more relevant knowledge and far more time to devote to it. But there may be corporate resource constraints or other interactions between divisional strategies. More important, corporate top management will want to retain some control over the divisional SIDs (unless the company is really run just as a holding company), at the very least to ensure that reasonably appropriate disciplines and criteria are applied and that authority delegated to the divisions is not putting the whole enterprise at risk.

In this paper we have explored various ways in which corporate top management resolves this issue. With the hlep of staff groups, especially planning and finance, top management can impose formal systems and procedures on the processes of *planning* and *capital budgeting*. In addition, senior managers are themselves *directly involved* up to a point and can in principle intervene at any stage. Finally corporate management has other less direct ways of controlling the *organizational context* within which SIDs are made. These four interrelated mechanisms have been discussed in the previous four sections. Here, we briefly review the conclusions.

Formal planning

Managers often use the terms 'corporate planning' and 'strategic planning' interchangeably. For clarity, we avoid the term 'corporate planning' here, preferring to distinguish between 'group strategic planning' (at overall corporate level) and 'divisional strategic planning'.

On this basis, most strategic planning in the firms we studied was at divisional level. In our view this rightly reflects that genuine competitive advantage stems from fairly specific product-market details (Barwise et al., 1987a). Conversely, most group planning was administrative and financial, bringing together the various strategies emerging from the divisions to a whole which was basically a simplified version of the sum of their parts. Even within the divisions, strategies were more 'emergent' than 'deliberate' (Mintzberg and Waters, 1985), although this partly depends on the unit of analysis: each SID may have been part of a longer-term strategy within the mind of its initiator. But in terms of the strategy which was revealed to outsiders – including those from head office – it was hard to view the SIDs we tracked as being the implementation of an explicit prior strategy.

However, there is an element of chicken and egg here. Most of the opportunities had been discussed previously, but events or the process of planning may have caused recognition of a particular threat or opportunity. Similarly, different SIDs within a particular part of the business are often highly interrelated, and there is great ambiguity about project boundary definitions. Finally, most SIDs will typically be justified in part by referring to selected aims or objectives from the divisional strategic plan. But our impression was that these plans were rightly left fairly flexible, so that almost any SID could be supported by judicious reference to selected parts of the plan.

Generally then, explicit strategic planning, even at divisional level, seems to have had only a limited impact on the SIDs that were proposed and accepted. The influence of group strategic planning was minimal.

Capital budgeting systems

All three firms studied had well-etablished formal capital budgeting procedures. For instance, all three had capital budgeting manuals and all 'used' DCF. If we had conducted a standard survey, these three would have come out at the most systematic and sophisticated end of the spectrum. However, the reality was much more complex and less clearcut. In particular, detailed data from documents, observed meetings and interviews show the ambiguity of what is meant by 'using' a particular technique.

In practice, the manuals did not turn out to be 'live' documents. Furthermore, to a greater or lesser extent, all three firms made analytical errors in their application of appraisal techniques. Most of these were conceptual, for example, inconsistent treatment of sunk costs or terminal values, considerable ambiguity about the 'do-nothing' base case, using an inappropriate mixture of real and nominal cash flows and discount rates before and after tax, and failing to distinguish between accounting return (ROI) and DCF return (IRR) and between return on assets and return on equity. These conceptual errors are not minor technicalities, and some could introduce serious distortion.

The extent of forecasting was also quite limited. Typically, costs and benefits which were hard to justify were excluded from the financial analysis. Furthermore, forecasting had a political dimension. In all three cases the managers involved had a strong bias towards going ahead with the project. This does not mean that they were making consciously biased forecasts, but they were conscious of the temptation.

A closely related issue was deciding which costs and benefits were or were not included in the formal proposal. Thus a 'good' project was more likely to be loaded with (perhaps necessary) overhead costs (e.g. computer systems, office refurbishment). The 'final' forecasts were not seen as complete best-guess estimates, but as oversimplified and incomplete projections, giving a good enough financial return to justify the project.

The formal proposals can thus paint a fairly distorted picture of a project. What is less clear is how much (if at all) this matters. In no case did the project teams propose something that they believed was bad for the group, and all three projects appeared to be worthwhile on financial grounds. However, we are not arguing that the methods of financial appraisal are wholly irrelevant, and this leaves us with a worrying question-mark about whether the various 'wrongs' always do, in fact, cancel out to make a 'right'. Certainly one potential danger is that projects which offer little 'slack', but which are still worthwhile, might never be proposed. We found no evidence of this, but such evidence would, by definition, be hard to come by.

Again, formal capital budgeting systems, while ritualistic, did influence reality. They forced the players to be more explicit about their assumptions (and to a lesser extent about alternatives) both to themselves and in order to justify them to others. Although the financial analysis was partly 'added on afterwards', it did to some extent help guide decisions and negotiations, and reveal new concerns. The formal systems provided deadlines and helped force the project pace. They also gave a scheduled set of occasions for face-to-face communication aross multiple levels of the hierarchy. This, in turn, caused the project team to think through and agree a plan, build their personal commitment to its success and make the commitment formal and public.

Senior management's direct role

Because of the severe information and time constraints which senior management in large diversified companies faces in dealing with SIDs from the divisions, a number of previous writers have suggested that top management's main role should be indirect: developing appropriate planning and capital budgeting procedures, and setting the right organizational context. However, our research suggests that top management has an important direct role in SID-making, albeit a more complex one than simply exercising ultimate authority at a single and identifiable decision point.

Certainly, top managers' involvement in the SID-making process, including the final approval stage, was not regarded as a mere ritual either by the top managers themselves or by the project proposers. Members of the project team may have talked of 'rubber stamping' and were clear that various details in the proposals' assumptions and forecasts were unlikely to be picked up. But considerable effort went into the preparation of the formal submission, and the outcome was not seen as a foregone conclusion. In fact, one of our three cases was turned down at this stage, with a radically different and much smaller revised version subsequently being proposed and accepted a full year after the original proposal. Top managers' power is real and is seen to be so, and this includes the making and breaking of careers as well as the acceptance and rejection of proposals. Nor was this just a presentational issue. The need to gain acceptance – and to anticipate awkward questions – exerted a strong and explicit influence on the project itself and on the way it was analysed. In particular, anticipated questions of the form 'what options have you explored?' and 'have you considered . . . ?' did encourage the project team to look at options and issues they might otherwise have neglected. However, this was typically done only to the extent that seemed necessary to gain acceptance.

One way in which senior management reduced the information gap was for members of the top management group to specialize in particular areas of knowledge. Such specialization was partly by function, but was mostly in terms of involvement with specific divisions and business areas. In all three cases there were examples of the same people wearing both a group and a divisional hat, and dual-level hats were again very common lower down the hierarchy.

While the advantages of this are obvious, it carries its own inherent drawbacks, particularly right at the top. Obviously, as Bower (1970) has argued, by the time the divisional chief executive gets to the stage of proposing a SID at the group investment committee, his main role is as an advocate of his division and not as an objective judge of the proposal. Perhaps less obviously, if some other member of group top management has part-time responsibility for that division, finding out about projects at a much earlier stage, he will be seen as having a duty to ensure that the case proposed is good – otherwise he should have stopped it or had it modified. There is some conflict here between being well-informed and being objective.

The climate within which SIDs were made was strongly influenced by what the corporate top managers did. Their role in questioning and policing assumptions varied widely between companies, from limited to close involvement. Too much questioning would not only be time-consuming for all parties, but would also be demotivating for the project team and possibly distorting. Nevertheless, such questioning was seen as important in encouraging wider thinking about options, issues and justifications. As we have seen, some members of the project teams also saw value in having their commitment tested.

In all three cases, top management intervened by setting limits and deadlines, and in two cases by introducing extra project-specific criteria. Top management's wider role in making or influencing all senior appointments was also seen as a factor in the particular SIDs. Similarly, within the divisions, the setting up of the project team interacted with other decisions about management roles and promotions.

In principle, corporate top management has a further role in seeing that each division's strategy takes due account of the interests of other divisions and of the group as a whole. However, this seems to have been only a minor factor in the three SIDs we monitored.

Overall, direct interventions by top management were more widespread and influential than Bower (1970) and King (1975a) seem to have observed. One question still to be resolved is the extent to which these interventions were part of a coherent and systematic approach. We found little evidence of any real attempt to develop such an approach. However, a parallel study by Goold and Campbell (1987a,b), focusing on top management in large diversified UK firms, has found more signs of a coherent philosophy of top management intervention within each firm – with some marked differences between firms.

Controlling the organizational context

Bower (1970) put particular emphasis on top management's indirect role in setting the organizational context within which SIDs are made. Obviously, context is set and determined on a much wider set of considerations than simply SID-making, and, clearly, tracking a single investment in each of three companies gives very limited data for investigating the general influence of context. Nevertheless we encountered interesting suggestive evidence on the role played by three 'context' variables, namely organizational structure, measurement and reward systems and corporate climate.

In an SID-making context, we found that organizational structure mattered in at least three ways. First, divisions tended to want to grow within their boundaries, although this also implied that they might miss opportunities perceived as being outside their domain. Second, there seemed to be an inbuilt bias in favour of 'make versus buy', or vertical integration, in terms of bringing (or maintaining) activities within the internal domain of the division. Third, although all three projects impacted on other divisions, they tended to 'favour' the initiating division.

Performance measurement was another important issue. Two of the project teams seemed concerned not to promise too much, so that divisional performance would, if possible, improve steadily from year to year and, above all, produce no nasty surprises. This is why the SID proposals in these two cases included enough benefit to gain acceptance rather than spelling out all the anticipated benefits. In all three cases the individual players identified strongly with the performance of their own business units and, although there was in no case a direct formal link with their salaries, they seemed to view their own prosperity and promotion prospects as closely linked to the business unit.

We have few direct data on the elusive concept of corporate climate or 'atmosphere'. Perhaps the strongest indicator of climate to the individual players was the behaviour of senior management. However, one factor which was frequently mentioned and appeared influential was the 'financial climate' within each corporation as a whole. In no case was there serious capital rationing, but in one company the financial climate shifted in the course of the project from one of saying 'do you really need all this capital?' to one of saying 'can't you think of any good way of investing more than this?'

Finally, growth seemed to be an important factor determining managers' morale. The very act of going ahead with new investment was seen as an extremely positive influence on divisional climate, particularly for an SID coming from a division in a mature or declining market.

Implementation as a key issue

Our research involved watching real people trying to influence outcomes, and make their part of the business grow – one aspect of strategy in the making. This in itself helped to emphasize that the key managerial need is for those who will make things happen. Implementation is not the end of the process, but the key overall issue. At the heart of the concept of distinctive competence is the fact that ideas must be feasible and must be within the capacity and energies of the particular managers concerned (Barwise et al., 1987a). In Bower's (1970) words, 'an operational definition of strategy requires a theory of implementation as a precondition'. Thus, in understanding SIDs, we need to recognize the importance of promises of action by those who can actually do things, and the extent to which the process encourages and reinforces commitment.

Given the real-time nature of our research, it is a matter for future observation as to whether the particular SIDs we tracked will become key strategic decisions for the organizations as a whole. Two of the three still have the potential for this. But whether this is achieved is down to the managers concerned, including top management, and, of course, to fortune.

Future research: towards the 1990s

We began this paper by pointing out how little is still known about how SIDs are made. Most previous research consists of generalizations from theory, particularly economics, with little empirical support apart from fairly crude surveys. Detailed studies of the process and analysis of how SIDs are made are few and far between. Our literature review in the first section thus revealed considerable gaps in what is known. As we look towards the next decade, how much can clinical case-based research of the kind represented in this paper help fill these gaps?

Future research on decision-making will still include theoretical as well as empirical work. Indeed, the potential contributions from such fields as option theory and agency theory have been documented elsewhere (Barwise et al., 1987a). However, much theoretical work on decision-making has, in the past, focused on artificially defined problems and on 'how to make optimal decisions on the assumptions of omnipotence and probabilistic omniscience' (King, 1975b). A key role for future empirical work is thus to help to inform theoreticians about the true nature of the decision-makers' problems as seen from the perspective of the actors.

The need for clinical case research

Looking forward to the forms of empirical research which are likely to achieve this, we can see few alternatives. Empirical research in management typically falls into one of three broad categories: database research, surveys and clinical case studies. For SID research, database studies are clearly infeasible, given the confidential qualitative situation-specific nature of the data required. Similarly, we cannot expect to arrive at any reasonable understanding of SID-making, let alone be in a position to provide prescriptive advice, if we resort to crude surveys. Our own research has shown how misleading such surveys would have been if they had been applied to our three sites, and we have no reason to believe that this result is anomalous. The fundamental problem with surveys is that, although the sample is larger, the data are much more superficial and are not necessarily 'harder' in the sense of being more valid.

In looking to the future, therefore, it would appear that only clinical case research can capture the level of detail required to improve our understanding of SID-making in organizations. But what should be the prime focus and nature of such future research?

We have argued in this paper that studies are required which focus on both process and analysis in enough depth to link the financial, strategic, organizational and individual perspectives on SID-making. To be able to understand and explain outcomes, future research needs to monitor and interpret these parallel, interracting and complex variables. Furthermore, research in this area is, in our view, likely to provide more insight if it embraces multiple perspectives, rather than adopting the tunnel vision of a single discipline or trying to develop a single over-arching analytical framework.

In this respect, our own research is still incomplete, since this first paper concentrated on only one perspective on SID-making, namely the impact of formal systems and the senior management hierarchy. Our immediate future research agenda is to use the three other perspectives listed in the first section to analyse the data from the three SIDs we tracked.

Limitations

The ability to explore such multiple perspectives derives from the richness of the data obtained in clinical case research. The obvious drawback is that the small sample and situation-specific nature of the data make it difficult or dangerous to generalize. This is particularly true of our own research since we have deliberately looked at SIDs made in large diversified private sector firms. Some of the features of SID-making we have observed will be a function of the size and structure of the firms, and other aspects may be purely situation specific. To clarify these issues, further research is required in both similar and alternative settings. Encouragingly, work is already in progress to this end (Butler et al., 1987).

Our focus in this paper has been specifically on SID-making. The focus on a 'key decision' was useful in giving a recognizable unit of analysis to both the researchers and the company, and helped to bound the problem in a manageable way. However, this boundary was somewhat arbitrary and reflected a particular assumption about the validity of the 'decision-making' construct. In research terms, it made it harder for us to set the SID in the context of relative importance versus what else was happening. Thus issues of, for instance, time allocation of key executives versus other pressing commitments could not easily be explored. Future research which seeks to combine 'event-orientated' clinical case studies with longitudinal and historical research (Pettigrew, 1985) would help to overcome these difficulties and provide complementary insights.

While we commend future research in this area, the dearth of earlier work seems no coincidence. Clinical case work, longitudinal historical studies and indeed any detailed research into strategy formulation in action is notoriously difficult and time-consuming. Not only are there serious problems of access and of internal and external confidentiality, but the problems of gathering, handling and analysing large amounts of qualitative data cannot be underestimated. From our own experience, such research is inefficient if conducted on a part-time basis, if undertaken in teams of much more than two and unless analysis is carried out in parallel with data collection. Yet few experienced researchers can afford the luxury of working full-time on such studies. Thus while we would welcome more research of this type, we suspect that it will continue to be a minority activity. This, of course, places an important responsibility on researchers to ensure that their data are retained in disaggregated form so that others can at least in principle have access to it later. Sadly, most previous researchers have failed to do this, making it impossible to re-examine their data to test alternative interpretations.

Two final issues

As researchers, this leads us to two final issues, which we believe will remain central concerns for this type of research in the 1990s. First there is the need for the very process of research to be at least reflective and at best 'reflexive'. Reflectivity is a desirable characteristic not only for the practitioner manager but also for the researcher attempting to understand managerial behaviour (Schon, 1983). Indeed, we concluded that our own research project itself raised many of the process issues that we had observed in the investment decisions that we were researching. The issue of the handling of complex and detailed information, the roles of those notionally managing the project (who were inevitably occupied with a whole range of other activities), the frustrations of those actually conducting the fieldwork, the flexible nature of deadlines and commitments, and the overall issue of frameworks and boundaries were all issues which arose forcibly in the research project itself. Indeed, our research projet could itself be viewed as a potential SID for the members of the research team, and in due course we aim to document this 'fourth case' and some of the parallels we observed with the projects we were monitoring.

Second, there is the issue of how to represent and communicate the knowledge and understanding that emerges from qualitative case research. As management researchers we are constrained by the social mores of the academic world, and some valuable results of research are therefore hard to communicate through traditional channels. As our reference list reveals, much interesting earlier work in this area lies hidden in unpublished or inaccessible sources. Yet if we believe in dissemination, we should regard this with sadness and as a challenge for future researchers to overcome.

Acknowledgement

This research was supported by funding from the Centre for Business Strategy, London Business School.

References

Ackerman, R.W. (1968). 'Organisation and the investment process: a comparative study'. Doctoral Dissertation, Harvard Business School, Boston, MA (unpublished).

Aharoni, Y. (1966). *The Foreign Investment Decision Process*. Boston, MA: Division of Research, Harvard Business School.

Allison, G.T. (1969). 'Conceptual models and the Cuban missile crisis'. *American Political Science Review*, **63**(3), 689–718.

Barwise, T.P., Marsh, P.R., Thomas, K. and Wensley, J.R.C. (1986). 'Research on strategic investment decisions'. In *Strategic Management Research: A European Perspective* (eds H. Thomas and J. McGee). Chichester: J. Wiley.

(This paper was originally presented at the Conference on Research in Strategic Management, Brussels, Belgium, June 1984.)

——, Marsh, P.R. and Wensley, J.R.C. (1987a). 'Strategic investment decisions'. *Research in Marketing*, 9, 1–57.

——, ——, Thomas, K. and Wensley, J.R.C. (1987b). 'An empirical study of strategic investment decisions'. Unpublished report, Centre for Business Strategy, London Business School.

Berg, N.A. (1963). 'The allocation of strategic funds in a large diversified industrial company'. Doctoral Dissertation, Harvard Business School (unpublished).

Berry, A.J. (1984). 'The control of capital investment'. *Journal of Management Studies*, 21(1), 61–81.

Bower, J.L. (1970). *Managing the Resource Allocation Process.* Boston, MA: Division of Research, Harvard Business School.

Burton, R.M. and Naylor, T.N. (1980). 'Economic theory in corporate planning'. *Strategic Management Journal*, 1(3), 249–63.

Butler, R.J., Davies, L., Pike, R. and Sharp, J. (1987). 'Strategic investment decision making: complexities, politics and processes'. Paper presented at the British Academy of Management Conference, University of Warwick, 13–15 September 1987.

Buzzell, R.D., Gale, B.T. and Sultan, R.C.M. (1975). 'Market share – a key to profitability'. *Harvard Business Review*, 53, 97–106.

Carsberg, B. and Hope, A. (1976). *Business Investment Decisions Under Inflation.* London: Institute of Chartered Accountants.

Carter, E.E. (1971). 'The behavioral theory of the firm and top level corporate decisions'. *Administrative Science Quarterly*, 16, 413–28.

Copeland, T.E. and Weston, J.F. (1983). *Financial Theory and Corporate Policy* (2nd edn). Reading, MA: Addison-Wesley.

Goold, M.C. and Campbell, A. (1987a). 'Strategic management styles'. (This book, Chapter 5.)

—— and —— (1987b). *Strategies and Styles: The Role of the Centre in Managing Diversified Corporations.* Oxford: Blackwell.

Granada Television (1975). *Decision Oil* and *Decision Steel* (ed. R. Graef).

Hedley, B. (1977). 'Strategic planning and the business portfolio'. *Long Range Planning*, 10, 9–15.

Hickson, D.J., Butler, R.J., Cray, D., Mallory, G.F. and Wilson, D.C. (1986). *Top Decisions: Strategic Decision-Making in Organisations.* Oxford: Blackwell.

Kanter, R.M. (1984). *The Change Masters: Corporate Entrepreneurs at Work.* London: Allen and Unwin.

Kennedy, J.A. and Sugden, K.F. (1986). 'Ritual and reality in capital budgeting'. *Management Accounting*, February, 34–7.

King, P. (1975a). 'Is the emphasis of capital budgeting theory misplaced?' *Journal of Business Finance and Accounting*, 2(1), 69–82.

—— (1975b). 'An investigation of the process of large scale capital investment decision making in diversified hierarchical organisations'. Doctoral Dissertation, Cambridge University (unpublished).

Klammer, T. (1972). 'Empirical evidence of the adoption of sophisticated capital budgeting techniques'. *Journal of Business*, **45**(3), 387–97.

—— and Walker, A.C. (1984). 'The continuing increase in the use of sophisticated capital budgeting techniques'. *California Management Review*, **26** Fall, 137–48.

Marsh, P.R. and Brealey, R.A. (1974). 'The use of imperfect forecasts in capital investment decisions'. In *European Finance Association 1974 Proceedings* (ed. B. Jacquillat). Amsterdam: North Holland.

McIntyre, A.D. and Coulthurst, N.J. (1985). 'Theory and practice in capital budgeting'. *The British Accounting Review*, **17**(2), 24–70.

Mintzberg, H.D. (1987). 'Crafting strategy'. *Harvard Business Review*, **87**(4), 66–75.

—— and Waters, J.A. (1985). 'Of strategies, deliberate and emergent'. *Strategic Management Journal*, **6**, 257–72.

——, Raisinghani, D. and Theoret, A. (1976). 'The structure of unstructured decision processes'. *Administrative Science Quarterly*, **21**(2), 246–75.

Morgan, G. (1986). *Images of Organisations*. Beverly Hills, CA: Sage.

Pascale, R.T. (1982). 'Our curious addiction to corporate grand strategy'. *Fortune*, January 25, 115–16.

—— (1984). 'Perspectives on strategy: the real story behind Honda's success'. *California Management Review*, **26**(3), 47–72.

Peters, T.J. and Waterman, R.H. (1982). *In Search of Excellence*. New York: Harper and Row.

Pettigrew, A.M. (1973). *The Politics of Organizational Decision Making*. London: Tavistock Publications.

—— (1985). *The Awakening Giant: Continuity and Change in Imperial Chemical Industries (ICI)*. Oxford: Blackwell.

Pike, R.H. (1983). 'A review of recent trends in formal capital budgeting processes'. *Accounting and Business Research*, **51**, 201–8.

Pinches, G.E. (1982). 'Myopia, capital budgeting and decision making'. *Financial Management*, **11**(3), 6–19.

Porter, M.E. (1980). *Competitive Strategy: Techniques for Analyzing Industries and Competitors*. New York: Free Press.

Rockley, L.E. (1973). *Investment for Profitability*. London: Business Books.

Rudden, E.M. (1982). 'The misuse of a sound investment tool'. *Wall Street Journal*, November 1.

Scapens, R.W., Sale, J.T. and Tikkas, P.A. (1982). *Financial Control of Divisional Capital Investment*. London: Institute of Cost and Management Accountants.

Schon, D.A. (1967). *Invention and the Evolution of Ideas*. London: Tavistock Publications. (First published as *Displacement of Concepts*. London: Tavistock Publications, 1963).

—— (1983). *The Reflective Practitioner*. New York: Basic Books.

Sihler, W.W. (1964). 'The capital investment analysis and decision process at the plant level of a large, diversified corporation'. Doctoral Dissertation, Harvard Business School (unpublished).

Wensley, J.R.C., Barwise, T.P. and Marsh, P.R. (1983). 'Strategic investment decisions'. Paper presented at the AMA Educators' Conference, Dearborn, MI, August.

Williams, B.R. and Scott, W.P. (1965). *Investment Proposals and Decisions.* London: Allen and Unwin.

Wind, Y. and Robertson, T.S. (1983). 'Marketing strategy: new directions for theory and research'. *Journal of Marketing*, **47**(2), 26–43.

5
Strategic management styles

Andrew Campbell and Michael Goold

Corporate structures are in a state of flux. The recent spate of mergers and take-overs is bringing together previously independent businesses within larger and larger parent companies. But, at the same time, management buy-outs and divestitures are restoring independence to subsidiaries of other groups. Some argue that the large diversified company is the most effective form of industrial organization.[1] Others claim that small, independent companies gain nothing, except overhead, from their membership of such groups.[2] The research into whether multibusiness companies or single-business companies are the most successful is profoundly inconclusive.[3]

These issues have recently been brought to a head in the UK in a series of contested bids for major public companies. Is Hanson Trust a better parent for Imperial's businesses than UB would have been? Should BTR have received support in its bid for control of Pilkington's businesses? What role will the centres of these different companies play, and which will create the most value? It is the ability to give a convincing answer to the last of these questions that frequently decides the outcome of a bid. One ex-Imperial manager told us that he believed that the root cause of the take-over by Hanson was confusion about how the centre could add value to the businesses in the group. 'In my recollection', he said, 'the problem at Imperial had nothing to do with the stock market or the businesses. It stemmed from an inability to articulate what the role of the centre was.'

To cast light on these questions we have recently completed research into the role of the centre in a cross-section of large British firms. We have addressed questions that have been the subject of research by others, such as:

how the centre allocates scarce resources (people and money) between business units, divisions and groups;[4]
how much autonomy business units are given over operating and

strategic decision (Vancil, 1979; Vancil and Green, 1984; Hamermesh and White, 1984);

how key management systems such as the financial control system or the compensation system are tailored to the objectives of the company (Vancil, 1973; Sathe, 1982; Eccles, 1983);

how strategy development is managed, including the creation of centres of strategic initiative (Strategic Business Units) and the design of the strategic planning system (Ansoff, 1979, 1984; Hofer and Schendel, 1978; Andrews, 1980; Lorange and Vancil, 1977; Lorange 1979).

Most of the previous research has been focused either on a particular aspect of the centre's management task or on the SBU level. Our purpose has been to take a holistic view on how, whether and when the centre adds value to the businesses in its portfolio. By looking at the complete management task of the centre and by focusing explicitly on the central activities rather than the SBU activities, we have been able to develop a framework for analysing the role of central management.

In this paper we describe the results of our research project which documented the management systems and philosophies of 16 multibusiness companies in the UK. The research recorded eight different management styles – ways of managing from the centre – and concluded that three styles are most common among successful companies. Each of the three popular styles has strengths and weaknesses. None of the three appears to be universally superior. Our research does not support the widely held view that there is some ideal of 'strategic management' (Gluck et al., 1980).

The research implies that managers should be more aware of the different style choices and of the strengths and weaknesses associated with each style. With this knowledge managers will be better able to choose a management style that fits their organization and business circumstances, and shareholders will be better equipped to decide which management team should be given the job of running their business.

The study

The research programme involved interviewing managers, documenting systems and analysing publicly available as well as internally privileged performance data. The companies in the sample were chosen mainly because they were successful multibusiness companies to which we could gain in-depth access to interview managers. Some were chosen because we had a direct contact with the company; others, such as BTR and

Table 5.1 Participant companies

Company	Main Activity	Sales in 1986 (£ million)	Rank in Times 1000
BP	Oil	34 247	1
ICI	Chemicals	10 136	5
GEC	Electricals	5 252	14
Hanson Trust	Diversified	4 312	17
BTR	Diversified	4 019	20
Courtaulds	Textiles and chemicals	2 261	45
BOC	Gases and health care	1 944	55
STC	Electronics	1 933	56
Cadbury Schweppes	Confectionery, soft drinks	1 839	58
UB	Foods	1 818	61
Tarmac	Construction	1 718	65
Plessey	Electronics	1 429	79
Lex Service	Distribution	1 111	104
Vickers	Engineering	691	149
Ferranti	Electronics	595	169
Imperial	Tobacco, food, drinks	Acquired by Hanson Trust	

Source: *The Times 1000, 1987–88*. London: Times Books, 1987.

GEC, were selected because of their reputation for unusual management systems and philosophy. The initial sample included only six companies, and this was subsequently expanded to 16 over a period of three years (table 5.1).

In each company we spoke to managers at the centre, at the division level and at the business unit or profit centre level. In some companies we spoke to 20 or more managers; in a few we interviewed less than 10. The interviews were wide-ranging discussions held against a broad agenda which included the following:

how are decisions made in your organization?
how does the centre manage the business?
what value does the centre add to the business units?

The interviews focused on the perceptions that managers had and on examples and events they described. In some cases different managers had different interpretations of an event or a management system. But in most cases managers at the centre and at lower levels were in agreement about the management approach being used by the centre.

To supplement our interviews we asked each company to complete a questionnaire with specific quantitative and qualitative data. We also carried out independent analysis of the company's financial and strategic performance.

Measures of central influence

Our initial expectation was that there are better and worse ways of executing the central office role and that our research would be able to point to the right way. We quickly realized that different companies use very different management approaches and yet are equally successful. We were observing central management teams who tried to influence their subsidiary companies in very different ways. We also observed different levels of influence.

We noted that the centre exerts influence through a wide range of mechanisms: the organization structure, the planning process, informal discussions, the norms and values of the centrally imposed culture, the capital approval process, the targets used, the centre's reaction to poor performance, the role of staff departments at the centre and many more. All of these mechanisms emit signals to the organization. These signals influence the behaviour of managers in the subsidiaries and as a result can influence the decisions taken, and the motivation and effectiveness of employees.

To make sense of the data we needed to be able to categorize and classify different kinds of central influence. We chose two dimensions – two types of central influence – around which to group our data: planning influence and control influence. We chose these two dimensions because we believe that they most accurately capture the data we were analysing. They are also closely related to the concepts of planning and control used by Chandler (1962) and Williamson (1975), both of whom have examined the roles and added value of the central management group.

Planning influence

Planning influence is exercised where the centre is directly involved in shaping individual business decisions.

In some companies central management has a major influence in devising important proposals at the business unit level:

If you have a concentration of businesses where they present big chip bets for capital expenditure or R & D, and the life cycle of these is four or five years, I cannot see how you can justify your pay unless you are deeply involved in decision-making,

pointed out Dick Giordano, Chief Executive of BOC (and, incidentally, amongst Britain's highest-paid chief executives). In other companies central managers limit their involvement to sanctioning or vetoing proposals put to them:

We see it as essential that all initiatives are sponsored by the divisions. If you have a centrally determined group strategy you have a different management philosophy. So long as the centre is not taking the crucial investment initiatives, it can focus on its monitoring and sanctioning functions

explained Graeme Odgers, Group Managing Director of Tarmac.[5] In each case the centre has influence, but the nature and degree of the influence differ. We have described BOC's approach as having a high level of planning influence and Tarmac's approach as having a low level of planning influence.

There are a number of means through which planning influence can be exercised.[6] Central managers can encourage business units to come forward with certain types of proposals by *setting the direction* of the organization as a whole. They achieve this through the following:

central strategic themes such as the 'service excellence' banner used by the Lex Service Group to guide the policies of all their businesses;

strategic thrusts or objectives for particular businesses, such as 'expand in the US' or 'go international'. An example is Cadbury Schweppes's publicly stated objective of becoming the world's leading non-cola carbonated soft drinks company.

Whether through the formal management processes or through informal contacts, central managers can also influence the thinking of business units by *asking probing questions* in planning or budgeting review sessions, or by making *specific suggestions* about how plans and proposals could be improved. Another important means of influencing the proposals put forward by managers is by *recasting the organization structure*. By grouping some businesses together or by keeping them apart the centre can encourage or discourage coordination between businesses. Also, a matrix structure can be used to raise or lower the influence of product versus customers versus geographical priorities. Central managers can also influence the thinking behind business unit strategies as a result of the *resource allocation* decisions they make. These decisions will be noted by business unit managers as signals of the intentions of their bosses. Past decisions are an important guide to what is likely to be acceptable in the future.

Planning influence is, therefore, imparted both through informal discussion and through formal management processes such as the strategic planning process, the budget-setting process and the capital approval process.

Control influence

Control influence concerns the centre's reaction to results achieved in comparison with planned targets, and the way that this indirectly influences business strategies.

In some companies the annual financial budget is viewed as a contract between the centre and the business unit. Failure to deliver will result in severe pressure on the unit's management team and can frequently lead to management changes. In other companies the centre reacts more flexibly, recognizing that a particular set of financial results may be mainly a reflection of the business environment and not necessarily a report card on the unit managers.

In reacting to results the centre obviously considers more than the financial performance of the business. For example, it also takes into account the strategic performance of the business and changes in skills, culture or attitudes. However, the most effective dimension along which to distinguish between management styles appears to be the importance that the centre attaches to annual financial targets. At one extreme, financial budgets dominate the control process: 'We peer at the businesses through the numbers', commented a manager at GEC. At the other extreme, budgets play only a supporting role, taking their place alongside a range of other longer-term more strategic measures of performance:

In businesses with long-term financial pay-offs we have to control through strategy. We learn from last year's strategic decisions and control next year's strategy and actions. If a manager is going to buy property in Indonesia, we can measure whether he has done it. The thing we can't measure is whether it was a good commercial decision. We won't know that for five or more years

explained Sir Peter Walters, Chairman of BP. We have labelled the GEC approach tight financial control and the BP approach flexible strategic control. We have also described a third category – tight strategic control – which is a combination of the other two styles.

Control influence is exercised through three processes: target setting, monitoring performance and following through with incentives and sanctions. Targets and broad business objectives are set and agreed in the strategic planning and budget-setting processes. Monitoring against these objectives is carried out in periodic reviews of actual versus planned results – a time when the unit managers may be required to explain variances and state how they are going to correct them. Finally, incentives are applied against results. These can be financial, career related or psychological, and help to make targets matter to individual managers. In BTR, where budget targets are particularly important, a division head said: 'I would give up £10 000 of my salary to be able to be sure at the beginning of the year that I will be ahead of budget at the monthly review meetings when we review performance against plan'.

Strategic management styles

Using these two dimensions, we have defined eight different strategic management styles – eight ways in which the centre can relate to the business units. In figure 5.1 we identify the eight styles on a grid that has the level of central planning influence on the vertical axis and the nature of control influence on the horizontal axis. The level of planning influence by the centre varies from high to low, paralleling, in a sense, the scale from centralized to decentralized. The control influence axis is divided into three categories reflecting three different positionings. The differences are best explained in the context of the three main styles described below. Inevitably this framework simplifies the nature of the relationship between the centre and the business unit, but we have found

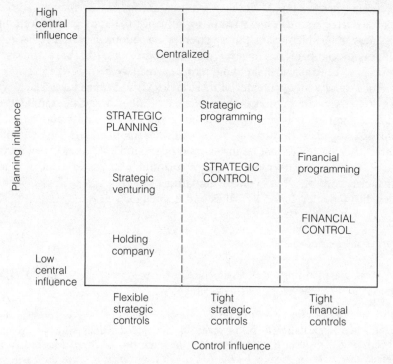

Figure 5.1 Strategic management styles.

Table 5.2 Company styles

Strategic planning	Strategic control	Financial control
BOC	Courtaulds	BTR[c]
BP[a]	ICI	Ferranti[c]
Cadbury Schweppes	Imperial Group	GEC
Lex[b]	Plessey	Hanson Trust
STC[b]	Vickers	Tarmac
UB[a]		

[a] Strategic venturing for some businesses
[b] Strategic programming attempted, but not sustained
[c] Tends towards financial planning

it to be a useful way of communicating differences and explaining the variety of style possibilities that exist. Table 5.2 shows how we classified the companies in our sample.

In our research, we found it possible to distinguish between companies with different levels of planning influence. At one extreme are *centralized* companies in which central managers in effect take all the major decisions themselves. At another extreme are *holding companies*[7] whose central managers make no attempt to influence the strategic thinking of business units. Neither of these extremes was adopted currently by any of our 16 companies. However, several companies had been through periods of centralized or holding company management in the past.

Since those with experience of these styles view them as unsatisfactory, we do not propose to discuss them further.[8] Rather, we shall examine the middle ground where top-down and bottom-up contributions are blended together in varying ways. All the companies in our sample currently have styles that lie in this middle ground. We have labelled the three most popular styles strategic planning, strategic control and financial control. They have similarities to the three management classifications developed by Miles and Snow (1978).[9]

Strategic planning

In strategic planning companies the centre believes that it should take the lead in the development of strategy:

It's a charade to pretend in this era of corporate democracy to decentralize the right and responsibility to be involved in strategic decisions widely into the organization. Down at the business level there are two or three decisions each decade that make or break a business. Do you really want to leave the business manager alone to make these?

explained a senior manager in one strategic planning company.

The centre orchestrates an extensive strategic planning and capital approval system, and uses these processes to influence the thinking of business unit managers and to make suggestions. This has the advantage of allowing the centre to provide active support to business units and to coordinate their strategies. From the perspective of the unit, however, the centre may be seen as too highly involved and bossy. One division manager in a typical strategic planning company commented: 'In this organization, if you ask the CEO for advice, you'll get an instruction'.

These companies frequently have organization structures that promote coordination between businesses and permit central influence to be exercised. Strong staff groups (such as BOC's central technical function) provide functional inputs, and overlapping responsibilities, as in BP's matrix structure, reduce the ability of the unit to act without consultation. The organization structure therefore serves to bring out different views on strategy, but it also blurs and limits the authority and autonomy of the business unit.

The centre's attitude to short-term financial targets matches its concern with strategy. Financial targets are important, but strategic objectives are more important. Sir Hector Laing at UB explained: 'If things are going wrong you identify with the management and help them out. At these times, control should get more friendly, not more fierce.' Poor performance in the short term can be tolerated if larger strategic issues are at stake. This applies particularly where the strategy is ambitious, risky or has a long-term pay-off.

This control philosophy supports the innovators and risk-takers, but as a result it loses some objectivity. Because the centre has been involved in forming the strategy and taking the decisions, it is then hard to hold business unit managers to account if the strategy does not perform as expected. As Dick Giordano of BOC put it: 'The greatest mistake I made was as a result of one manager who fell in love with his business and got me to fall in love with it too'. Giordano underlined the difficulty of achieving tight control in companies that stress the importance of long-term strategic progress: 'This is probably one of the most difficult challenges. How do you have milestones that measure strategic progress without allowing excuse making from business managers'.

Strategic control

Strategic control companies devolve the responsibility for strategy to strong division managers and devote more attention than strategic planning companies to annual financial performance. The philosophy of central managers is different too. Sir Christopher Hogg of Courtaulds described his role as 'a detached but sympathetic and knowledgeable 100 per cent shareholder', and Sir John Clark of Plessey captured the essence of the relationship between the centre and the business units when he said 'You can't hire a dog and bark yourself'.

As with the strategic planning style these companies have extensive strategic planning systems, but their purpose is different. They are used to raise the quality of thinking of business unit managers and to pinpoint weak links in the chain. The centre does not push its own viewpoint. It focuses on asking probing questions and uses the planning staff, as Sir David Plastow of Vickers said, 'to put ferrets down holes'. The headquarters is likely to be small in these companies, and the organization structure places clear responsibility on the senior line manager in charge of each business area. Resources are often allocated between businesses based on portfolio planning techniques. However, unlike strategic planning companies, the centre's role is more passive. Proposals are made by business unit managers and sanctioned by the centre, based on the strength of the financial case and the strategic potential of the business.

The centre's reaction to results is more balanced than in strategic planning companies. The centre is likely to set both strategic and financial targets with each business unit manager. Achievement of these targets is viewed as important and the centre controls tightly against them. In strategic control companies, control becomes fiercer when targets are not met, and business unit managers recognize that their performance is not closely involved in shaping business unit strategy. The centre can be more demanding about performance and incentives than under the strategic planning style.

The tightness of the centre's control is, however, limited by the nature of the targets. Strategic targets are often qualitative and less susceptible to objective measurement. Moreover, strategic and financial targets can conflict. Market-share targets can sometimes only be achieved by reducing margins. Return-on-capital targets can sometimes only be achieved by cutting out marginal export business. In these circumstances management has to strike a compromise between strategic and financial targets. Achieving the right balance between financial controls and strategic plans is never easy for these companies and can create conflicts for business unit managers. For example, although long-term strategy may nominally be recognized as the prime concern, the more important and tangible incentives often relate to the achievement of short-term budget targets.

The ambiguity that characterizes the management task in many strategic control companies was well expressed by one division head. He told us that, when he was appointed four years earlier, he had asked the corporate chief executive officer (CEO) whether the company was an industrial group or a financial conglomerate. 'Now', he said, 'the question still seems relevant and the answer is always: "Ask me again in six months' time".'

Financial control

Financial control companies place the responsibility for strategy development even more firmly on the shoulders of business unit managers and rely heavily on the budget process for exercising influence. The centre does not wish to be involved in formulating business unit strategy and therefore it does not formally review strategic plans. Instead it concentrates on short-term budgetary control. This philosophy was well described by a manager at Tarmac: 'The danger is that managers may have their eyes on the horizon when there are pot-holes in the road ahead'.

To ensure that business unit managers are focused on the 'pot-holes in the road ahead', the centre devotes most of its planning energy to the annual budgeting process or, as BTR calls it, the profit-planning process. 'We call it a profit plan not a budget, because it is about making money, not spending money'.

Substantial effort is also devoted to the capital approval process. Hanson Trust, for example, insists that all capital requests greater than £500 in the UK and $1000 in the US require Lord Hanson's signature. The message to unit managers is clear: 'It is not your money, it belongs to the shareholders. If you want to invest, you must show justification'. The criteria for approving proposals are based on the proposal's financial attractiveness and on the strength of the management team concerned. The 'strategic' importance of the business or the individual proposal is not considered. Moreover, the centre believes that its role is purely to sanction or turn away proposals and not to shape or initiate them. This philosophy of decentralization was underlined by one manager, who said: 'You should never tell a business unit manager what to do. If you feel you have to tell him, you know that it is time to replace him'.

Unlike strategic control companies, these companies do not see themselves as allocating a fixed amount of capital between businesses. In fact they do not consider capital a scarce resource: 'We make sure that we are in a position to fund all good proposals. One of the key tasks of the centre is to ensure that we have the funds available', explained one manager. This involves maintaining access to the capital markets so that money can be raised as needed.

Since the centre devotes little energy to trying to influence particular decisions, its main emphasis is on controlling against results. Here the budget-setting process is vital. The objective is to get the business unit to put forward a tough but achievable profit target that will provide both a high return on capital and year-on-year growth. Tarmac call this process putting the business on the 'high wire'. Once the budget is agreed, and it may take two or three iterations to gain agreement, it becomes a contract – a promise between the centre and the unit. Each month results are compared with the budget, variances are discussed and remedial action is expected. As Graeme Odgers explained:

If the business unit managers don't deliver they should feel very bad. They should feel that they have failed themselves, failed us and that life is awful. On the other hand if they succeed, they feel like winners. They are basking and they are rewarded, although the reward is mainly in the mind.

The fact that the 'reward is mainly in the mind' is an interesting feature of these companies. Some, like Hanson Trust, have large bonus schemes that can amount to as much as 100 per cent of salary, but in the main these companies rely on psychological incentives. The business unit manager sets himself stretching targets and feels like a winner when he achieves them. It is this sense of achievement that is the strongest motivating factor.

The penalties for failure, however, are severe. Those failing to meet budget may be given another chance or they may not: 'They might last six months into the year', commented Malcolm Bates at GEC, only slightly exaggerating GEC's emphasis on financial performance. Inevitably, this environment is less encouraging for strategies that involve high risk or long-term investments:

We are a fairly low-risk organization. To get us to take the sort of risks inherent in this proposal (to invest in plant to produce specialist equipment for the oil industry) we would need to be looking at an 18-month payback

explained a group chief executive in BTR.

In summary, the three main styles – strategic planning, strategic control and financial control – are part of a continuous scale. At one end is a style where the centre is highly influential in forming plans and recognizes that annual financial performance may have to be subordinated to strategic objectives. At the other end is a style where the centre avoids interfering in decisions but insists that agreed financial targets must be met. The differences in types of people, culture and atmosphere between these extremes are dramatic, and yet successful companies exist with different styles. In the next section we shall describe the strengths and weaknesses of the three main styles. First, however, we should briefly mention three less popular styles that appear on our conceptual chart in figure 5.1.

Strategic venturing is a style in which central managers decentralize strategy development to the business units and react flexibly to annual financial performance. This style has similarities with the holding company style. The difference is that less autonomy is given to business unit managers. The style is analogous to that of a venture capital company where the parent makes a long-term commitment with the intention of interfering only in extreme circumstances. Active support is provided and results are closely monitored, but the parent does not try to shape the strategy of the entrepreneur or insist that annual profit targets are adhered to. None of the companies in our research sample used this style exclusively; major industrial companies tend not to be comfortable in treating the bulk of their portoflio on such a hands-off basis. However, we found that the style is used in parts of BP and UB, particularly in newer businesses, where the centre has less detailed knowledge of the key issues and is willing to delegate substantial authority to local manage-ment to build businesses for the long-term future.

Strategic programming is the style that many corporate level managers intuitively feel is right. It combines a high level of central influence in planning and developing strategy with a balanced approach to control. Targets are set in both financial and strategic terms, and control against these targets is tight. Some companies, notably STC and Lex, have attempted this style but they have now moved away from it because of the practical difficulties. These companies found it hard for the centre both to be closely involved in taking decisions and to remain sufficiently detached to set and control against clear targets. They also encountered some difficulties in motivating business unit management where the centre was so closely involved. Lex has expressed this trade-off most clearly. It has publicly stated that it is trying to move from a philosophy of 'control' by the centre to one of 'commitment' from the business units. The tight control required in strategic programming is particularly difficult to combine with the sort of ambitious strategies which often emerge from close central involvement in strategy development.

Financial programming is a variant of financial control. BTR and Ferranti are two companies that attach very high importance to annual financial targets, but they combine this short-term financial orientation with a centre that chooses to be more involved in planning than is the case with the other financial control companies. Both BTR and Ferranti have a three-year medium-term plan. They also have more involvement in decision-taking: for example, in BTR the centre is frequently influential in pricing decisions and in Ferranti the centre reviews and approves all private venture research and development projects. Nevertheless – and this is the key feature of the style – it is made clear that decisions and responsibility rest ultimately with the business units and not with the centre.

Of these three less popular styles, two – strategic venturing and strategic programming – do not appear to be sustainable for a whole company. The third, financial programming, is really a variant of financial control. We have therefore concluded that the practical style choices lie on the diagonal from the top left to the bottom right in figure 5.1.

Adding value

Each of the three main styles has important strengths and each has flaws; each adds value to the businesses in the portfolio, but each can also subtract value as well. This implies that central managers should choose the style that best matches their situation. The art of managing large multibusiness organizations may therefore be the art of matching the management approach with the circumstances of the business. As an aid to helping managers choose between the three styles – strategic planning, strategic control and financial control – we shall describe the strengths of each style and we shall note the weaknesses that can lead to subtracted value.

The strategic planning style

The strategic planning style has three important strengths that can add value. The first is that it encourages a more comprehensive search for the best strategy for each business. Proposals from the business units will be challenged and supplemented by the centre. Additional ideas may emerge from other businesses or staff units whose responsibilities overlap with the business in question. These new perspectives prevent the business unit from accepting its prevailing strategy without question, and ensure a wider discussion of alternatives.

A second strength of the style is that it encourages strategies that are integrated across business units. Close involvement of central managers, strong corporate staff functions and organization structures with overlapping responsibilities make it possible for coordination between units to be established. This is often necessary in linked business areas, as Dominic Cadbury, the Chief Executive of Cadbury Schweppes, told us:

In confectionery and soft drinks, our core businesses, I am trying to ensure that we are maximizing our opportunities for synergy. Making sure we are transferring skills, product knowledge and sharing assets.

Or, as Sir Kenneth Corfield of STC remarked:

In businesses such as electronics, we are making sure that divisions help each other. One may have to forgo things so another can get on better.

The third – and perhaps the greatest – strength of the style is its ability to create and support bold and ambitious business strategies. Strategic planning companies are most effective where the business units are striving to gain advantage over competitors – where the units are trying to win. Because the centre provides strategic leadership and has a view about the direction the business unit should be following, it is more possible for a unit to put forward bold plans to increase its market position in line with the centre's objectives. 'We would never have been able to pursue such an ambitious strategy as an independent company', is a comment we received from a number of business unit managers in strategic planning companies. Moreover, because the centre has a set of strategic objectives, units can focus development efforts in support of these objectives without being overly concerned about the short-term financial impact of their decisions. Strategic leadership from the centre encourages business units to focus on building competitive advantages that support the central thrusts and acts as a buffer to capital market pressures. At its best, there is a shared purpose between the centre and the unit that creates a common motivation to build up the core business areas.

The results of the strategic planning companies – BP, BOC, Cadbury's, Lex, STC, UB – provide evidence of these strengths. Strategic planning companies have the highest level of organic growth of the three groups (figure 5.2). Furthermore they appear to make a larger number of bold long-payback decisions than companies with other styles. BP have invested heavily in minerals, coal, nutrition and a number of other areas such as electronics, recognizing that immediate returns may be low. BOC has ploughed resources into strengthening its worldwide position in gases. It has also built a major position in health care and made large capital investments in the carbon graphite electrode business. Cadbury's, Lex, STC and UB have all made important investments in the USA, each in different ways, recognizing that returns may be temporarily low or volatile but believing that a US position is essential for the long-term strength of their core businesses. Sir Hector Laing of UB told us: 'In my

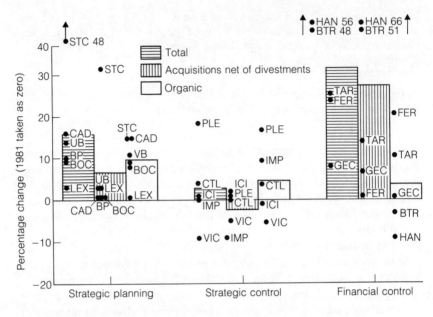

Figure 5.2 Average yearly fixed asset growth, 1981–1985 (from *Datastream Annual Reports*). The growth statistics have been drawn from *Datastream* using the following definitions:

net earnings per share (EPS)

$$= \frac{\text{net earnings for ordinary}}{\text{average weighted capital, fully adjusted}}$$

total sales = UK sales to third parties
+ exports from UK (including overseas subsidiaries if only described as exports in accounts – otherwise overseas sales excluded from exports)
+ overseas sales (overseas subsidiary sales to third parties – sometimes inclusive of intercompany sales if not defined in accounts)
– intercompany sales
– associate company sales
– value-added tax if included in turnover (mainly retail companies)
– other duties and taxes (excise and sales-related taxes paid)

experience it takes about seven years to build a viable business in today's competitive environment'. And Sir Kenneth Corfield of STC commented: 'Sometimes you need to go along with a development for five to seven years before getting any business'.

In a given business, strategic planning companies are more likely to choose the ambitious expansive option rather than the cautious option. For example, STC, Plessey and GEC have all been competitors in manufacturing electronic components for defence and telecommunications systems. STC (the strategic planning company) decided that it should have a major presence in components to compete successfully in the worldwide telecommunications market. Management therefore decided to build businesses in Europe and the USA, and to move into the production of integrated circuits. Plessey (the strategic control company) also believed that a presence in components would be a benefit to its telecommunications and defence businesses. However, faced with a shortage of capital and acknowledging a weak positon in components, management decided to specialize rather than expand and, at one point, even considered selling the component division. GEC (the financial control company) had no preconceived rationale for being in the components industry. Since the profit returns in the industry were cyclical and remained low overall, GEC limited its position in many component products or avoided investing in them in the first place.

We therefore believe that the strategic planning style is most effective where the need is for a wide search for optimum integrated strategies to build businesses with long-term competitive advantage.

However, these strengths are accompanied by drawbacks. The extensive planning process can become cumbersome, frustrating and costly, particularly when many managers are trying to stamp their own view on the outcome. The line management of the business units can then become demotivated, feeling that their responsibility for strategy choice has been attenuated and that they have little personal ownership of the decisions being made for the businesses nominally in their charge. It is in these circumstances that 'advice' can come to seem like 'instructions', with the result that business managers become protective about their decisions. 'The secret is not to have to spend too much time defending your own policies and implementation decisions from corporate intervention', we were told by one division manager in a strategic planning company.

Secondly, decisions that require extensive consultation tend to be reached slowly, causing the business units to become less flexible in response to local market needs or fast-changing conditions. This, together with looser controls, can lead to delayed reactions to adversity.

The quality of central influence can also vary. In particular, when the distance between the centre and the market is too great, central managers can lose touch with the business and steer on the basis of an understanding of the environment that is faulty or out of date:

The chairman sees himself as a strategist – especially concerning collaboration and acquisitions. He tends to throw out ideas. His understanding of the business may be rather weak however, so some ideas can appear strange.

'Bold' investments can then become overambitious risky strategies that result in major setbacks.

The strategic planning style therefore brings more dangers of serious reverses. Cadbury's, Lex and STC have all experienced setbacks in their expansion strategies that have led to earnings decline for the company as a whole, and BP, BOC and UB have suffered heavy losses in some of their business-building ventures. The style can also mean that losing strategies are supported for too long. It is possible in these companies to find businesses or divisions that have performed poorly for five or ten years, but where business unit managers are still asking the centre for one more chance to 'get the long-term strategy right'.

These problems are particularly evident in highly diverse portfolios, where the centre has great difficulty in acquiring a depth of strategic understanding concerning each of the businesses in the group. Accordingly, the strategic planning companies have tended to focus increasingly on a few core businesses, like BOC in gases and health care. They have also divested many businesses that did not fit into their core areas.

In summary, the strategic planning style appears to be most effective in homogeneous portfolios and for building businesses, particularly where global or integrated strategies are needed. However, it is a costly time-consuming style that can demotivate managers, and the lack of detachment of central managers can cause the company to attempt overambitious strategies or to follow a losing strategy for too long.

The financial control style

The financial control style is almost a mirror image of the strategic planning style. Its key source of added value is the increased motivation and pressure that it creates to improve financial performance. Targets are clear and unequivocal, investment paybacks are kept short, performance is monitored carefully and variances against plan invoke swift and decisive central action. Rather than providing a buffer to financial pressures from the City, the financial control style represents a more efficient and penetrating discipline than the capital markets. All of this results in better profit performance, at least in the short term.

The results of the companies in our sample – BTR, Ferranti, GEC, Hanson and Tarmac – support this relationship. On average they have higher profitability ratios – return on sales and return on capital – than companies with the other two styles (figure 5.3). They are also more active than companies in the other style groups in rationalizing poorly performing businesses and turning around new acquisitions than companies in the other style groups. The style is therefore strong in

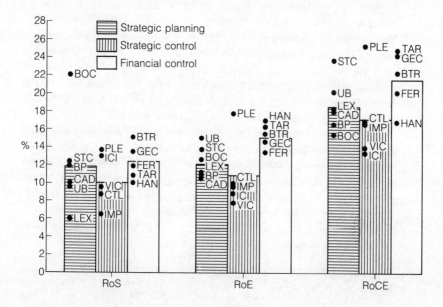

Figure 5.3 Four-year profitability averages, 1981–1985 (from *Datastream Annual Reports*). The profitability ratios have been drawn from *Datastream* using the following definitions:

return on shareholders' equity (RoE)

$$= \frac{\text{earned for ordinary (fully taxed)}}{\text{ordinary share capital + reserves − goodwill + deferred tax}}$$

return on capital employed (RoCE)

$$= \frac{\text{pre-tax profits (including assocs.) + interest charges}}{\text{total capital employed + borrowing repayable within 1 year − goodwill}}$$

trading profit margin (RoS)

$$= \frac{\text{trading profit}}{\text{total sales}}$$

RoE, RoCE and RoS are expressed as percentages. Trading profit is the net profit before depreciation is deducted, operating profit is the trading profit less depreciation and pre-tax profit is the operating profit plus non-trading income less interest.

pressing for improved short-term results. However, it also has a number of other less obvious strengths.

1 Because year-on-year *improvements* in profits are required, business managers are given an incentive not to sacrifice future years to achieve a single unsustainable profit surge.

2 Because there is unforgiving enforcement of demanding targets, failing strategies are challenged forcefully. The centre may do little

to assist in identifying alternative strategies, but they do provide the impetus to break business managers out of an inappropriate strategy pattern.

3 Because profit responsibility is devolved to the lowest levels, general management experience is given early to a large number of potential high fliers. Those who succeed reach the top only after extensive general management experience. Those who are less suited to the general management task are identified early, and weeded out before much damage is done to the company as a whole.

4 Because clear and demanding targets are set, managers who reach their objectives have a greater sense of achievement. 'Survivors' in the financial control system know that they have been tested against the toughest benchmarks of performance and have succeeded. This gives them the self-confidence to push forward with their businesses as they see fit, in the expectation that they will be able to continue to deliver. This is referred to in Tarmac as a 'winners' psychology. Graeme Odgers put it this way:

> Pure logic would argue that a management team would set a low budget because life will be easy. However, when they do put in a low budget, we make them feel that they have let the side down. We make them feel that they are not ambitious to be part of the first team. On the whole, we have more problems in the other direction. The management have so much belief in themselves that they want to go in too deep. They may fall into the trap of thinking that they can do anything.

5 Because a 'winners psychology' is created amongst the general managers of the business units, the quality of the dialogue with the centre is improved. Business management with a track record of 'delivering' will argue their views more openly and with less concern to please the boss. They are confident that their progress in the company depends on the results they achieve, not on their eloquence in plan review meetings.

A further strength of the financial control style is that it is effective in a highly diverse portfolio. To adopt the financial control style, the centre does not need an intimate knowledge of the competition and the market-place of each unit. The responsibility for strategy development is wholly decentralized, and the centre concentrates on control against established ratios that can be compared across many different businesses without requiring detailed product or market knowledge at the centre. The emphasis on financial targets and ratios therefore makes it easier to manage diversity.

However, the financial control style also has its weaknesses. It is biased against long-payback investments and strategies that build advantages in the long term. At a minimum this makes the style vulnerable to aggressive committed competitors and causes problems in businesses which do intrinsically require long lead times. From a strong position in rubber belting, BTR did not aggressively follow the trend to plastic belting (which captured more than 50 per cent of the market), in large part because of the strength of the competitors' moves. They chose instead to develop a niche position in steel cord belting. Tarmac were ready to sell their oil exploration and production business because the decisions were large and highly risky, and therefore difficult to manage within an annual budget cycle. Anthony Alexander of Hanson Trust described one business that approached the centre with a proposal to produce a promising new generation of products which, however, had a seven- to eight-year payback period: 'We found this difficult to deal with at the centre. The business was sold shortly after'. Pushed to extremes, the style can lead to milking a business for purely short-term gains and to excessive risk aversion concerning investment and development expenditures.

The consequence for the financial control company is that major growth tends to depend more on acquisitions than on organic developments. Despite the highly successful acquisition record of companies such as Hanson and BTR, there are limits to how far growth based on acquisition can be taken. At Hanson's current size, there are now very few potential targets that would make a major impact on their results, so that further significant acquisition-based growth will be hard to achieve. Viewed nationally, it can also be argued that acquisitions create less real wealth than organic investments.

Secondly, extreme decentralization makes it hard to gain the potential benefits of synergy between business units. In part this problem can be solved by redefining business units so that two linked businesses are viewed as one. But the philosophy of the style works against putting businesses together. It is more normal for these companies to tear businesses apart in the quest to weed out low profit activities. With some notable exceptions, few units in financial control companies are involved in attempting to build major coordinated global positions. It is more normal for them to be focused on segments or niches, and to avoid integrated strategies across a broad business area. Finally, rigorous control processes reduce flexibility. In businesses where circumstances change rapidly, blind adherence to last year's budget targets may preclude more adaptive strategies that take advantage of events as they unfold. Where controls become a strait-jacket, opportunities can be missed.

The financial control style is therefore most powerful in drawing maximum performance out of managers in extensive portfolios of established businesses. However, it can inhibit innovation and risk-taking. This means that growth tends to come from acquisition and profitability improvement rather than from organic business building.

The strategic control style

The strategic control style aims for a balance between strategic planning and financial control. In theory, the style has the potential to obtain all the added value of the other two styles and none of the weaknesses. In practice, however, there are tensions in the style which make it perhaps the hardest to execute successfully.

The main strength of strategic control is that it achieves a balance between the objectives of building a business and maximizing financial performance and avoids the excesses of the other two styles. The key features of the style all support this balance. Business unit managers are measured against both financial short-term objectives and strategic measures or milestones. The capital approval processes use both financial and strategic criteria to allocate resources between projects, and are frequently backed by a portfolio planning system that categorizes businesses by their strategic importance. In accordance with this, some business units will be labelled growth areas where long-term investment is required to build and develop the products, while others are labelled as cash generators where the objectives are more financial and less strategic. Finally, these companies delegate strategy development to business and divisional levels, but have a thorough planning system to ensure that business unit managers are taking both a strategic and a financial view of their businesses. The process is mainly directed at raising the quality of thinking in the business unit, but it also serves to set the strategic and financial targets that are part of the balanced control process. The results of the strategic control companies – Courtaulds, ICI, Imperial, Plessey and Vickers – show how this balanced planning and control process performs. In general it results in lower organic growth rates than are obtained by strategic planning companies, but at the same time it causes substantial improvement in profitability ratios (figure 5.4).

Some of the business units undoubtedly pursue long-term strategies aimed at building major positions. For example, the Pharmaceutical Division of ICI and the International Paints Division of Courtaulds are among the greatest international success stories in British industry, and have built up their positions using systematic long-term investments. However, there have been relatively few important new initiatives. Major investments and acquisitions, which are so important to the business-building strategies of the strategic planning companies, have been much rarer in the strategic control companies. Extensive investigations of possible acquisitions have been made, but few have come to fruition.

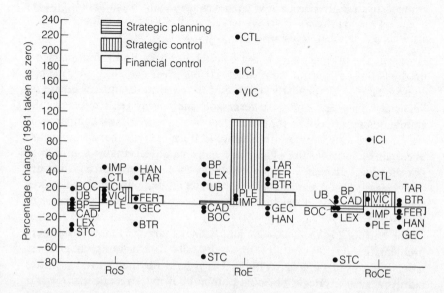

Figure 5.4 Change in profitability ratios, 1981–1985 (from *Datastream Annual Reports*).

Equally, the drive to raise performance in less profitable businesses has been less ruthless than under the financial control style. As with strategic planning companies, 'strategic' arguments (or excuses) have allowed some less profitable businesses to continue to operate at basically unsatisfactory levels of return for extended periods. It took Imperial Group over five years finally to bite the bullet and dispose of the Howard Johnson chain, which had so depressed their corporate earnings in the early 1980s. A balance is therefore achieved between long-term strategy and short-term profit, but in achieving this balance compromises have to be made and the appropriateness of the balance can sometimes be called into question.

A second major strength of the strategic control style is that it enhances the motivation of business unit managers by giving them more responsibility and by making them more accountable. Decentralization of strategy is not always comfortable for the centre, but it can provide significant benefits down the line. The Chairman of a Vickers Division, describing his attitude to freedom and responsibility, argued as follows:

In giving freedom, it's a bit nerve-racking at times because you feel you're not in control, not in charge. But the result is that they take more initiative and they perform better. And they feel responsible for their actions, whereas if you at the centre always ask questions, always try and monitor things very carefully, you get a reaction that they're not really responsible for the decisions, that you're really controlling things and so if it goes wrong, it's as much your fault as it is theirs.

However, the responsibility and accountability of business unit managers in the strategic control companies is less clear-cut than in financial control companies, precisely because of the need to balance strategic and financial objectives, and long-term and short-term goals. In fact, the ambiguous nature of the control system in strategic control companies is one of the main weaknesses of the style. Business unit managements are uncertain about priorities. This can result in an overcautious approach to fast-growing businesses and an insufficiently tough approach to mature businesses. The balance between strategic and financial objectives complicates the task of business unit managers and reduces the clarity of objectives.

The balance between strategic and financial targets is made even more problematic on account of the difficulty of defining objectively measurable strategic goals. This makes it hard for the centre to control tightly against strategic objectives, thus allowing strategic excuses for poor performance. The centre's lack of conviction also rubs off on the business unit managers. One manager commented:

Tight control was and is needed. But it does discourage risk-taking. Managers get kicked hard if they go for risky innovations and fail. So the tendency is for the more risky investments to drop out of the plan and as it gets turned into the budget.

At its worst the style can become an ineffective form of financial control. The only real measures of performance become financial; and yet managers devote time to a planning process that adds cost but little value. Alternatively, the ambiguity of control objectives and the difficulty of defining strategic control measures can lead to a political assessment process in which achievement of planned objectives takes second place to impressing the boss.

A third feature of the strategic control style is that it can cope with a diverse portfolio of businesses in different sorts of competitive environments. The whole idea of 'strategic' controls is that they should be tailored to the needs of each business, while the decentralization of strategy development places the main onus for managing the business on local management. However, the ability to cope with diversity creates its own problems if it is taken too far. Too much diversity of businesses can lead to superficiality in the planning process. One manager complained that in his company there are 'a whole series of rakings over at different levels, but all of them too shallow'. The centre may be stretched across too many businesses to judge the potential of each. By misunderstanding businesses, the centre can pick the wrong strategic objectives. This will cause businesses to underperform and will demotivate the unit management.

Therefore, although strategic control can be the most balanced style, it has within it certain ambiguities and tensions. It has the potential to handle a diverse portfolio of businesses and to help them to tune their strategies to their specific circumstances, but the success of companies adopting this style depends on how well they handle the ambiguities.

Conclusions

In our research we have identified three major different relationships between central managers and business unit managers – three strategic management styles for the centre. Each style can add value, but its strengths are often balanced by offsetting weaknesses (tables 5.3–5.5). We have concluded that there is no one right style – no single ideal way for the centre to manage a diversity of business units. Instead, a choice must be made between basically different styles. We believe that these different styles exist because of certain tensions implicit in the role of

Table 5.3 Strategic planning

Key features	Added value	Subtracted value
Complex coordinated structure	Wider discussion of issues	Less individual responsibility and authority
	Synergy	
Extensive strategic planning process	More thorough search for best strategies	Less freedom of action
		Slower decisions
Strong central leadership	Bolder strategies	Less 'ownership' by business
	Shared purpose and commitment	Less objectivity by centre
Long-term criteria	Building core businesses	Slower reactions to adversity
	'Buffer' to capital market	Less clear targets
Flexible controls	More tenacious pursuit of long-term goals	Subjective assessments
	More innovative responsive strategies	Less accountability

Table 5.4   Financial control

Key features	Added value	Subtracted value
Separate profit centres	Simplifies task Early general management responsibility	No coordination, synergy
Budgetary planning	Higher standards Challenges strategies that will not deliver Avoids 'pot-holes'	Distracts from strategic issues
Business autonomy	Advice, not instructions	No cooperation, no 'help' for businesses
Short-term criteria	Clearer criteria 'Efficient' internal capital market	Missed opportunities
Tight controls	Faster reaction More motivation Winners psychology	Less flexibility and creativity

corporate management. In our work, we found many managers who argued for the following:

strong leadership by the centre;
coordinated strategies that take account of a variety of viewpoints;
thorough and careful analysis of decisions;
long-term thinking;
flexibility in strategy.

Equally – and sometimes amongst the same managers – there were advocates of the following:

freedom and autonomy for business managers who are closest to the action;
clear personal responsibilities and accountabilities;
entrepreneurial speed of response to market opportunities;
emphasis on short-term performance;
tight control of actual results versus plans.

Both these lists of guiding principles have their attractions. Yet they are, to a greater or lesser extent, in conflict with each other. Central leadership, if it has any teeth, must inhibit business autonomy; coordinated strategies must detract from clear personal accountability; thorough planning precludes entrepreneurial speed of response; long-term thinking and goals will compromise short-term performance pressure; flexibility in strategy is at odds with precise adherence to planned objectives.

Table 5.5   Strategic control

Key features	Added value	Subtracted value
Decentralized profit centres Divisional coordination	Little by centre	No central coordination
Extensive strategic planning process	Raises minimum standards of thinking and analysis Challenges habits of mind	Constraining
Long- and short-term criteria	Acceptance of longer-term investments Balanced objectives	Ambiguous objectives
Tight controls	More motivation to perform	Risk aversion Subjective balancing of objectives

Therefore no style can hope to succeed simultaneously in all dimensions. Each of the styles we have identified can be seen as a choice of certain sources of added value at the expense of others which are incompatible. The weaknesses of each style follow inevitably from its own strengths. This means that the task of corporate management is to select a style whose strengths are vital and whose weaknesses are of less consequence, given the nature and needs of the businesses in the portfolio. Is it worth sacrificing tight control and individual responsibility in order to build up selected long-term core businesses under the strategic planning style? Do the benefits of clear goals and devolved responsibility under a financial control style outweigh the dangers of risk aversion and short-term thinking? Are we willing to handle the ambiguity of strategic control in order to achieve a balanced approach across a diverse portfolio? These are the types of question that the central team must address. They can be finally resolved only after taking account of the particular characteristics of the businesses in each company's portfolio and of the people in the management team. However, a clearer appreciation of the trade-offs involved will improve the chances that the corporate centre will add value to the businesses under their charge, rather than subtracting value from them.

Our research has reopened an agenda for central management that was first documented by Alfred Chandler and Alfred Sloane. Most of the current literature focuses on the business or SBU level, or, where it does address the role of the centre, on the subject of corporate strategies. Little research is focused on the *management process* of the corporate centre.

Future research therefore has a wide canvas to cover. The most urgent task is to validate the categorizations – the styles we have used to describe our sample. Do these styles capture the behaviour patterns in a broader sample? Do they exist in a similar form in companies with headquarters in other countries such as the USA, Germany or France? Can others confirm that different styles cause different decisions to be made and lead to different results? Do managers recognize themselves and their companies when offered these style descriptions? We hypothesize that the answer to all of these questions is yes, and we believe that there are researchable issues.

By developing a questionnaire it should be possible to test a larger sample of UK companies. The questionnaire would also help to assess whether these categories have meaning for managers. Continued interviewing with companies that do not easily fit the mould, such as Unilever or Coloroll or Hillsdown, will also help to test the robustness of the style's framework. Any extension of the work to companies with headquarters outside the UK would almost certainly need to be done by a team of researchers from the country in question for language, access and cultural reasons. However, a similar programme of interviews and analysis in overseas companies would substantially expand the base of this research.

The impact of style on decisions is probably the most critical issue. If the different styles do not lead managers to make different decisions given the same circumstances, the categorizations are not useful. But this is the hardest research to undertake. The same circumstances never exist. The researcher must look for patterns and biases from a stream of decisions. We took the anecdotes and descriptions of decisions from our interviews and from annual reports. This gave some 70 decision examples for each style type. On a crude categorization it was apparent that the financial control companies have a greater number of short-term decisions and the strategic planning companies talk more about long-term decisions. However, we would need to have a random sample of the complete decision set and a means of categorizing differences such as payback period or size to be comfortable with the conclusion. The research is difficult but not infeasible.

An alternative research methodology would be to use managers from companies with different styles and put each team through a similar decision case study. This kind of laboratory work has been used to assess the decision-making impact of different national cultures (Kaur, 1987) and could be used in a similar way for this research.

The second urgent task is to identify what kinds of situations best fit each of the styles. Our research implies that each style needs to be matched with the business situation – a contingency theory of headquarters management. In *Strategies and Styles* (Goold and Campbell, 1987) we push our thinking on this issue as far as we can. We hypothesize answers to such questions as the following. How many styles can the centre operate at one time? How quickly can style be changed? What are the critical ingredients of the business situation that should be matched to the style? Answers to these questions can be confirmed only by further research documenting case studies. There appears to be no alternative to the lengthy process of developing more case studies which are more detailed to validate these hypotheses.

Notes

1 The rapid increase in diversification since the war (Channon, 1982; Rumelt, 1974) would suggest that the diversified firm must have some advantages. If it did not, then 'survival of the fittest' would have prevented this trend from occurring.
2 Academic research to quantify the benefits of diversification has been inconclusive. Studies of specific diversification and acquisition moves (Kitching, 1967, 1974; Biggadike 1979).
3 For a summary of the litrature and a recent UK study see Grant et al. (1986).
4 See for example, Porter (1980, appendix A) for a summary of the two main techniques of portfolio analysis. Important studies of resource allocation decisions include Bower (1970), Pettigrew (1973), King (1975) and Marsh et al. (1988).
5 Graeme Odgers is now Deputy Chairman of British Telecom. In general, our comments in this paper refer to the period during which we carried out the fieldwork for this research, which ended early in 1986.
6 Marsh et al. (1987) describe the nature of interventions made by the centre in the decisions they studied. It is evident that the business units take the centre's sanctioning authority seriously. They identified eight ways in which the centre intervened. These interventions appear to be similar to the planning influence interventions we have identified. The two studies have used different language, but are describing the same reality.

Our language	Marsh's language
Setting the direction	Imposing specific criteria
Making specific suggestions	Testing for commitment
Asking probing questions	Questioning assumptions
Recasting the organizational structure	Controlling the organization context
	Appointing senior managers
	Protecting group and other divisions' interests
	Wearing two hats

7 The term 'holding company' is used by Williamson (1975), who argues that diversified firms can allocate capital more efficiently than the outside capital market provided they have appropriate planning and control mechanisms. He refers to firms with such mechanisms as M-form (multidivisional) enterprises. Divisionalized firms which lack the requisite planning and control mechanisms are referred to as H-form (holding company) enterprises.

8 A much fuller description of all the styles and of the findings from the research is given in Goold and Campbell (1987).

9 In one of the most perceptive and useful recent attempts to integrate strategy thinking and the analysis of management processes, Miles and Snow (1978) also stress the way in which certain combinations of strategy, structure, systems and people go together. They draw distinctions between ways of managing that have some analogy with our strategic planning, strategic control and financial control classifications, although their focus is on the business unit rather than the corporate level. Miles and Snow identify prospectors (businesses that are constantly seeking market opportunities for new products), defenders (businesses that concentrate on optimizing their performance in existing product markets) and analysers (businesses that analyse the changing competitive environment to determine whether and when to match competitors' new product or optimization moves). Miles and Snow believe that the whole administrative context and structure tends to differ between these strategic orientations. Although the analogy with our conclusions is by no means complete, it is interesting that they propose two philosophies which are polar opposites (prospectors and defenders) and one which is a combination of them (analysers). This is reminiscent of our contrasts between strategic planning and financial control, with strategic control as an intermediate position.

References

Andrews, K. (1980). *The Concept of Corporate Strategy*. Homewood, IL: Irwin.

Ansoff, I.H. (1979). *Strategic Management*. New York: Macmillan.

—— (1984). *Implanting Strategic Management*. Englewood Cliffs, NJ: Prentice-Hall.

Biggadike, R. (1979). *Corporate Diversification*. Boston, MA: Division of Research, Harvard Business School.

Bower, J.L. (1970). *Managing the Resource Allocation Process*. Boston, MA: Harvard Business School. (Republished in 1986.)

Chandler, A.D. (1962). *Strategy and Structure: Chapters in the History of Industrial Enterprise*. Cambridge, MA: MIT Press.

Channon, D. (1982). 'Industrial Structure' *Long Range Planning*, October, 15(5), 78–93.

Eccles, R.G. (1983). 'Control with fairness in transfer pricing'. *Harvard Business Review*, November–December, 63(6), 149–56.

Gluck, F., Kaufmann, S. and Walleck, A.S. (1980). 'Strategic management for competitive advantage'. *Harvard Business Review*, July–August, 60(4), 154–61.

Goold, M. and Campbell, A. (1987). *Strategies and Styles: The Role of the Centre in Managing the Diversified Corporation.* Oxford: Blackwell.

Grant, R.M., Jammine, A. and Thomas H. (1986). 'Diversification and profitability: a study of 305 British manufacturing companies 1972–84'. Research Paper 25, Centre for Business Strategy, London Business School.

Hamermesh, R.G. and White, R.E. (1984). 'Manage beyond portfolio analysis'. *Harvard Business Review*, January–February. **64**(1), 103–10.

Hofer, D.W. and Schendel, D. (1978). *Strategy Formulation: Analytical Concepts.* St. Paul, MN: West Publishing.

Kaur, S. (1987). 'Culturally bounded rationality'. Dissertation, Henley Management College (unpublished).

King, P.F. (1975). 'An investigation of the process of large scale capital investment decision making in diversified hierarchical organisations'. Doctoral Dissertation, Cambridge University (unpublished).

Kitching, J. (1967). 'Why do mergers miscarry?' *Harvard Business Review*, November–December, **47**(6), 84–101.

—— (1974). 'Winning and losing with European acquisitions'. *Harvard Business Review*, March–April, **54**(2), 124–36.

Lorange, P. (1979). *Implementation of Strategic Planning.* Englewood Cliffs, NJ: Prentice-Hall.

—— and Vancil, R.F. (1977). *Strategic Planning Systems.* Englewood Cliffs, NJ: Prentice-Hall.

Marsh, P., Barwise, P., Thomas, K. and Wensley, R. (1988). 'Managing strategic investment decisions'. In *Competitiveness and the Management Process* (ed. A.M. Pettigrew). Oxford: Basil Blackwell.

Miles, R. and Snow, C. (1978). *Organizational Strategy, Structure and Process.* New York: McGraw-Hill.

Pettigrew, A.M. (1973). *The Politics of Organisational Decision Making.* London: Tavistock Publications.

Porter, M. (1980). *Competitive Strategy.* New York: Free Press.

Rumelt, R.R. (1974). *Strategy, Structure and Economic Performance.* Boston, MA: Division of Research, Harvard Business School.

Sathe, V. (1982). *Controller Involvement in Management.* Englewood Cliffs, NJ: Prentice-Hall.

Vancil, R.F. (1973). 'What kind of management control do you need?' *Harvard Business Review*, March–April, **53**(2), 75–87.

—— (1979). *Decentralisation: Management Ambiguity by Design.* New York: Dow Jones–Irwin.

—— and Green, C.F. (1984). 'How CEOs use top management committees'. *Harvard Business Review*, January–February. **64**(1), 65–73.

Williamson, O.E. (1975). *Markets and Hierarchies: A Study in the Economics of Internal Organisation.* New York: Free Press.

6
Managing the executive process

Iain Mangham

A short time ago, I attended a retirement dinner for the divisional managing director of a major UK company. There were some 30 to 40 of us present acknowledging his 28 years of 'service to the company'. Paul, as I will call him, had been responsible for a substantial part of the group's turnover and, in earlier years, for the larger share of its profits. In the past four years, a new strategy had been devised, a new structure agreed, new senior posts filled, new markets identified, new products developed, factories had been rationalized and 4000 people had been made redundant. Nevertheless the division turned in substantial losses in each of these years and Paul, who had been severely ill, was going early at 50 years old.

At my end of the table, some of the executives – until 24 hours before, members of his team – were running a book on the possible length of his valedictory address. I suggested a time much shorter than anyone else (15 minutes to their 40 and 50 minutes) and was quizzed about it: 'Do you know what he is going to say?' On affirming, falsely, that I did, the follow-up came quickly: 'Have you talked to him about it? If so, let's hope you had the same influence as you have had in the past. One of us is bound to win in that case.' Some of us were going down with him; I had spent the last four years working with Paul and his team and am closely identified with his failure 'to turn the company around'.

What follows is an account of what I have learned about managing the executive process from that experience, from the experience of working intensively with four other teams over the past 10 years, from my own time as a senior manager in both industry and the university, from talking to managers around the world and from reading what others have to say about the process. Some of what I have to say is anecdotal. I make no apology for that; most of us learn everything we need to know about how to operate in an organization from the stories that we tell and are told. Those of you who are uneasy with such an approach – probably most of you who lay claim to being academics – will be relieved to know that much of what I have to say will be in terms recognizable to you if not normally acceptable to you. I shall begin by delineating the nature of the executive process – the area of study which is of interest to me – I shall discuss how it can be studied, concentrating on an outline of what I think I know about it, and conclude, inevitably, with some comments on the need for further research.

Chester E. Barnard wrote the seminal work on executive function and process and it is to that that I turn first for my definition. For the most part, what he has to say by his own admission is 'laboured, abstract and abstruse'. However, his central concern is clear. For him – and, with important qualifications, for me – an organization is a 'system of consciously coordinated activities or forces of two or more persons'.

Those familiar with my work will recognize that my qualifications will centre around terms such as 'systems' and 'consciously coordinated' – more of that later. The essential executive functions, according to Barnard, are 'first, to provide the system of communication; second, to promote the securing of essential efforts; and third, to formulate and define purpose' (Barnard, 1938). The functions of the executive relate to all those aspects of work essential to the vitality and endurance of an organization, and its concern ought not to be with the work *of* the organization but the specialized work of *maintaining* it in operation.

The executive functions which Barnard enumerated have, of course, no separate concrete existence. They are part of the *process* of organization as a whole which is much less easy to specify. Indeed, Barnard ducks it and so shall I. The genuinely creative side of organization is coordination: the securing of the appropriate combination of activities to produce whatever it is the organization is in business to produce – widgets, hula-hoops, spacecraft, students, research or whatever. This mysterious balancing – the 'feel' for what is appropriate, the ability to be an all-round good manager – is essentially non-technical in character. What an effective executive requires is an ability to hold it all together, a sense of things as a whole, a persistence in subordinating the parts to the whole, and an ability to discriminate what is important and strategic from that which is not. Since little of this can be measured and most of what occurs in organizations is in dynamic and complex flux, what is important is 'judgement' or 'feeling'.

So my interest is in what it is that senior managers functioning as executives do to coordinate their activities and those of others in the organization. How is it that they 'sense' what is necessary and appropriate and how is it that they set up communication, secure essential effort, and formulate and define purpose? Through what process do managers as executives arrive at organizations through the 'modification of the actions of the individual' and how do they 'facilitate the synthesis in concrete action of contradictory forces, reconcile conflicting forces, instincts, interests, conditions, positions and ideals'? (Barnard, 1938). This is an area of interest which, as Barnard himself was the first to acknowledge, is recognized rather than described and is known by its effects rather than by analysis.

Some 50 years have elapsed and we still do not know a great deal about what top managers do and still less about executive function and executive process. My concern has been, and is, with the handful of senior executives who usually surrounded the chief executive officer (CEO), and they and their activities are my focus since they, above all others, are responsible for the functions I have outlined above and the survival of the enterprise depends upon their skill. I take this interest to be a matter of consequence; too much of what passes for research into management is concerned with aspects of it that can be quantified rather than features that are important. The executive process is central to the success of the company; without teamwork at the top the organization has a bleak future. McDonald (1972) captures the essence of my positon in his statement:

If the power center at the top is in chaos, what hope has the rest of the corporation for constructive action? Business cannot go on as usual. Limp, anxious and vulnerable, the organization is unable to react effectively to new threats. As the contagion spreads, even distant departments are soon infected with pettiness, personal rivalries linked to different leaders, and arbitrary rulings of little logic or importance.

Levels of analysis in the studying of executive process

As Doise (1986) points out, it is possible to distinguish at least four levels of analysis in the study of behaviour in organizations. The first is concerned with psychological or intrapersonal processes: what happens at the executive level is depicted as the result of the way an individual construes and organizes his or her experiences of the world. The focus is on finding out what individual managers do at this level – the 'I proved I could do it to screw Henry Ford' type of biography (ghosted or not). A second level of explanation looks beyond the individual to the dynamics of the interpersonal and intrasituational processes. In this kind of explanation certain factors are seen to be important to behaviour and are capable of being manipulated. From this perspective, for example, since certain skills are required to operate an effective team, optimum groups (it is argued) can be constructed (Belbin, 1981). A third type of explanation recognizes that extrasituational factors may be of conse-quence in interaction. No one comes naked to the conference table; each of us trails a reputation, a position or whatever, and these factors (which are variously identified) affect performance in a group. Finally, a fourth level of explanation begins much further out, a long way from the individual, with an analysis of broad concepts covering society in general and attempts to show how, for example, ideologies lead to different ways of behaving.

It is, of course, nonsense to claim that each and every study of executive process can be assigned clearly to one or other of these levels of analysis. However, the distinction is useful in that it helps to see the particular emphasis of a piece of work. What follows is located somewhere at the third level and should not be confused with studies which adopt a different level of analysis. I am making no claims that what I am offering is of a higher order or is somehow better than other approaches, nor that it is unaffected by them; I am simply declaring that my emphasis is upon the executive process as a group or team activity, influenced by factors such as individual skill, position, reputation and, importantly, ideology.

Scripts and performance

Chester Barnard was not primarily a scholar, although his book has the hallmarks of a scholarly tome: it is lengthy, ponderous, turgid, full of definitions and qualifications, wordy and quite extraordinarily difficult to read. He clearly got a number of things wrong: he talks of purpose but not of choice and of the individual but not of persons, and he says little or nothing about the executive group. However, he does stress the unarticulated side of the executive process – top management as an art:

In the common-sense, everyday, practical knowledge necessary to the practice of the arts, there is much that is not susceptible to verbal statement – it is a matter of know-how . . . It is necessary to doing things in concrete situations. It is nowhere more indispensable than in the executive arts. It is acquired by persistent, habitual experience and is often called intuitive. (Barnard, 1938)

It is acquired by persistent, habitual experience and is often called intuitive. So it is. Most executives, much of the time, act intuitively, that is to say without reflection, because what they do is to realize performances with which they are familiar. Most actions at a senior level, as elsewhere, repeat well-rehearsed patterns and most attempts at executive coordination are no more than variations on well-worn themes. Sometimes, of course, there is, as Barnard declares, a matter of *know-how*; sometimes, perhaps often, given the fall-out rate for organizations (Starbuck, 1983), there is a matter of *not-know-how*.

Elsewhere, I have used the term 'script' to highlight the fact that a great deal of everyday behaviour inside and outside organizations is run off without a moment's reflection. We behave spontaneously within the frameworks that we have all grown to know and love. A script – in the sense that I am using it – refers to a circumstance in which (a) the situation is specified, (b) several players have interlocking roles to play and (c) the players share an understanding of what is to happen (Schank and Abelson, 1977; Mangham, 1986, 1987; Mangham and Overington, 1986). There are scripts for behaving in a supermarket, for conducting oneself appropriately at a cocktail party, for interviews, for lovers, for funerals, for eating out or in, for conferences . . . executive meetings. March and Simon had a similar concept years ago:

Situations in which a relatively simple stimulus sets off an elaborate programme of activity without any apparent interval of search, problem-solving, or choice are not rare. They account for a very large part of the behaviour of all persons, and for almost all of the behaviour of persons in relatively routine positions. Most behaviour, and particularly most behaviour in organizations, is governed by performance programmes. (March and Simon, 1958)

Organizations effectively amplify this general human tendency to create scripts – stereotyped sequences of events – because the executive function is to coordinate, control and direct. To do this they frequently create scripts that are activated by job assignments, clocks and calendars (Starbuck, 1983). Consequently, figures are provided for review in a standard format by such and such a date, plans are constructed and submitted on approved forms by another date, appraisals are conducted in the appropriate fashion by yet another date and so on. Thus members of organizations are induced to act unreflectively most of the time. Clearly there are qualifications to a statement as bald as this: some organizations are more bureaucratic than others, older ones more set in their ways than newer ones, and successful operations are more prone than the less successful to attempt to establish a routine for success (Starbuck, 1985). These are clear exceptions to the rule, but the script concept can and does serve to describe most of the behaviour that is observable in organizations of all shapes and sizes.

It is this persistent habitual performance of scripts which constitutes the know-how of organizations and it is this know-how that leads them into trouble. It gradually becomes not-know-how: either they fail to see that they are in trouble and need to reorientate, or they see it, recognize the need and are unable to reorientate. They are trapped in scripts largely of their own making, endlessly performing to a diminishing audience until the shutters come down.

Make no mistake about it, scripts are powerful determinants of behaviour. Not only do they channel action, they channel perception, since they constitute in and of themselves ways of seeing. *Intuitively* I know that such and such a proposal is wrong since it violates some of the basic tenets of the received cognitive framework. From within a particular script, some acts are literally unthinkable; incrementalism – mild variation – is the order of the day. It is the very nature of the script. Some executives are occasionally aware of the danger and deliberately seek to challenge received scripts:

ICI chairman, Sir John Harvey-Jones, when I asked him whether he thought MBAs tended to be bumptious, said he liked young people to be bumptious. 'Organizations should be driven from the bottom and the task of the top is to encourage the maximum amount of creative conflict. So we have to learn to harness creative energy. Business school graduates assist the process and should be used appropriately . . . '

So far, so good – but he cannot avoid a key qualification:

'But, mind you, if the graduate brings all the theory without the humility to learn from experience, then we have trouble!' (Bull, 1987)

And the last thing we want, of course, is trouble. For the greater part of the time senior executives, no less than others, act consistently and avoid trouble in that their actions resemble preceding and successive actions: one executive meeting is much like another and repeats familiar scripts. This consistency arises not because any one or more of us strives consciously to follow the pattern, but rather because the setting for our performances appears to remain stable and because we have been trained from an early age to improvise around familiar scripts. The reflective practitioner, even at executive level, is a contradiction in terms.

It is not my present purpose to discuss how such scripts may be taken apart and rewritten (Mangham, 1988). In this paper, I am more concerned to describe what scripts obtain at this level of the organization and to suggest how and why they persist. To do this, I need to introduce the idea of improvisation.

It will not have escaped notice that the framework I use derives from the theatre: roles, characters, scenes, scripts, settings, rehearsals, performances and now improvisation. The latter refers to the circumstance in which we behave more or less in line with some underlying referent. There is a continuum of possibilities for our behaviour between the extreme hypothetical limit of 'pure' improvisation and 'pure' composition, and between the situation in which everything is created afresh without reference to any other pattern and one in which every line and gesture is programmed for us. These limits, of course, are never obtained in live performance because no improviser (even in so-called 'free' improvisation) can avoid the use of previously learned material, and no re-creative performer can avoid small variations specific to each occasion (Pressing, 1984; Preston, 1987).

Central to improvisation is the concept of what elsewhere I have variously termed subtext, protoscript, schema or referent. I now prefer the last-mentioned term. The referent is an underlying guiding idea or issue specific to a given piece which is used by the improviser to facilitate the generation and editing of his or her improvised behaviour. Much of the variety of improvisation observable in the theatre or in music comes from the many different types of referent which can be used. Theatrical actors may be asked to improvise around a story, an emotion, a musical theme, an animal, a quality of movement, a character, an attribute or a social situation – virtually any coherent image which allows the improviser a sense of engagement and continuity. In social and organizational life, we do find improvisations around, for example, characters and mood, but, for the most part, senior executives engaged in executive work appear upon my limited sample to improvise around relationships, and two referents in particular stand out: authority and fraternity.

I shall briefly discuss the distinction between content and relationship before I look more closely at these referents. I follow Bateson (1972) and Watzlawick et al. (1967) in claiming that exchange – every message which passes between individuals – has a 'content' and a 'relationship' aspect. The content dimension is present to carry information, whereas the relationship dimension refers to what I have defined elsewhere as the metacommunication or emblematic aspect of the message in which interactants mutually define and display their relationship. When actors in the theatre rehearse a play, they are concerned with both content and relationships but recognize that the former always and inevitably informs the latter. As on the stage, so in social and organizational life: it is difficult to think of any message sent by one person to another that does not in some way also carry a commentary on the relationship between those involved (Knapp, 1978). Even the finest of linguistic minutiae (form of address, verb tense, language intensity, tone of voice) evidence relational definition (Brown and Levinson, 1978). 'Gentlemen, shall we begin?'

I assume, for present purposes, that referents exist in all groups, but are hardest to detect in groups in which the manifest content is itself relatively coherent and internally consistent. When a group of executives are talking about something technical, we might assume that that is all that is happening, but there is always something more. The referent is not likely to be within the social actor's awareness. From his or her point of view, the discussion is about technical matters. An observer, however, whether he or she is an outsider or someone else within the situation, is able to grasp the underlying issue. Once he or she 'sees' the core issue, aspects of the session which might appear diverse, contradictory or meaningless gain coherence and meaning (Whitaker and Lieberman, 1964).

The content of what a group of executives is discussing may concern results, budgets, formal planning or their expenses, but the referent is frequently a matter of relationships (rarely openly discussed) – a matter of who can do what, am I in or out of this group and related questions of where do I stand with regard to my colleagues. There is nothing else to observe in the executive process than technical activities and improvisations around issues of authority and fraternity.

What then is authority? There is the rub: it is easier to apprehend than to comprehend. To grasp its essence, I need to resort once more to anecdote and to link it with some ideas deriving from Sennett (1980). The image of authority which sticks in my mind comes from working for an all-too-brief span with a senior executive in a company. Some executives have a presence which is larger than life; they have a kind of star quality about them which, as it were, hedges them about with an aura of competence and invites deference. The company had a number of such characters chosen, some of us would declare mockingly, for their height and looks, groomed in the company charm school and set to guide us lesser spotty mortals. Fred had some of these characteristics but not all of them: he was tall, good-looking and well-spoken, but he did not move with his own following spot; he did not signal delight in himself as some of the others did ('if he were an ice cream he would eat himself'). He was a relaxed individual and gave the impression of being in complete control. He was apparently totally self-assured and appeared not to need to raise his voice either to convince himself or others. He was certainly not authoritarian; he encouraged ideas and clearly reflected upon them before deciding the most appropriate course of action.

Some executives raise the voice, become involved in contests over authority and direction, and cajole, threaten and exhort. Fred did none of this (or, at least, I never experienced it). With him there was no coercion, no threat; simply a senior executive trying to help me sort the problem out – someone who was helping me to do my job better. It was not evident then, but is now, that in many cases (by no means all) doing the job better meant doing it Fred's way because he knew and guided me, in a relaxed but none the less effective manner, to the correct solution.

It should be clear that I liked Fred, but that he also inspired a form of fear in me. I remember being in a meeting with him when I had decided to leave the company for a career as an itinerant academic. He was 'disappointed' but understood my decision and had only been concerned that my spell with the company which he had persuaded me to join had not adversely affected my academic pretensions. This particular meeting, involving several executives, was important and, since my mind was elsewhere, I did not perform particularly well; I did not screw it up totally but I was not up to standard. At one point, Fred looked across at me and said very quietly and very carefully, 'Perhaps you would take us through this last bit again, Iain. I am not sure that you convinced too many of us of the necessity of this investment'. I was not living up to my reputation and he was not going to let me or anyone else get away with sloppy work. I made a proper job of it the second time around.

So what are the elements of authority? Relaxed, self-assured, experience and knowledge, superior judgement, ability to set standards and cause others to meet them, undogmatic, ability to impose a non-demonstrative discipline. And integrity – the sense that Fred's authority was disinterested and was guiding and reassuring me; it was not an expression of domination, I had no sense of being exploited, manipulated or manoeuvred. I was a willing recipient of something that I took to be solid, stable and geared towards my needs and my overall welfare.

By now, some of you may be feeling distinctly uncomfortable; despite my disclaimers, you will have perceived something malign or exploitative in the relationship. You may have ascribed naivety to me and be concerned that my spaniel-like attachment to Fred was a consequence of previously poor relations with my father, inadequate potty training or whatever. Or, you may grant that my upbringing was right and proper save that it did not equip me for the cynical manipulation of an expert in human relations whose primary motive, however well disguised from me, was the pursuit of self-aggrandizement and/or company profit. If you harbour such doubts, or variants of them, fine; you are exhibiting exactly the ambivalence about authority which I take to be characteristic of much of what passes for everyday interaction in organizations. Our present condition is that we fear authority; we anticipate that others and perhaps even ourselves will use whatever brief authority we have to do harm or, at best, simply serve a self-interest. The issue of authority is basic to interaction at the executive level. Most of the executives with whom I have worked have wished to be in authority – not simply to dominate their colleagues nor to be subject to them but to have their position willingly accepted or themselves to go along willingly with someone else. A great many actions can be seen as relating to ambivalence about authority. Each of us seeks to provide, or have provided for us, guidance, security and stability; simultaneously, many of us doubt our own ability and/or that of other people to provide these goodies.

The bond of authority which informs the executive process everywhere is constituted from images of strength and weakness – the need for leadership and the rejection of it. Fraternity – the other referent – is based upon the sense of belonging, the concept of 'us', often as opposed to 'them' and occasionally as opposed to 'me'. Authority and fraternity connect me to my colleagues but each also binds me to them; I need to participate in authority and I need to nurture and be nurtured, but if I am to survive as an individual I fear enslavement. I need to belong and to share with others, but I do not wish to be possessed by them. Both referents are important, but I shall confine my remarks to aspects of authority. A full discussion of both authority and fraternity can be found elsewhere (Mangham, 1988).

A deep ambivalence about authority is the hallmark of our times (Sennett, 1980). In reflecting upon this, it is as well to remember that authority is not a thing, it is a social function – something we jointly elaborate and then behave towards as though it were something other than a construction. Authority is the image of strength, stability and security that we erect around an institution or an individual. Once upon a time (or so the fairy tales would have us believe), we were content to submit to authority voluntarily; now we are more prone to challenge it. Sennet (1980), in a powerful essay which informs much of my own thinking, notes that the dilemma of our time is that we are attracted to strong figures and that we construct images of authority which we consider illegitimate. We desperately create the Iacoccas, McGregors, Edwardeses and Thatchers, and immediately deny the ground upon which we place them. Having created a hero or heroine, we swiftly move to make them villains and fools.

In an odd sort of fashion we need to create images of strength and to deny them. We use powerful figures as touchstones against which we define ourselves; many a group of executives such as that around Paul (the retiring CEO) is held together by the very disaffections members feel for each other and the leader. This paradoxical state of affairs takes a number of forms (Mangham, 1988); three examples will probably illustrate its complexity. Teams such as Paul's may improvise around authority in scripts which reflect disobedient dependence, idealized authority and fantasies of rejection (Sennett, 1980). Elsewhere (Mangham, 1986 and 1988) I have illustrated the kinds of scripts which embody disobedient dependence. For example, George, one of Paul's colleagues, spent a great deal of his time in meetings bewailing the poor performance figures and accusing himself and others of dereliction of duty: 'We all ought to be fired'. He did this against a background of knowing that Paul did not like to hear negative comments, and he continued to do it until explicitly told not to, at which point he reluctantly conformed. He believed that such a performance signalled his independence. It did not; it was a manifestation of his dependence. He challenged Paul in order that he, George, would be told what to do. Clearly this did not constitute open dependence but for all that, it was dependence. George needs the authority figure to confirm or deny his approach; he is nothing without Paul, although he is reluctant to own such an interpretation.

Other members of Paul's executive were keen to tell me, each other and, on occasion, Paul himself what a mess he was making of the job of leading them. All of us took succour from Paul's shortcomings; we exaggerated them as we repeated stories about his spectacular incompetence and indecisiveness. After a couple of years, his ineptitude assumed legendary proportions and yet we all continued to interact with him; no executive declared it to be beyond a joke and none of us quit the company. We needed Paul as a negative from which we could print our idealized positive of authority. The image that we constructed around him (and that he clearly had a part in) was such that it served to show us what we were missing whilst simultaneously being such that we were able to cast all of our shortcomings upon it. Paul, for his part, considered the image to be unjust and so considered his colleagues as ill-informed or, at best, inexperienced in leadership. Thus each of us locked into each other's image and danced to the music of our times.

Sometimes members of Paul's group indulged in fantasy and, on occasion, imaginary plots to remove him. The fantasy was one of rejection. What would it be like if Paul were to leave? Could we manage without him? How much better would it be? It was clear at these times that things would be much better and that the sooner he went the better for all concerned. On the occasions when the cabal met to plot his downfall 'for the sake of the company' there was speculation about a world without him – a dream world in which all ills had been cured and all wrongs rectified. Nothing came of these moves because we needed him; Paul was the measure of all things that were and could be. He was our central preoccupation, and whether our improvisation took the form of disobedience, idealization or fantasized rejection, he was the central focus. Like many another executive team, we were tied to him and he to us.

This brings me back neatly to the concept of bonds. You will have observed that I referred earlier to authority and fraternity as bonds. I followed Sennett in choosing the term 'bond' since it expresses at one and the same time a sense of uniting and constraining; it also conveys for me an emotional rather than a legal contractual arrangement. I am particularly anxious to highlight this aspect of the definition since I hold (in common with but a few others) that individuals, groups, organizations, institutions are emotionally rather than cognitively bonded. To the lay mind, there is something visceral and preconscious about emotion which accords well with the ideas of script and improvisation that I have outlined above. Interactions in organizations, as elsewhere, are intuitive; they are reflections of know-how rather than matters of planning and strategy. Erving Goffman notwithstanding, most of us, most of the time, do not consciously seek to manipulate our colleagues; this is not to deny the possibility of such behaviour but rather to assert that it is more honoured in the breach than the observance. Much of what passes for the executive process is, ultimately, concerned with authority and fraternity and, at one level or another, overt or covert, is likely to be a matter of emotion. Much of what we experience as emotion, to paraphrase Kemper (1978), results from 'real, imagined or anticipated outcomes in social relationships'; virtually every effect-laden interaction we observe at executive level in organizations can be seen as relating to matters of authority and fraternity, whether or not these referents are directly addressed.

Clearly there are a number of qualifications to be made to such a position and I have made them elsewhere (Mangham, 1988); for the moment, I wish to do no more than assert that the two key referents in the executive process are authority and fraternity, and that feelings – powerful determinants and inhibitors of particular actions – are generated by changes or the threat of changes in patterns of authority and fraternity. Furthermore, since authority and fraternity both constrain and unite us as social actors, the stability we may experience around such issues is at best fragile and subject to constant threat.

What has all this to do with managing the executive process? It may or may not be fascinating to be told that every executive action relates, ultimately, to a concern for authority and/or fraternity, but how does that knowledge help us to distinguish between one executive group and another? To answer that, I must outline another aspect of improvised performances.

As I have said, matters of authority and fraternity influence the executive process in my team but, as in any other form of improvisation, they are not constructed *ab initio*. Social actors make sense of their present circumstance in the light of how they have previously performed and how they might perform in the future; interaction is at one and the same time happening now, retrospectively and prospectively. Most executive groups have a past and some of them have a future. There is then likely to be a discernible shape to these interactions; at any one time, one or other of the referents is more salient than the other. At some times in the development of the group, fraternity is a fundamental concern; at another time authority is more important. Having said that, it must be remembered that, given the ambivalent attitudes we each of us have to the bonds, either or both may become salient at any time.

None the less, executive groups can be seen to go through (and return to) aspects of authority and fraternity in a relatively distinct fashion. New executive groups or those with an infusion of new members will have fraternity as the primary referent; older groups may be marked by a relatively ready acknowledgement of authority and a marked degree of interdependence, or may be 'arrested' at a counterdependent stage where covert disputes about authority are the hallmarks of their interaction.

A number of 'ideal' groups can be identified. In new (or restructured) groups the issue of fraternity is at the centre of their interactions. Who am I to be in this team? What must I do to be included? What must I do to prevent myself from being overwhelmed by others? Each social actor hopes to find a place for himself/herself which will mean a minimal loss of definition of whom they take themselves to be. Relations between individuals at this stage are quite superficial. Information which they exchange about themselves is largely innocuous and may or may not confirm reputations which have preceded them. The energy that is on display goes into defining who I am: I have a reputation for incisiveness, humour or whatever (or wish to gain one), and this is the time to display it. At this stage members rarely listen to one another but they do listen carefully to themselves. As a performer in this group, I am more concerned about what being in implies than I am about authority. I am more likely to go along with the leader because he or she has an established identity; he or she is the CEO, the chairperson or whatever. So concerned am I about dealing with fraternity issues that I am likely readily to defer excessively to the leader and to expect him or her to take full responsibility for the group task. 'You are the boss, you tell me what to do' is the message, although it is rarely expressed so crudely and overtly.

As Srivastva et al. (1977) note, this stage may sound 'boring and trivial', but it is an important part of the development of an executive group. Marking out one's claim to identity is, paradoxically, the primary step towards fraternity. Here I am and this is what I wish to be taken for. Are the rest of you happy to accept me? Am I happy to accept you? If not, how do we adjust to each other?

The latter part of this is probably a second distinct stage of executive group development when matters of authority gradually become more dominant. This is me. Who can I link with and how can 'we' deal with the leader who may or may not have gone along with our earlier desires for strong leadership? If he or she has, then members may become uneasy with 'blind obedience'; if he or she has not, then members may wish to attribute the lack of movement to his or her 'failure' to direct their efforts.

A third stage may follow in which identities and links between individual members are now more or less stable (although not necessarily optimally satisfying from the perspective of each single member) and expressions of dependence and counterdependence are giving way to concepts of shared authority. At this juncture, members are not worried at being possessed by others or enslaved by authority. It is, not surprisingly, a stage marked by a great deal of confrontation over roles and expectations. Although rarely expressed openly, matters of authority become the focus when goals and standards are discussed. However, fraternity is delineated in signs of integration of the group and in the expressions of openness, trust and an empathy in concern for colleagues (Slater, 1966).

Indeed, the final stage marks a return to fraternity with the emphasis upon a state of complex interdependence. Members of the group recognize that they are both highly differentiated and tightly integrated around task issues. They demonstrate cooperative interdependence between themselves and between themselves and their leader. The leader contributes towards task accomplishment according to his or her expertise, as does everyone else in the team; each and every member places a top priority on successful task accomplishment and, as a whole, the group can deal openly and productively with matters of authority and fraternity. They can acknowledge and handle differences at the same time as they can express support and affection for each other.

The key aspect of managing the executive process is knowing what stage your particular group or team is going through (table 6.1). That is far from simple because (a) the ideal types depicted are seldom observable in the pure state and (b) the manager seeking to discern what is happening is, whether he or she likes it or not, inevitably and inextricably a key part of the executive process. Authority is closely related to his or her actions and reactions and, not surprisingly given what I have said earlier about scripts, many find it difficult to understand what may be occurring, let alone recognize their own part in it. To be told, as Paul was (remember him, recently retired) that one's vacillation and one's inability either to share authority with one's colleagues or to assume it for oneself is a direct cause of one's inability to function as an executive is, as can be imagined, a matter of considerable emotion. All the technical help in the world – strategies, market analyses, structures and new appointments – can do nothing for a company if it remains unable to 'reconcile the conflicting forces, instincts, interests, conditions, positions and ideals' of its constituent members. An executive group, which, trapped in its own scripts and improvisations, cannot itself operate effectively, is in no position to sort out the problems of the rest of the organization.

Table 6.1   Stages of executive group development

Stage	Basic referent for behaviour	Characteristics of behaviour
1	Fraternity	Self-promotion; 'this is me' display; isolated individuals; everyone for themselves; leader orientated; high level of dependence
2	Fraternity–authority	Coalitions; alliances; some concern for who else is present; some counterdependence; covert hostility to leader
3	Authority–fraternity	Relatively stable alliances and coalitions; sorting out of roles and expectations; little concern about membership
4	Fraternity	Complex interdependence; members both highly differentiated and highly integrated around task; cooperative interdependence between all including leader; matters of authority and fraternity dealt with openly.

Adapted from Srivastva et al. (1977).

Paul (and his somewhat less than merry men) is not unique, nor is he (or they) perverse or wicked. He and they were trying to do a good job but, like many another team, were victims of the fictions they created, sustained and elaborated. Despite much noise to the contrary, we cannot point to much success in helping such groups rewrite the scripts; authority and fraternity are such fundamental issues and so bound up with emotion that intervention is fraught with problems. Having executives talk about these issues (Argyris, 1985, 1987; Mangham, 1978, 1988) is neither easy, as is occasionally implied, nor does it lead necessarily to different patterns of behaviour.

So where does this leave us? I have attempted to show that there is more, often much more, to company success than factors such as a bias for action, closeness to the customer, autonomy and entrepreneurship, productivity through people, hands-on, value-driven, 'sticking to the knitting', simple form, lean staff and loose–tight properties (Peters and Waterman, 1982). Without an effective executive process, there can be no realization of these factors. The problem is that we do not know enough about what constitutes an effective executive process. In this area, as in so many areas of what passes for management science, we lack the concepts for articulating what is going on.

Excellent study techniques, precise instruments, impressive statistics and even a close acquaintance with the subject under study are preconditions for the advancement of a science. They are, however, of limited value without the anchorage and order that can come about only through the elaboration and continual articulation of concepts. As Kant said 200 years ago, 'Perception without conception is blind; conception without perception is empty'. A concept enables us to pin down some element of experience, and to make it the subject of separate investigation and theoretical speculation. The weaving together of concepts is the process by which any one of us may arrive at systematic knowledge; there can be no real advance in knowledge without a larger framework. Too much of what purports to be management science consists of technicians dabbling with restricted and specific problems; real social scientists do it systematically.

One problem with social science in general and management studies in particular is the vagueness of its concepts. What we mean by morale, productivity, efficiency and effectiveness, let alone excellence, is anyone's guess. It is probably inappropriate to attempt to be too rigorous at this stage of the development of the field of management research. Perhaps we should settle for that which Blumer terms a 'sensitizing concept':

Whereas definitive concepts provide prescriptions of what to see, sensitizing concepts merely suggest directions along which to look . . . They rest on a general sense of what is relevant. (Blumer, 1969).

Parsons (1968) has something of the same kind in mind when he writes of Cooley's analysis of the socialization process that he, Cooley, was neither rigorous nor much concerned with methodology. What he did show, however, was

. . . . creative ideas about what to look for – especially things which common sense has either overlooked or considered to be so commonplace as to not present serious problems of interpretation.

'Authority' is, I believe, one such creative idea, a sensitizing concept, something to which we ought to devote more attention.

If we are to advance our understanding of management, we must be prepared to challenge much of what purports to be research around the subject. A great deal of it lacks any theoretical base, little of it appears to be even aware that such a base is necessary if a science is to develop and virtually none of it makes any attempt to take even the first step towards such a science by elaborating present concepts or developing sensitizing ones. Ideas such as those offered by Peters and Waterman (1982), sneered at as they are by many of us, derive directly from the literature;

we may well envy the packaging, but we should not despise the content for it is the product of our efforts. We clearly need to do better; we need to reapply ourselves to the fundamentals and not rush headlong into seeking to impress others with our knowledge. Neither we nor the managers know what it is to manage; some know how to do it but none of us can adequately conceptualize it, let alone pass it on to others.

Unless we can make some of the know-how susceptible to verbal statement, the outlook for all of us is bleak. Paul and his colleagues will remain in the dark as to why it is they failed to operate effectively, and organizations will continue to go out of business. It is nonsense in such a context to talk of a massive expansion in management education. What is needed is a massive expansion of knowledge; unless we know what it is we are talking about, there is little point in simply speaking louder.

References

Argyris, C. (1985). *Strategy, Change and Defensive Routines*. Marshfield: Pitman.
—— (1987). 'A leadership dilemma: skilled incompetence'. *Business Economics Review*, 1, Summer.
Barnard, C.E. (1938). *The Functions of the Executive*. Cambridge, MA: Harvard University Press.
Bateson, G. (1972). *Steps to an Ecology of Mind*. San Francisco, CA: Chandler.
Belbin, R.M. (1981). *Management Teams: Why They Succeed or Fail*. London: Heinemann.
Blumer, H. (1969). *Symbolic Interactionism*. Englewood Cliffs, NJ: Prentice-Hall.
Brown, P. and Levinson, S. (1978). 'Universals in language usage: politeness phenomena'. In *Questions and Politeness* (ed. E.N. Goody). Cambridge: Cambridge University Press.
Bull, G. (1987). 'Who wants to be an MBA?' *Expression*, September.
Doise, W. (1986). *Levels of Explanation in Social Psychology*. Cambridge: Cambridge University Press.
Kemper, T.D. (1978). *A Social Interactional Theory of Emotion*. New York: Interscience.
Knapp, M. (1978). *Social Intercourse*. Boston, MA: Allyn and Brown.
McDonald, A. (1972). 'Conflict at the summit: a deadly game'. *Harvard Business Review*, 50(2), 59–68.
Mangham, I.L. (1978). *Interactions and Interventions in Organizations*. Chichester: Wiley.
—— (1986). *Power and Performance in Organizations: An Exploration of Executive Process*. Oxford: Blackwell.
—— (1987). 'A matter of context'. In *Organizational Analysis and Development: The Social Construction of Organizational Behaviour* (ed. I.L. Mangham). Chichester: Wiley.
—— (1988). *Effecting Organizational Change: Further Explorations of the Executive Process*. Oxford: Blackwell.

—— and Overington, M.A. (1986). *Organizations as Theatre: A Social Psychology of Dramatic Appearances*. Chichester: Wiley.

March, J.G. and Simon, H.A. (1958). *Organizations*. New York: Wiley.

Parsons, T. (1968). 'Cooley and the problem of internalization'. In *Cooley and Sociological Analysis* (ed. A.J. Reiss). Ann Arbor, MI: Free Press.

Peters, T.J. and Waterman, R.H., Jr. (1982). *In Search of Excellence*. New York: Harper and Row.

Pressing, J. (1984). 'Cognitive processes in improvization'. In *Cognitive Processes in the Perception of Art* (ed. R. Crozier). Amsterdam: North-Holland.

Preston, A.M. (1987). 'Improvising order'. In *Organizational Analysis and Development: The Social Construction of Organizational Behaviour* (ed. I.L. Mangham). Chichester: Wiley.

Schank, R. and Abelson, R. (1977). *Scripts, Plans, Goals and Understanding*. Hillsdale, NJ: Lawrence Erlbaum.

Sennett, R. (1980). *Authority*. London: Secker and Warburg.

Slater, P. (1966). *Microcosm*. New York: Wiley.

Srivastva, S., Obert, S.L. and Neilsen, E. (1977). 'Organizational analysis through group processes: a theoretical perspective'. In *Organizational Development in the UK and USA* (ed. C.L. Cooper). London: Macmillan.

Starbuck, W.H. (1983). 'Organizations as action generators'. *American Sociological Review*, **48**(1), 91–102.

—— (1985). 'Acting first and thinking later: theory versus reality in strategic change'. In *Organizational Strategy and Change* (ed. J.M. Pennings). San Francisco, CA: Jossey Bass.

Watzlawick, P., Beavin, J.H. and Jackson, D.D. (1967). *Pragmatics of Human Communication*. New York: Norton.

Whitaker, D.S. and Lieberman, M. (1964). *Psychotherapy and the Group Process*. New York: Atherton Press.

7
Managerial work: a diagnostic model

Sudi Sharifi

Introduction

Managerial work has been described in various ways. There are very few multidimensional studies of managerial work, and very few concepts which would describe it in terms of the means by which and the contexts within which managers learn.

Over the last four decades the industry of management training and development has been founded upon assumptions about what managers do. The concern has been to translate the features which constitute 'effective management' into forms and techniques of management training. This paper begins with an examination of the relationship between theorizing about the practice of management and management practices. It is argued that management and organizational theorizing contains conventional and predictable cliches and rephrased concepts. A major implication of such 'conceptual redundancy' for management training and development is the degree of congruence between theory and practice and the 'ideal' measures of effectiveness, and hence the extent to which the questions 'what are managers actually doing?', 'what do they think they are doing?', 'what should they be doing ideally?' and 'what they could be doing practically?' are brought together in such theorizing about managerial work.

The impact of management theory on management practice (via management training and education) has been minimal (Weick, 1979; Peters and Waterman, 1982) simply because it falls short of illustrating the contexts within which managerial practices are situated. This paper puts forward a set of concepts and contexts related to managerial learning in order to develop a diagnostic model of management. Such a model can be viewed as an initial step towards developing a prospectus for training managers. It can also serve as an analytical tool for investigating the nature of managerial practices. The model is the outcome of an extensive literature search and empirical work (Sharifi, 1985a).

The first part of this paper focuses on a brief critique of these studies; the second part concentrates on the conceptual basis of the diagnostic model.

Managerial work

The studies selected for this paper are based upon different theoretical assumptions and can be viewed as complementary to each other in furthering an understanding of managerial work (table 7.1). Each of these studies illustrates one aspect of managerial work. In this paper they are designated and reviewed according to the terms that reflect the aspects of managerial work upon which they have focused:

managerial work as 'how managers spend their time';
managerial work as 'what managers do';
managerial work as 'how managers make choices';
managerial work as 'how managers manage meanings';
managerial work as 'how managers build networks';
managerial work as 'what successful managers do'.

Managerial work as 'how managers spend their time'

During the past 35 years studies of managerial work have created a paradigm which concentrates on observing managers' activities and taking note of the time they spend on each activity. The classical accounts of managerial work i.e. functions and roles, prescribed by Fayol (1948) and others have been discarded as being empirically unsubstantiated. These studies, despite their focus on how and with whom managers spend their time, have produced static pictures of management activities. As descriptions of managers' 'time-spending' patterns some of these studies set the background for the growth of the recent 'time-management' industry. Time budgeting and effective use of time have become measures of performance and thus of central concern to managers.

Managerial work as 'what managers do'

In the early 1970s Mintzberg's (1973, 1975) observation of 'what managers were really doing' was an attempt to illustrate the gap that existed between theory (i.e. the classical functions or folklore of management) and practice (i.e. activities observed by Mintzberg). He presented the 'real' image of managers' jobs in the form of roles that they performed and an 'ideal' image of what managers should be doing in

Table 7.1 A taxonomy of perspectives of managerial work

Perspective	Core ideas	Implications
What managers do (Mintzberg, 1973)	No POSDCORB (planning, organizing, staffing, directing, coordinating, reporting and budgeting)	Training for managerial roles Resource allocation
How managers spend their time (Stewart, 1967, 1976a,b; Burns, 1964; Horne and Lupton, 1965)	FOUR (formulating, organizing, unifying and regulating) Time dictates the pattern of work and contact Art is recognition of choices	Training for different skills . . .
How managers make choices Stewart, 1978a,b; 1982; Child, 1972)	Managers have choices over time and contact Managers exercise strategic choices and hence evaluate events	Recognize choices to be effective Concept development?
How managers manage meaning (Pettigrew, 1973; Dalton, 1959; Marglin, 1976; Newby, 1977)	Conflict is a typical state Organizations as systems of political action Hierarchies and symbols created by managers	Assertiveness and protective mimicry? Intuitive skill training
What successful managers do (Kotter, 1982a,b)	Successful managers are born and made General managers are specialists They have different personal charms Influence strategies	Education What and why of work Different situations
What successful organizations do (Peters and Waterman, 1982)	Adroit at responding to environmental changes Action stimulated, entrepreneurial defender, people orientated	Train for action and experimentation Test McKenzie's 7Ss Develop new skills

order to enhance their performance. Mintzberg used a pre-coded diary, i.e. a work study method, in his observations and characterized managerial work as brief, varied and fragmentary. Thus he refuted the established image which portrayed management as a set of coherent and rational practices.

There is little evidence in Mintzberg's database that managers do not plan. If he expected a 'scientific' approach to planning this might not be detected from observation. Studies of the development of managerial hierarchies, for instance, have shown that managers do plan and assume responsibilities and roles regarding the allocation of resources (Chandler, 1977). Mintzberg's classification of managers' roles is barely distinct from the classicists' functions. Furthermore, they imply planning, controlling and organizing. Although Mintzberg took account of the organizational context and environment of managers' activities in his classification of managers' roles, he did not note managers' constructs which produce such environments and form their interpretations of environmental characteristics.

Managerial work as 'how managers make choices'

These studies have concentrated on varying characteristics of managers' activities. For instance, Stewart (1967, 1976a,b, 1982), using such time criteria as the duration of activities, periodicity and deadlines, developed a demand–choice–constraint framework. A set of work and contact patterns emerges showing that managers have choices regarding their time budgets. Constraints emerge as a result of the analysis of context, i.e. the what, how, when and who of the job. They include items such as skills, attitudes, group and organizational pressures etc. However, Stewart has emphasized that managers do not think analytically and are unaware of their choices. Nevertheless, her conceptualization of a demand–choice–constraint framework remains acontextual and therefore does not provide any explanation of managers' 'projected acts', i.e. planned choices and motives (Cullen, 1972). Choice implies control (cf. Stewart, 1982) and control mechanisms by which the equivocality in the situation is reduced and managerial projects are realized.

In contrast with Stewart's choice framework, Child's (1972) concept of 'strategic choice' considers partly the dynamics of managers' decision-making activities. It illustrates that exercise of choice by managers, the assessment of opportunities and constraints, and the formulation of strategy and organizational forms are interlinked. The core of the concept shows that managers' evaluation of environmental events and other actors' expectations are influenced by the organization's dominant ideology which also affects the choices of organizational form and measures of effectiveness.

Child's concept of strategic choice supports the 'thinking aspect' of managerial practices which is discussed in this paper. This discussion draws on Weick's (1979) concept of organizing as 'thinking practices'. It emphasizes the ways in which managers develop assumptions and expectations about the contexts of their actions and how these assumptions are shared by the members of their role set.

Strategic choice also indicates that the variabilities in managers' understanding of the situation are resolved at the evaluation–choice phase in which a preferred interpretation of environmental events is adopted. It shows that managers have discretion in their interpretation of environmental events, and thus their perception of events becomes focal to strategy formulation. Child portrays an integrated and rational choice–evaluation phase in a decision-making process and hence underplays managers' political manoeuvring and lobbying of their role set about the interpretation of environmental characteristics and choice of organizational form. His conceptualization of managers' intentions, differences in interest and preferences is unclear and unfinished.

Managerial work as 'how managers manage meanings'

Some writers on managerial practices (Silverman, 1970; Clegg, 1975; Newby, 1977) have discussed the mechanisms by which strategies and decisions made by the 'dominant coalition' are pursued. Their focus is on managers' intentions in dominating members of their organization through the process of 'meaning management'. Although studies of managerial activities and time-spending patterns (Mintzberg, 1973; Stewart, 1976b) consider contact patterns and interpersonal roles, their conceptions of the 'how' and 'what' of managers' jobs undermine the complexity and differentiation that characterizes managerial processes and thus the 'why' of managers' jobs. As Pettigrew (1973, 1979) has argued in his study of decision-making processes, definition of situations and allocation of resources by organizational actors develop within the temporal and internal political contexts. In this paper it is argued that the political context of managers' actions, particularly their decision-making activities (i.e. choice, evaluation and adoption), implies an underlying continuity encompassing the process (Dalton, 1959). In other words, if the political manoeuvrings of organizational actors are noted, there will be continuity rather than fragmentation in managerial activities.

Pettigrew (1985) describes continuity in organizational actions as the existence of dominating frameworks of thought ('recipes' according to Schutz (1967) or 'dominant ideology' according to Child (1972)) which determine the nature of relationships and procedures in organizations. It should be noted that Pettigrew's concept of the temporal context is developed within his longitudinal and 'over-time' approach, on the basis of which he has examined the life span of decisions. This can be differentiated from the concept of temporality in this paper which emphasizes *in-times* analysis of managerial practices and considers organizational temporal context as a spread of experienced past events, perceived present events and anticipated future events. It is argued here that certain events recur, strategies evolve and organizational forms are reconstructed through managers' political manoeuvrings.

Managerial work as 'how managers build networks'

An attempt to analyse managerial activities in terms of interactions and interpersonal relations can also be seen in the work of Kotter (1982a,b) who describes and prescribes factors which contribute to a manager's success. Kotter has demonstrated that managers do not work in easily identifiable environments and there are no formal or systematic managerial tools. He has argued that managers 'managed' the uncertainties and got things done through agenda setting and network building. Managers' agendas (or action sheets) contain their plans and priorities which are fulfilled through network-building activities. Network building means identifying people who satisfy a need and then developing cooperative relationships. Kotter's concept of network building is an apolitical presentation of managerial political activities. In the process of 'symbolic communication' Kotter erroneously depicts members of the manager's role-set as deferential, cooperative, persuaded and dependent. Therefore he disregards the 'logics of action' (Karpik, 1978) of actors involved in the process, i.e. the principles which shape their reactions. Such a depiction can degenerate into a morass of managerial characteristics. Overall his writings are largely atemporal accounts of managers' activities and, crucially, his description of agendas excludes event time.

Managerial work as 'what successful managers do'

According to Kotter a combination of factors such as personality traits, job characteristics and family background have to be present if a manager is to be successful. Success is measured as the sales turnover of the company. Peters and Waterman (1982) have presented the art of management in successful American companies using similar measures of economic health as well as some growth measures and a degree of innovativeness. Their 'distilled' interpretations are given in eight basic principles: a bias for action, staying close to customer, autonomy and entrepreneurship, productivity through people, hands-on, stick to the knitting, simple form and loose–tight properties (Peters and Waterman, 1982, pp. 13–15).

An alternative interpretation of these principles will show managers of these successful companies as customer- and achievement-orientated doers who operate within schisms and pyramids, defending their business niches through MBOs and establishing all-embracing values. It will be recognized that the principles for success as prescribed by Peters and Waterman are motherhood concepts and rephrased classicist conceptions of management. As in the case of the empirical generalizations of the 'what managers do' school, the concepts developed by Peters and Waterman are not culture free and yet disregard cultural differences. A question mark remains over the extent to which the following are true:

'productivity through people' resolves industrial relations hiccups;
'hands-on' value-driven strategies allow for changes in technology and other resources, competition and unexpected events;
the 'Japanization' of management styles will ensure individuals' organizational commitment and identity, particularly in situations where individualism is rewarded.

Peters and Waterman assume that the direction of causation is from the principles identified to success whereas the opposite could easily be true: principles could be the outcome of success.

Summarizing comments

In summary, this critical evaluation of orthodox perspectives of managerial work shows that unidimensional and acontextual perspectives present an inadequate account of what managing is about and what managers are doing. The folklore of overburdened and time-pressured managers developed in these studies only emphasizes time and contact management and undermines managers' strategic and analytical thinking. Moreover, despite the claim of the work study school, the classical theorizing of management functions, such as Gluick's (1937) POSDCORB (i.e. planning, organizing, staffing, directing, coordinating, reporting and budgeting) has not been deposed. In other words, managerial roles presented by the new orthodoxy are no different from the managerial functions proposed by classical theorists. Moreover, their characterization of managerial work as fragmentary neglects the continuity that underlies managerial activities through political manoeuvring, networking and through-times and of which managers are aware. It is necessary to identify the ways in which these characteristics can be translated, transferred and made accessible to practising and embryonic managers. Table 7.1 summarizes the characteristics of managerial work according to the schools of thought discussed above.

Alternative focus

The existing orthodoxy in theorizing about managerial work has been criticized within a perspective which assumes that managers' practices are embedded in the temporal and political contexts of their organizations. Therefore, in discussing 'what managers are doing', the structuring influences of these contexts are emphasized. On this premise a diagnostic model of management is developed which subsumes three managerial situations. The model and these situations are based on a review of various studies of organizations, managers and their jobs, as well as a theoretically driven empirical study of practices of four sets of managers in four different settings (Sharifi, 1985a). These situations take account of both the observable and non-observable activities of managers. Non-observable activities are translated intentions, motives, feelings realized in the format of managers' agendas, portfolios, plans, gossiping, networking and ordinary hypocrisy.

The situations within which managerial practices are located are discussed in the following sections. These are thinking, temporal and intentional situations. It is shown that managers build sense-making and decisional models which contain their individual and organizational recipes, include past, present and anticipated future events, and indicate their intentions regarding the direction of their decisions.

Thinking practices

Managers are engaged in mental activities and analytical thinking (cf. Stewart, 1982). They make assumptions about environmental events and have expectations regarding the outcome of their practices. Their assumptions and expectations constitute the templates for their sense-making of events and may transform their established templates. 'Template' here is described as a guiding system which includes a set of definitions of events, decision outcomes and activities. Each template can have defined parameters (e.g. label of the activity or event, time span of the activity, actors involved, their roles, expected outcomes . . .). Organizational templates may be known to certain members, which implies commonality of their reactions to an identified event. Templates may be used by actors to routinize and rationalize unfamiliar situations or unexpected outcomes. Managers can impose a known template upon a situation as an overlay in order to reveal the configuration of the courses of action which can be taken. For example, in a study of the activities of managers in a component-manufacturing firm, it was shown that the prediction of a forthcoming recession in the construction industry (a major user of their products) was a template used by the production and marketing managers and their co-workers. It triggered off a set of alternative courses of action: they could maintain the production level and increase their stock, or reduce the production level to meet the anticipated drop in demand, or find an alternative buyer (Sharifi, 1985a).

There are other concepts which imply a similar process: these include recipe and contextual norms (Schutz, 1967; Spender, 1980), cause maps (Weick, 1979; Jenkins, 1981; Bougon, 1983), meaningful structures (Schutz, 1967; Weick, 1979), theories of action (Argyris and Schon, 1978) and structural poses (Gearing, 1958; Clark, 1985). For instance, according to Schutz, recipe is a typical means for sense-making; it is a means for expression as well as interpretation. Alternatively, as Spender (1980) argues, recipes are managers' generalizations about the appropriate course of action which may keep their business viable. Recipe is grounded empirically in the contexts of managerial activities, and so it is influenced by managers' experiences. Similarly, cause maps indicate formation of a stock of information which is repeatedly encountered.

These concepts share certain characteristics with respect to the nature of managerial work:

they structure managerial activities;
they are shaped by the past experiences of managers/organizations;
they encourage habitual interpretation of events;
they enable as well as constrain managers' sense-making of their environment.

A basic implication of these characteristics is that less reflective thinking occurs. The absence of reflective thinking can lead to rehearsal of a set of recipes or selection and retention of familiar organizational adaptive postures (i.e. routinized reactions and adaptation). In other words, if the environment is changing, a routinized process, such as application of familiar recipes to the situation, may lead to a decline in the performance of the organization. The concept of template, however, will include the editing of the existing recipes through reflection on past events and the unintended consequences of a selected course of action. Indeed, these concepts illustrate aspects of the organization's adaptive cycle. However, their viability is reduced as they assume rationality in managerial practices. Clearly there is more 'rationalization' and thus retrospection and justification in what managers do.

The word 'template' is used in order to highlight the way in which managers' perceived patterns of relationships between events are transformed into rules and codes. The reflective thinking underlying this process encompasses the rationalization of the decoding stage. To portray managers as 'thinking-doers' here is to revisit the theorizing of the classical and Carnegie schools. It implies that managers are aware of the choices and constraints regarding the contexts of their activities and that they avoid uncertainty by utilizing their established repertoire of responses and thus creating more familiar circumstances.

Their repertoire may include conservative responses. There will be a gradual change within continuity and hence organizational inertia (Aldrich, 1979) and slowly evolving strategies (Pettigrew, 1973; Miller and Friesen, 1980). This conservatism reflects the extent to which managers are loaded with their past experiences and organizational events (i.e. their past-loadedness). Therefore the variety of responses in their repertoire will be an indication of the conditions within which the organization is founded and the time that the manager joined the organization (Stinchcombe, 1965). For instance, a decline in the performance of the organization can be analysed by considering the templates which are imprinted in its early life and the extent to which they are repeatedly referred to as the shared ways of doing things. The components of the manager's organizational life may therefore remain unchanged even though changes in the environment are perceived. For example, in the case of the *Saturday Evening Post*, Hall (1976) has shown that, in the more successful days of the paper, the established template contained the relationship between the amount of space allocated to advertising, the level of costs and the extent of readership. For a period of time recurrence of events and desired outcomes validated the template. However, when the situation changed (with respect to the readership and market niche) the template in use proved to be pathological and, as Hall has argued, led to the demise of the newspaper. In view of the core argument of this paper and the points already discussed, the thinking practices of managers can thus be seen as establishing templates. Managers and their role set are collectively involved in this process via their mutual information loading, their scheduled and unscheduled meetings, corridor chats and visits to the shop-floor.

Time context

It is argued here that managerial practices in terms of establishing templates are embedded in times, i.e. they are developed with regard to a spread of past–present–future events. Events are therefore taken as the key time dimension for describing what managers do. Within such a framework, managers' habitual interpretations indicate recurrence of events and outcomes. Conversely, adaptation is described as reconstruction of events and identification of disjunctures, i.e. managing discontinuity (perceived need for change or disjuncture) within continuity (rehearsal of established recipes or reproduction of recipes).

Templates may therefore contain non-conservative items and disjunctive elements: certain events encourage discontinuity. Managers may depart from familiar established approaches to the allocation of resources and tasks. These are often decisions of a strategic nature which also require a search for novel resource pools and negotiations amongst the managers' role set. The following example from a study of a set of managers, i.e. administrators and planning officers in a health authority (Sharifi, 1985a,b), elaborates this argument. These managers were involved in the design and commissioning of a new district general hospital in the UK. There were formalized ways of designing, planning and commissioning hospitals, supported by consultative documents, and a standard design package, which contained various parameters from ratios of functional departments to operating systems and structural relationships, was available. The design blueprint provided them with preconstructed operational objectives and practices. However, past experiences of these managers in planning hospitals constituted their basic template. The hospital would be built on a 'green-field site', an element which the administrators used, via their lobbying and networking, to challenge the established methods of planning and commissioning. They altered the parameters imposed by the design package and inserted new rules in the operating system regarding the relationship between the medical staff and the health authority. For these actors the site and the design package set out the points of departure from the established practices regarding some aspects of commissioning. Other aspects, such as staffing ratios, were routinized via preset formulae and remained unchanged. The past experience of these actors included the economies of scale of the 1970s and the rise of the National Health Service, whereas the present situation implied recession and required cost-effective measures and further cuts in resources were anticipated in the near future. These events structured what these managers were doing.

The thinking and temporal aspects of managerial work are illustrated in figure 7.1. It is shown that managers' definitions of present situations and theorized/assumed survival paths are influenced by the established templates and are embedded in the temporal context of their organization.

Some studies of managerial work (Clark, 1975, 1985; Sharifi, 1985a) have shown that managers search for a variety of events which can be placed on trajectories, irrespective of their settings. Each trajectory shows the relevance of the event to a situation. It also includes the intervals between events, their duration and their periodic recurrence.

It is argued that managers label events according to the pattern and

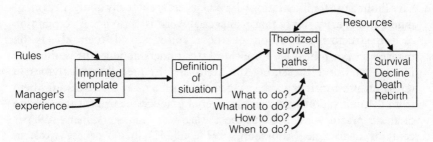

Figure 7.1   Temporal embeddedness of managerial practices.

nature of the activities that they initiate and the resources they sensitize. For instance, an expected event has the following characteristics:

it requires application of a familiar practice;
it includes activities which have well-defined paths and ends;
it has a recurrent pattern or is periodic;
there are episodes with known durations and intervals;
it includes more mechanical reaction.

An unexpected event may be characterized as follows:

it requires analytical thinking;
no familiar scenarios exists in the repertoire;
anticipated future events are not realized.

An expected–unexpected event implies the following:

managers will search for it;
it allows deliberate editing;
there are contingency plans.

Such concepts as 'past-loadedness' and the organization's 'founding conditions' (Dill, 1962) are significant in illustrating the process by which events are identified and labelled by managers. If managers are exposed to a limited number of scenarios, and so experience limited variations of events, they may fail to recognize a specific event or may anticipate recurrence of an event and activate a response which may produce the undesired outcome (hence bounded rationality).

Orthodox studies of managerial work (Stewart, 1976a,b; Mintzberg, 1973) have disregarded the time context in their analysis. Their diary and observation methods either deny repetition or show recurrence within the unitary framework of clock time. The attributes of clock time (i.e. its duration and sequence) may seem attractive for producing 'one-minute managers'. However, its being free or severed from events and its precision have limited use for illustrating what managers are actually doing. Fragmentation and brevity imply that managerial work is episodic. A recognition of the structuring function of these episodes and their effects on managers' portfolios is more focal to understanding the nature of managerial work. Presenting durations and frequencies of activities in terms of interruptions in the manager's working day and isolating them from the motivational basis of managerial practices disregards the essence of these practices. We should be asking why managers spend '39 per cent' of their time (Mintzberg, 1973, p. 241) in a working week in scheduled meetings.

Intentionality

This context shows the intentionality in which managers' practices are embedded. Intentionality can be seen as managers' portfolios which include their projects, future acts and preferences. This does not imply that managers have clearly defined goals or objectives. Rather, there are situationally identified objects which are shared to the extent that tactics and strategies for achieving them are continually discussed in managers' meetings and corridor talks. The continuity underlying managerial practices is shown in the patterning of managers' interactions and their relationships with individuals and groups in their organizations.

Karpik's concept of the 'logics of action' throws some light on this argument. He defined the logics of action as 'principles around which individuals organise their activities and behaviour' (Karpik 1978, p. 47). Logics of action motivate goal-seeking goal-attaining behaviour in organizational 'actors'. Across this domain managerial situations are described as multi-actor arenas where actors continually bargain over means (strategies) for attainment of their goals. The arena houses a number of coalitions which change over time. The politics (policy outcomes) are the results of these activities.

The main point in considering political manoeuvring by managers is to highlight the collective and intersubjective character of managers' sensemaking models and to de-emphasize managers' networking or political machination as an end in itself. Within times (continuity) managers and their role-set may deliberately edit and adjust the existing rules and assumptions (intended discontinuity). It has been argued elsewhere that in such situations managers frequently reproduce and reconstruct templates (Sharifi, 1985b). These deliberate editing activities are related to the events spotted by managers and their colleagues, as was the case in the example of the hospital administrators referred to in the previous section.

Diagnostic model

Briefly, recent studies of managerial practices and analysis of structuration processes (Giddens, 1984) have shown that managerial work activities are embedded in thinking, temporal and intentional situations. These situations are simultaneous and interconnected, and as a whole, they have the following characteristics:

1 they indicate the continuity underlying managerial practices;
2 they show how managers and their role-sets learn;
3 they demonstrate the empirical nature of their learning;
4 they show that discontinuity is intended editing of the established templates or recipes.

Figure 7.2 illustrates these situations and shows where the studies discussed stand with reference to the theoretical framework of this paper.

Situated activities of managers are also described as model building which entails their actions, reflections and learning. There is a set of 'what if . . . and then . . . ' assumptions that managers test empirically in relation to perceived events.

These situated practices are included in the proposed diagnostic model shown in figure 7.3. The model is a simplified version of how managers make sense of their surroundings. It assumes that managers are 'thinking-doers', whether they are managing recurrent or routine events (assumed less thinking) or managing an erupted present or managing

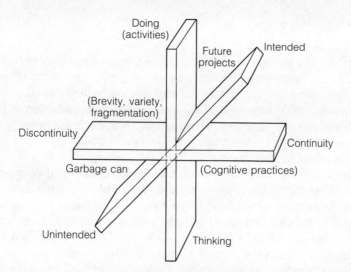

Figure 7.2   Situations of managerial work.

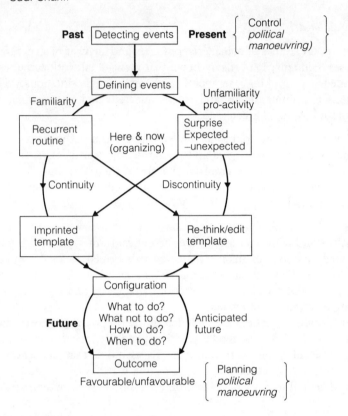

Figure 7.3   The diagnostic model.

surprises. The model can also be described as 'managing by experience' (MBE), i.e. managers' decisions on the appropriate course of action regarding anticipated future events are embedded in their past experiences, their awareness of the present situation and their access to the organization's repertoire of responses. Another assumption is that managers' experiences are empirically and contextually grounded. MBE may therefore include instances of hurtful learning.

The model also shows that managerial work includes goal-directed and goal-seeking activities. Managers and their role-set rationalize their actions by looking forwards and backwards in time, searching for events in order to manage their portfolios and reduce the perceived uncertainty in the situation. Surely the future is relatively unknown, and when managers face surprise events they will refer to the organization's imprinted template as their initial coping strategy in searching for a familiar response. The established responses will be edited or adjusted if

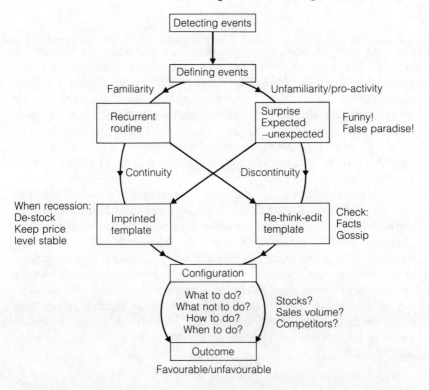

Figure 7.4 The diagnostic model applied to the activities of managers in a component-manufacturing firm.

managers perceive that they will not produce the desired outcome. The 'rationality' originates in their past organizational experiences (i.e. their past-loadedness) and they will have to be content with generalization regarding a forward-looking perspective. Figure 7.4 shows the model with reference to some templates and configurations which underlined the activities of managers in a component-manufacturing firm (Sharifi, 1985a).

Implications

The diagnostic model and the situations discussed in this paper have major implications for the theory and practice of management.

Theory

Over the past 15 years the main development within the domain of orthodox management theory has been its focus on observable activities of managers as an attempt to weave theory and practice together. Within the framework of the model presented in this paper the claims of the 'what managers do' school have been dismissed in view of their inadequacy in grasping the situated practices of managers. Characterization of managerial work as fragmented and varied is based on 'snapshots' of what managers are doing; the contexts of their activities are neglected.

The concepts and contexts included in the diagnostic model show that the 'activity' school portrayal of fragmentary episodes can be represented as the ways in which managers develop and maintain rites and rituals (Sharifi, 1985a,b). Within the framework of this paper, fragmentation can be interpreted as managers' allocating blocks of time to organizing and controlling resources. Therefore the 'temporal situation' and 'event time' resolve the fragmentation puzzle by showing the recurrence of events and disjunctures, and demonstrating that managers and their role-set are involved in decision-making activities which include detection of events within the frame of reference to their organizations.

Practice

The model aims at coupling the theory and the practice of management. Therefore it is argued that the theoretical concepts included in the model, such as templates, events and recurrence, are incorporated in the foundations of managers' tactical and strategic approaches. They present managers with a vantage ground for understanding their tactics and strategies. Managers can apply such concepts to their experiences and thus structure them.

The model also highlights the point that the three situations embedding managerial work activities influence the extent of opportunities and choices for managers to build their repertoires. In other words, managers' practices set the prospectus for their learning and development. It indicates that managers' theorizing about their work environments and their coping strategies is fed back into their sense-making systems and forms a set of enabling as well as constraining analytical tools for future incidents. Indeed, managers' awareness of their recipes and the degree that these recipes are routinized and institutionalized (and hence taken for granted) is central to the effectiveness of their adaptive behaviour.

The implications for managers' learning are therefore in the identification of their organization's shared templates and sense-making systems and the way in which they are established and edited. Intuitive and intentional aspects are included in their learning. The model elucidates the situational dilemmas that managers encounter and the ways in which they may insert their projections in their detection of events. It therefore aims to de-emphasize a sterile approach to the development of managers' thinking skills. It is suggested that managers' performance can be a joint function of their awareness of concepts and contexts embedding the model and their ability to apply them to their experiences, thus analysing and structuring them. A provisional course outline based on this assertion is shown in figure 7.5.

The course as shown is based on the model and consists of some conceptual and practical questions. It aims at providing insight into the complexities of managerial situations: managerial recipes, events and political manoeuvring. The central theme will be 'choice and time structuring' in order to demystify the pictures of managerial work created by the pragmatic approach of some management training and time-management courses. Day One of the programme will concentrate on managers' choices, i.e. setting up their decision priorities and identifying time-wasters and time-savers. This will refer to networking as saving time – a future orientation in contrast with the time-management approach. The concept of 'event time' will be introduced in the form of a case exercise. Day Two will continue with the emphasis on the political manoeuvring and negotiations which underly the process of detecting events. Time management will be discussed with reference to the structuring function of time. It will be shown how managers (a) peg their day around a set of structuring episodes such as meetings, tours and visits, and (b) allocate chunks of time to planning within the timetables of their organizations. The content of the course is expected to increase managers' awareness of the contexts of their activities and the structuring implications that they have for their performance.

In conclusion, the model emphasizes the constructs of 'time' and 'event' and considers managers as entrepreneurial technocrats who impose structure upon unstructured situations and initiate discontinuity. It is a means for managers to probe into the perceptual boundaries of their organization. Events as the key time dimension show the significance of managers' rolling agendas in the adaptation process.

Acknowledgements

My thanks are due to Neil Anderson and Johann Riedel, Aston Management Centre, Rosemary Stewart, Templeton College, Oxford, Terry Thornley,

DAY ONE

10.00 – 10.30 Introduction, Orientation

10.30 – 12.30 Choices for managers
Adjustments; ordering of decisions

12.30 – 13.45 Lunch

14.00 – 15.30 Choices and constraints
Time-wasting
Time-storing

15.30 – 16.00 Coffee

16.00 – 17.00 Syndicate exercise
Event time

18.30 – 20.00 Dinner
Thought for the evening
Others' choice
Others' time

DAY TWO

9.00 – 10.30 Choices and political manoeuvring
Managers' role set in the
process of detecting events

10.30 – 11.00 Coffee and reflection

11.00 – 12.30 Time template
Choice and proactivity
Recurrent versus surprise
(Continuity versus discontinuity)

12.30 – 13.45 Lunch

14.00 – 15.30 Time structuring
Planning, chunking and pegging

15.30 Coffee
Course review

Figure 7.5 A provisional translation of the diagnostic model into a two-day management training programme.

Huddersfield Polytechnic, John Burgoyne, Lancaster University and Howard Aldrich, University of North Carolina, for their comments on earlier versions of this paper.

References

Aldrich, H.E. (1979). *Organisations and Environments*. Englewood Cliffs, NJ: Prentice-Hall.
Argyris, C. and Schon, D. (1978). *Organisational Learning: A Theory of Action Perspective*. Reading, MA: Addison-Wesley.
Bougon, M. (1983). 'Uncovering cognitive maps, the self-Q technique'. In *Beyond Method: Strategies for Social Resaerch* (ed. G. Morgan). London: Sage.
Burns, T. (1964). 'What managers do'. *New Society*, 4(17), 8–9.
Chandler, A.D. (1977). *The Visible Hand: The Managerial Revolution in American Business*. Cambridge, MA: Harvard University Press.
Child, J. (1972). 'Organisation structure, environment and performance: the role of strategic choice'. *Sociology*, 6, 1–22.
Clark, P.A. (1975). 'Time reckoning systems in modern Western organisations'. Presented at *34th International Conference, Society for Applied Anthropology* (mimeograph).
—— (1985). 'A review of the theories of time and structure for organizational sociology'. In *Research in the Sociology of Organisations* vol. 4 (eds S. Bachrach and S.M. Mitchell). Greenwich, CT: JAT Press.
Clegg, S. (1975). *Power, Rule and Domination*. London: Roultedge & Kegan Paul.
Cullen, I.G. (1972). 'Space, time and the disruption of behaviour in cities'. *Environment and Planning*, 4, 459–70.
Dalton, M. (1959). *Men Who Manage: Fusions of Feelings and Theory in Administration*. New York: Wiley.
Dill, W.R. (1962). 'The impact of environment on organisation development'. In *Concepts and Issues in Administrative Behaviour* (eds S. Mailick and E.H. Van Ness). Englewood Cliffs, NJ: Prentice-Hall.
Fayol, H. (1948). *General and Industrial Management*. London: Pitman.
Gearing, E. (1958). 'The structural poses of the 18th century Cherokee villages'. *American Anthropologist*, 60, 1148–57.
Giddens, A. (1984). *The Constitution of Society*. Cambridge: Polity Press.
Gluick, L.H. (1937). 'Notes on the theory of organisation'. In *Papers on the Science of Administration* (eds L.H. Gluick and F.L. Urwick). New York: Columbia University Press.
Hall, R.I. (1976). 'System pathology of organisation: the rise and fall of *Saturday Evening Post*'. *Administrative Science Quarterly*, 21, 185–211.
Horne, J.H. and Lupton, T. (1965). 'The work activities of middle managers, an exploratory study'. *Journal of Management Studies*, 2(1), 14–33.
Jenkins, R. (1981). 'Thinking and doing: towards a model of cognitive practice'.

In *The Structure of Folk Models* (eds L. Holy and M. Stuchlik). New York: Academic Press.

Karpik, L. (ed.) (1978). *Organisation and Environment: Theory, Issue and Reality.* London: Sage.

Kotter, J.P. (1982a). *The General Manager.* New York: Free Press.

—— (1982b). 'What effective general managers do'. *Harvard Business Review,* November–December, 60, 156–67.

Marglin, S. (1976). 'What do bosses do? The origins of hierarchy in capitalist production'. In *The Division of Labour: The Labour Process and Class Struggle in Modern Capitalism* (ed. A. Gorz). Hassocks, Sussex: Harvester Press.

Miller, D. and Friesen, P.H. (1980). 'Momentum and revolution in organisational adaptation'. *Academy of Management Journal,* 23(4), 591–614.

Mintzberg, H. (1973). *The Nature of Managerial Work.* New York: Harper and Row.

—— (1975). 'The manager's job: folklore and fact'. *Harvard Business Review,* 53, July–August, 49–61.

Newby, H. (1977). *The Deferential Worker: A Study of Farm Workers in East Anglia.* Harmondsworth: Penguin.

Peters, T.J. and Waterman, R.H. (1982). *In Search of Excellence.* New York: Harper and Row.

Pettigrew, A.M. (1973). *The Politics of Organizational Decision-Making.* London: Tavistock Publications.

—— (1979). 'Strategy formulation as a political process'. *International Studies of Management and Organisation,* 7(2), 78–87.

—— (1985). *The Awakening Giant: Continuity and Change in ICI.* Oxford: Blackwell.

Schutz, A. (1967). *The Problem of Social Reality, Collected Papers I.* The Hague: Nijhoff.

Sharifi, S. (1985a). 'Managing the future: a theoretical and empirical examination of fragmentation and continuity puzzles'. Doctoral Thesis, Aston University Management Centre (unpublished).

—— (1985b). 'Studying managerial practices', Doctoral Working Paper No. 105, Aston University Management Centre, Birmingham, England.

Silverman, D. (1970). *The Theory of Organizations.* London: Heinemann.

Spender, J.-C. (1980). 'Strategy making in business'. Doctoral Thesis, School of Business, University of Manchester.

Stewart, R. (1967). *Managers and Their Jobs.* London: Macmillan.

—— (1976a). 'To understand the manager's job consider demands, constraints, choices'. *Organisational Dynamics,* 4, Spring, 22–32.

—— (1976b). 'Patterns of work and dictates of time'. *Personnel Management,* 8, June, 25–28.

—— (1982). 'A model for understanding managerial jobs and behaviour'. *Academy of Management Review,* 7(1), 7–13.

Stinchcombe, A.L. (1965). 'Social structure and organisations'. In *Handbook of Organisations* (ed. J.G. March). Chicago, IL: Rand McNally.

Weick, K.E. (1979). *The Social Psychology of Organising.* Reading, MA: Addison-Wesley.

Bibliography

Allport, F.H. (1954). 'The structuring of event: an outline of a general theory with application to psychology'. *Psychological Review*, **61**, 281–303.

Argyris, C. (1982). *Reasoning, Learning, and Action, Individual and Organisational.* London: Jossey Bass.

Barrett, W. (1968). 'The flow of time'. In *Time: A Collection of Essays* (ed. R.M. Gale). London: Macmillan.

Bougon, M., Weick, K.E. and Binkhorst, D. (1977). 'Cognition in organization: an analysis of Utrecht Jazz Orchestra'. *Administrative Science Quarterly*, **22**, 606–30.

Carlson, S. (1951). *Executive Behaviour: A Study of the Work Load and the Working Methods of Managing Directors.* Stockholm: Stronbergs.

Carlstein, T., Parkes, D. and Thrift, N. (eds) (1978). *Timing of Space and Spacing of Time*, vol. 1, *Making Sense of Time.* London: Edward Arnold.

Clark, P.A. (1978). 'Temporal innovations and time structuring in large organisations'. In *The Study of Time*, vol. 3. New York: Springer-Verlag.

Cohen, M.D., March, J.G. and Olson, J.P. (1972). 'A garbage can model of organisational choice'. *Administrative Science Quarterly*, **17**, 1–25.

Copeman, G.H., Luijk, H. and Hanika, F.C. (1963). *How the Executive Spends His Time.* London: Business Publications.

Crozier, M. and Friedberg, E. (1980). *Actors and Systems: The Politics of Collective Action.* Chicago, IL: University of Chicago Press.

Davies, J. and Easterby-Smith, M. (1984). 'Learning and developing from managerial work experiences'. *Journal of Management Studies*, **21**(2), 169–83.

Georg-Bros, R. (1982). 'Digital structure of social time and changing structures of biographical time: the case of the temporary workers'. Presented to the Ad hoc Group on the uses of Life-Stories for Social Research, 10th World Congress of Sociology, Mexico.

Giddens, A. (1976). New Rules of Sociological Method. London: Hutchinson.

—— (1979). *Central Problem in Social Theory: Actions, Structure and Contradiction in Social Analysis.* London: Macmillan.

Gurvitch, G. (1963). 'Social structure and the multiplicity of times'. In *Sociological Theory, Values and Sociocultural Change* (ed. E.A. Tiryakian). New York: Free Press.

Hales, C.P. (1986). 'What do managers do? A critical review of the evidence'. *Journal of Management Studies*, **23**(1), 88–115.

Hall, R.I. (1984). 'The natural logic of management: its implications for the survival of an organisation'. *Management Science*, **30**(8), 905–27.

Jaques, E. (1982). *The Form of Time.* London: Heinemann.

Jelinek, M. (1979). *Institutionalising Innovation: A Study of Organisational Learning Systems.* New York: Praeger.

Kurke, L.B. and Aldrich, H.E. (1979). 'Mintzberg was right!: a replication and extension of the nature of managerial work'. Paper presented at the 39th Annual Meeting of the Academy of Management, Atlanta, GA.

McCall, M.W., Morrison, A.M. and Hannan, R.L. (1978). 'Studies of managerial work: results and methods'. Technical Report 9, Centre for Creative Leadership, North Carolina.

Mant, A. (1981). 'Developing effective managers for the future: learning through experience'. In *Developing Managers for the 1980s* (ed. C.L. Cooper). London: Macmillan.

March, J.G. (1962). 'The business firm as a political coalition'. *Journal of Politics*, **24**, 662–78.

—— (1981). 'Footnotes to organisational change'. *Administrative Science Quarterly*, **26**, 563–77.

Marples, D.L. (1967). 'Studies of managers: a fresh start?' *Journal of Management Studies*, **4**, 282–99.

Merton, R.K. (1957). 'Role-set: problems in sociological theory'. *British Journal of Sociology*, **8**, 106–20.

Miles, R.E. and Snow, C.C. (1978). *Organisational Strategy Structure and Process*. New York: McGraw-Hill.

Morgan, G. (ed.) (1983). *Beyond Method: Strategies for Social Research*. London: Sage.

—— (1983). 'What is management? Notes toward a radical–humanist critique'. Presented at the Journal of Management Studies Conference, Manchester Business School.

Newell, A. and Simon, H.A. (1972). *Human Problem-Solving*. Englewood Cliffs, NJ: Prentice-Hall.

Rosen, M. (1983). 'Myth and reproduction: the contextualisation of management theory, method and practice'. *Journal of Management Studies*, **21**(3), 303–22.

Schackle, G.L.S. (1978). 'Time, choice and uncertainty'. In *Making Sense of Time* (eds T. Carlstein, D. Parkes and N. Thrift). London: Edward Arnold.

Shrivastava, P. (1983). 'A typology of organisational learning systems'. *Journal of Management Studies*, **20**(1), 7–27.

Toffler, A. (1971). *Future Shock*. London: Pan.

Urwick, L.F. (1943). *The Elements of Administration*. New York: Harper.

Weiss, J.W. (1981). 'The historical and political perspective of Lucian Karpik'. In *Complex Organisations: Critical Perspectives* (eds M. Zey-Ferrell and M. Aiken). Glenview, IL: Scott Foresmen.

Wilmott, H.C. (1983). 'Images and ideals of managerial work: a critical examination of conceptual and empirical accounts'. *Journal of Management Studies*, **21**(3), 349–68.

8
Marketing and competitive success

Michael J. Baker

In the opening paragraph of his widely acclaimed book *Competitive Marketing* O'Shaughnessy (1984) observes:

Success in business is success in a market. Firms go out of business not by closing factories but by unprofitable marketing. Firms usually enter a business by creating products (i.e. goods and services) but stay in business only by creating and retaining customers at a profit.

It has always been so, but it is only in the comparatively recent past (since the mid-1950s) that specific focus has been given to 'marketing' as the orientation and function which offers the best prospect of achieving competitive success. This focus has sharpened considerably in the past decade as national economies of every kind have struggled to cope with the consequences of the turbulent trading conditions which succeeded the oil crisis of the early 1970s. Today marketing is beginning to assume the characteristics of a universal panacea for all competitive ills. The purpose of this paper is to try and establish whether, in fact, marketing possesses any magical curative properties or is merely a placebo disguising other, as yet undefined, processes. In pursuit of this objective we examine first the factors which underlie the nature of competition together with some of the reasons why the basis of competition appears to have changed during this century. In that 'marketing' is perceived as a response to these changed conditions, some definition of the scope and nature of both the function and its philosophical underpinnings seems called for and is provided. Attention is turned next to the factors giving rise to the 'sharpened focus' referred to above, epitomized by the publication of a series of management best-sellers purporting to detail the critical factors, including marketing, which lead to competitive success. Perceived deficiencies in the often anecdotal analysis underlying these prescriptions provide the point of departure for a more rigorous attempt to establish the association between marketing and competitive success. Based on the findings of this survey (Project MACS) conclusions are drawn and recommendations are made.

Competition

It is a widely accepted proposition that the primary purpose and the function of an economy is to maximize the satisfaction of the persons comprising that economy through the most efficient utilization of the scarce resources at their disposal. Three elements are the key to this proposition – the concepts of satisfaction or effectiveness, of efficiency and of scarcity. Taking these in reverse order, the following observations seem apposite if we are to grasp why the relative emphasis upon these has changed radically within the last century and thereby resulted in significant changes in a fourth concept of competition.

Until comparatively recently the vast majority of mankind has accepted scarcity as an endemic fact of life. Indeed, this is still the case, although the existence of countries where plenty rather than scarcity is the rule has become widely known through developments in the media and communications. Because the basic necessities of life are in short supply, the world's great religions tend to share the common features of emphasizing frugality, sharing behaviour, fortitude in the face of adversity, and the prospect of an afterlife enjoyed in an environment overflowing with material comforts in which there will be an absence of pain and suffering. Depending upon the political organization of the society, the reality of scarcity and the prospect of surfeit were underlined by the existence of ostentatious displays of wealth by the state and/or church – living proof that scarcity could be overcome.

In the present century, and in the advanced industrialized economies, traditional concepts of scarcity founded upon the presence or absence of the basic requirements for survival – food, shelter and clothing – have had to be modified in face of the burgeoning output resulting from the application of science and technology to the process of production. By the 1950s social commentators as diverse as John Kenneth Galbraith and Vance Packard were cautioning against the excesses of materialism while the 1960s were to see numerous polemics (*Limits to Growth* (Club of Rome, 1970), *Small is Beautiful* (Schumacher, 1973)) pointing out that, while scarcity may appear to have been overcome in the affluent economies of the west, this was not the case. This point was underlined with great force by the energy crisis of the 1970s and the recession which it precipitated.

In simple terms efficiency means 'doing things right' and contains the implicit connotation that efficiency can be measured and quantified in such a way that it can be optimized under any given set of circumstances. In fact, this is so, provided that one can agree upon the objectives or outcomes which are to be pursued and achieved and the units of measurement which will be used to quantify such progress and achievement. Resolution of this problem lies at the very heart of economics and is central to the idea of the market, in which price is the mechanism that adjusts the balance between the supply of and demand for goods and services until equilibrium is attained. The manner in which this adjustment is achieved is defined as competition and may exist between producers of similar if not identical outputs (direct competition) or dissimilar and quite different outputs (indirect competition). In terms of direct competition a spectrum of competitive states anchored by monopoly at one end and pure or perfect competition at the other is seen to exist. Various shades of imperfect competition lie between these extremes.

Technically, and on the basis of a set of explicit assumptions to be found in any basic economics text, it can be shown that efficiency will be maximized under conditons of pure competition. Practically this can never be so for at least two basic reasons. In the first place consumers are not homogeneous, and in the second their preferences and behaviour are dynamic and change over time. Essentially the problem is one of defining 'satisfaction' which, we suggested earlier, is the essence of effectiveness which can be defined as 'doing the right things'. In other words, if we are concerned with maximizing satisfaction it follows that satisfaction determines what objectives are to be pursued, and it is the optimal achievement of these which results in efficiency in the technical economic sense. The problem is further compounded because not only does the consumer or demand side of the model depart from the ideal but so does the producer or supply side – success for whom implies exercising some control over the market and not being controlled by it. It follows that, while the idea of perfect competition has its attractions and, in fact, is a reasonable description of many simple non-advanced economies, its main value lies in its definition of a boundary condition which all producers and most consumers will wish to avoid because their concept of satisfaction is intrinsically subjective and dynamic and so is not amenable to theoretical models which see it as objective and static.

Because consumers have different perceptions of what constitutes satisfaction it follows that in their terms a 'competitive' market must offer variety and choice. For the producer this represents both a threat and an opportunity for, provided that he can endow his product with a comparative advantage, he will command the support of all those who perceive this. If he posseses no comparative advantage, then he will fail.

Under conditions of perfect competition products are assumed to be homogeneous – a not unreasonable assumption in underdeveloped economies where consumers have small incomes and are concerned with basic survival. The real problem is to acquire the 'mostest for the leastest' in terms of bread, potatoes, fuel, clothing or whatever. It follows that, assuming basic or non-differentiated products, the most obvious and compelling comparative advantage is a lower price. But lower prices can only be offered consistently if one enjoys a cost advantage over rival producers, and it is an accepted fact that a major source of cost advantages is the economies of scale. Thus if one assumes that products are or should be homogeneous, then it would seem to follow that one should pursue the economies of scale and so reduce costs and prices despite having to abandon one of the conditions of perfect competition which is the existence of many suppliers, of whom none can influence conditions in the market.

So far, so good. But, if pursued to its logical conclusion, the concentration of supply into an oligopoly or monopoly could lead to the elimination of choice and the absence of price competition to the long-run disadvantage of the consumer. It is because of this potential outcome that most countries have enacted anti-monopolistic legislation strictly controlling the degree of supply concentration which is permissible.

Given that monopoly is prohibited and perfect competition is to be avoided, in that it leaves the producer a price-taker rather than a price-maker, it is unsurprising that competition has become imperfect with producers gravitating towards one or other end of the spectrum depending on the trade-off between heterogeneity and scale economies. Basically, however, the basis of competition has shifted from one based on price for essentially similar products to one based on performance (or satisfaction) for differentiated products.

Returning to our opening quotation, it is clear that as long as suppliers create products which deliver customer satisfaction at a profit they will succeed. The validity of the statement is such that none would challenge it, and successful companies have competed on this basis for centuries without any explicit need for anything called 'marketing'. Clearly, businessmen have always succeeded if they can deliver what the customer wants at a satisfactory profit to themselves. The problem is that the shift in the basis of competition described above placed a premium upon 'knowing what the customer wants' at the very time when this was undergoing radical change which was emphasized and accelerated by the producers' own actions in offering greater variety. Thus in the twentieth century a variety of factors have resulted in producers losing touch with their customers at the very time when they needed to be getting closer to them. The salient factors are as follows:

1 a physical and psychological distancing between producers and consumers owing to the concentration of production into larger and more cost-effective units and the development of intermediaries to

service longer and more complex channels of distribution;

2 increased competition from *direct* substitutes owing to the growth and expansion of international trade;

3 increased competition from *indirect* substitutes as increasing affluence and discretionary purchasing power have increased the options open to consumers;

4 the accelerating rate of technological change which has increased the degree and extent of new product development, thus shortening product life cycles, rendering old products obsolete and offering greater variety and choice to consumers;

5 the development of a better educated, better informed, more sophisticated and more discriminating consumer.

These developments, and particularly the last mentioned, have resulted in a profound change in the relationship between the two parties to commercial exchange relationships – a change which was to come to a head in the 1950s.

The consumer revolt

Although 'materialism' has always attracted critics, their views largely fell upon the deaf ears of a population denied the excesses described. However, the increased affluence of the population of the advanced economies and the methods and practices adopted by manufacturers to exploit this opportunity changed all this.

Amongst the first popularist writers to attract wide attention was Vance Packard, whose *Hidden Persuaders* (Packard, 1957) promoted an Orwellian view that big business was brainwashing consumers into purchasing products that they did not really want. This was a major indictment of advertising and selling which of necessity assume a much larger role in determining the preference of a consumer faced with a wide selection of competing products with identical performance characteristics and prices. The 'big business is bad for you' theme was also promoted in *The Waste Makers* (Packard, 1960) in which he attacked some of the excesses and consequences of a materialistic society.

Packard's indictment was picked up with enthusiasm by Ralph Nader, whose *Unsafe At Any Speed* (Nader, 1966) was a chilling picture of uncaring car manufacturers who cut corners in product design and manufacture in order to swell the corporate coffers with scant regard for the lives of their customers. General Motors attempted to discredit Nader but only succeeded in losing a highly publicized court case from which Nader emerged as the hero of the consumer revolt.

More general criticisms such as Rachel Carson's *Silent Spring* (Carson, 1963), in which she described a world devoid of wildlife as a consequence of chemical farming, initiated a green movement which enjoys political representation in many governments and led, in 1986, to some rather frosty exchanges between the Prime Ministers of Norway and the UK. Concurrently, thinking businessmen began to pay heed to the groundswell of anti-materialistic sentiment and initiated their own inquiries into the implications of the consumerists' clarion call for fewer but better products offering greater value for money but with less profligate use of scarce resources. *Limits to Growth* (Club of Rome, 1970) may well have been the catalyst for a response to the latter requirement in the early 1970s, but an answer to the value-for-money lobby was already on its way from an unexpected source.

Rise of the phoenix

So much has been written about the West German and Japanese economies that only passing reference need be made here to the phenomenon of two economies devastated by war emerging from the ashes as the leading trading nations in the world.

While many would argue that almost total destruction of an economy creates a golden opportunity to reconstruct it, very few would possess the resolve to do so. After all, academics like myself frequently offer the advice that it would make sense to start agian with a clean sheet rather than attempt to patch up an ailing concern, but not many practitioners take up the suggestion even though the Japanese and German examples point to the long-term benefits of radical as opposed to gradualist solutions. However, our exemplars had no choice – it was either get on or go under – and the lesson to be learned is from what they did rather than from why they did it. In very simplified terms the *phoenix strategy* would seem to comprise the following steps:

1 Acquire the best available technology (it has been estimated that for an outlay of $3 billion in the 1950s Japan secured the rights to all the Western world's R&D and has used this as the foundation for its own investment).
2 Secure the home base – concentrate first upon the needs of the domestic market and set out to make what you can sell, i.e. a marketing orientation.
3 Offer the highest possible quality consistent with the asking price.
4 Accept that responsibility does not end when the product leaves the factory gate – ensure adequate channels of distribution and provide appropriate after-sales service.

5 Concentrate resources and do not overreach yourself, i.e. do not seek to enter a new market until you have developed the necessary infrastructure and support systems and have secured a dominant or leadership position in the markets you are in.

6 Be patient – seek to build long-term lasting relationships rather than make a quick profit.

7 Research your markets continuously and modify your offering to match changing needs, i.e. consolidate your position.

Taken together these steps represent an almost irresistible strategy founded on the basic rule for business success – build a better product than your competitors at an equivalent or lower price and make it readily available to consumers. If you follow this precept then, whether you make steel, machine tools, textile machinery, consumer electronics or whatever, you will succeed – a fact learned painfully in the UK as leading firms and even whole industries, like motor cycle manufacturing, were displaced from the market.

However, worse was to come – while the First World debated the implications of *Limits to Growth* the Third World acted upon it and began to ration basic raw materials, particularly oil, and so attacked the very foundations of Western materialism. This, more than anything else, initiated the instability, if not crisis, of the 1970s.

The rediscovery of marketing

With the growth of imperfect competition based upon product differentiation, itself facilitated by scientific and technological change, the possibility of oversupply in more competitive markets became a reality in the 1920s. The Depression of the 1930s and the Second World War delayed its impact as did the decade of post-war reconstruction which followed it. Throughout this period the major managerial emphasis fluctuated between sales and production depending on whether supply exceeded demand or vice versa. However, by the mid-1950s the pent-up demand of the war years and the reconstruction of war-damaged economies was largely complete, and it became clear that high-pressure salesmanship alone would be insufficient to cope with the output of an increasingly productive manufacturing industry. Faced with the daunting prospect of cut-throat price competition between producers of too many goods chasing too little money it became clear that an alternative approach was required and marketing was rediscovered.

As hinted earlier marketing is founded upon the essentially simple philosophy that you should make what you can sell. In practice businessmen have always sought to do this but, as our eclectic review of economic development has attempted to show, there has been a radical change in both the supply and demand functions (particularly the latter) with the result that the real needs of consumers have become much more complex and difficult to identify. While product differentiation represents an attempt to respond to the existence of differentiated demand, in so far as it reflects the *producers'* concept of what the customer wants, it can at best offer only a trial-and-error approach to competitive success, i.e. you develop a new product and see how it performs in the market place. This is consistent with the finding of a 1964 National Industrial Conference Board survey into the causes of new product failure which cited inadequate market research as the primary cause – in other words producers did not know what they were doing!

If one is to succeed in highly competitive markets where the consumer is faced with far more choices than he requires to satisfy his needs and expend his purchasing power, it follows that one needs a much better understanding of what gives consumers 'satisfaction'. While the concept of marketing had been articulated by McGetterick in the mid-1950s it was Levitt of the Harvard Business School who first addressed this central issue in his famous article 'Marketing myopia' (Levitt, 1960). Levitt had the following to say (the quotes are somewhat out of sequence):

Every major industry was once a growth industry. But some that are now riding a wave of growth enthusiasm are very much in the shadow of decline. Others which are thought of as seasoned growth industries have actually stopped growing. In every case the reason growth is threatened, slowed, or stopped is *not* because the market is saturated. It is because there has been a failure of management.

It is impossible to mention a single major industry that did not at one time qualify for the magic appellation 'growth industry'. In each case its assumed strength lay in the apparently unchallenged superiority of its products. There appeared to be no effective substitute for it. It was itself a runaway substitute for the product it so triumphantly replaced. Yet one after another of these celebrated industries has come under a shadow.

The failure is at the top. The executives responsible for it, in the last analysis, are those who deal with broad aims and policies. Thus:

The railroads did not stop growing because the need for passenger and freight transportation declined. That grew. The railroads are in trouble today not because the need was filled by others (cars, trucks, airplanes, even telephones), but because it was not filled by the railroads themselves. They let others take customers away from them because they assumed themselves to be in the railroad business rather than in the transportation business. The reason they defined their industry wrong was because they were railroad-oriented instead of transportation-oriented; they were product-oriented instead of customer-oriented.

Hollywood barely escaped being totally ravished by television. Actually, all the established film companies went through drastic reorganizations. Some simply disappeared. All of them got into trouble not because of TV's inroads but because of their own myopia. As with the railroads, Hollywood defined its business incorrectly. It thought it was in the movie business when it was actually in the entertainment business. 'Movies' implied a specific, limited product. This produced a fatuous contentment which from the beginning led producers to view TV as a threat. Hollywood scorned and rejected TV when it should have welcomed it as an opportunity – an opportunity to expand the entertainment business.

Today, TV is bigger business than the old narrowly defined movie business ever was. Had Hollywood been customer-oriented (providing entertainment), rather than product-oriented (making movies), would it have gone through the fiscal purgatory that it did? I doubt it. What ultimately saved Hollywood and accounted for its recent resurgence was the wave of new young writers, producers, and directors whose previous success in television had decimated the old movie companies and toppled the big movie moguls.

With devastating insight and pungent prose Levitt spells out the essence of a marketing orientation. It is an overriding concern for the consumer and a desire to look at products and services in terms of his perception of the derived satisfaction. As Levitt reminds us, 'People buy ¼″ drills – they want ¼″ holes'. If you make ¼″ drills, beware – the first firm to introduce a cheap safe laser gun which can cut holes in anything to any required size has put you out of business.

Almost 30 years later Levitt's analysis is as fresh as when it was first published. Consider the following; it should make familiar reading.

In the case of electronics, the greatest danger which faces the glamorous new companies in this field is not that they do not pay enough attention to research and development, but that they pay too much attention to it. And the fact that the fastest growing electronics firms owe their eminence to their heavy emphasis on technical research is completely beside the point. They have vaulted to affluence on a sudden crest of unusually strong general receptiveness to new technical ideas. Also, their success has been shaped in the virtually guaranteed market of military subsidies and by military orders that in many cases actually preceded the existence of facilities to make the products. Their expansion has, in other words, been almost totally devoid of marketing effort. Thus, they are growing up under conditions that come dangerously close to creating the illusion that a superior product will sell itself. Having created a successful company by making a superior product, it is not surprising that management continues to be oriented toward the product rather than the people who consume it. It develops the philosophy that continued growth is a matter of continued product innovation and improvement.

A number of other factors tend to strengthen and sustain this belief:

1 Because electronic products are highly complex and sophisticated, manage-

ments become top-heavy with engineers and scientists. This creates a selective bias in favor of research and production at the expense of marketing. The organization tends to view itself as making things rather than satisfying customer needs. Marketing gets treated as a residual activity, 'something else' that must be done once the vital job of product creation and production is completed.

2 To this bias in favor of product research, development, and production is added the bias in favor of dealing with controllable variables. Engineers and scientists are at home in the world of concrete things like machines, test tubes, production lines, and even balance sheets. The abstractions to which they feel kindly are those which are testable or manipulatable in the laboratory, or, if not testable, then functional, such as Euclid's axioms. In short, the managements of the new glamour-growth companies tend to favor those business activities which lend themselves to careful study, experimentation, and control – the hard, practical, realities of the lab, the shop, the books.

What gets shortchanged are the realities of the market. Consumers are unpredictable, varied, fickle, stupid, shortsighted, stubborn, and generally bothersome. This is not what the engineer-managers say, but deep down in their consciousness it is what they believe. And this accounts for their concentrating on what they know and what they can control, namely, product research, engineering, and production. The emphasis on production becomes particularly attractive when the product can be made at declining unit costs. There is no more inviting way of making money than by running the plant full blast.

Today the top-heavy science–engineering–production orientation of so many electronics companies works reasonably well because they are pushing into new frontiers in which the armed services have pioneered virtually assured markets. The companies are in the felicitous position of having to fill, not find markets; of not having to discover what the customer needs and wants, but of having the customer voluntarily come forward with specific new product demands. If a team of consultants had been assigned specifically to design a business situation calculated to prevent the emergence and development of a customer-oriented marketing viewpoint, it could not have produced anything better than the conditions just described.

Of course things have changed, as witness the phoenix strategy pursued by West Germany and Japan, but less so in the UK and USA, both of whom have experienced massive import penetration and declining exports of manufactured goods. The continuing emphasis upon R&D expenditure in defence industries in these countries has undoubtedly prolonged the dominance of a scientific and production orientation towards the market. So what is to be done?

Back from the brink

The first step in the treatment of any problem must be awareness that it exists in the first place and second that it is of sufficient consequence to merit careful analysis. While the first condition – declining competitiveness – has been apparent for several decades, it was only in the 1970s that the symptoms became sufficiently acute for them to be taken seriously. As in ageing or a wasting disease, initially one can compensate or adjust for loss of a capacity but eventually one is reduced to vital functions, the loss of which can only have one outcome.

Fundamentally, the basic economic problem of maximizing satisfaction from the consumption of scarce resources resolves itself into a question of the appropriate unit of analysis. The ideal theoretical solution would be to treat the whole world as a single economy and pursue the theory of comparative advantage to its logical conclusion through universal free trade. Nationalism, politics, culture, stage of economic development, barriers to trade etc. make this both impractical and unrealistic. However, enlightened self-interest rejects the other extreme of self-sufficiency and protectionism, and the compromise is a mixture of both free trade and protectionist policies with the emphasis depending on the economy's basic resource endowment. Thus the UK and Japan, with a limited resource base, opt for trade, while the USA is more self-sufficient and protectionist in its policies.

While it is true that Britain's share of world trade has been declining since the middle of the last century – at which time we accounted for almost 50 per cent and so, by definition, could not increase our share – the decline was comparatively slow and overwhelmed in volume terms by the absolute growth in world trade. However, consider what has happened since 1950: as Schott (1984) has pointed out, we then enjoyed a 25 per cent market share of the world trade in manufacturers but by 1966 this had declined to only 6 per cent. Perhaps the only consolation to be drawn from figure 8.1, which records this, is that for the last 10 years we have begun to hold our position better. Schott (1984) points out:

This loss in market share of world manufacturing appears to have largely gone to West Germany and Japan. During the 1950–81 period West Germany increased its market share of these world exports from 7 per cent to 18 per cent; and over the same period Japan increased its share from just 3 per cent in 1950 to 18 per cent in 1981.

Schott concludes that UK industry has lost its ability to compete in export markets for manufactured goods.

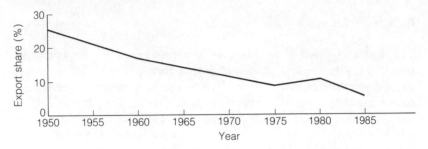

Figure 8.1   Export share of manufacturers' world trade. (*Source: Monthly Review of External Trade Statistics.*)

While declining export competitiveness is not good news, it would be of less consequence if the UK balance of trade was kept in equilibrium by a reduction in imports. Unfortunately, as figure 8.2 shows, the problem has been compounded by an increase in import penetration that has grown as rapidly as our export performance has declined. The consequence is a trade deficit for many products where previously we enjoyed a significant competitive advantage. Clearly, this situation has not developed overnight and there has been no shortage of investigation and reports identifying the problem, analysing its causes and prescribing courses of action to alleviate if not reverse the trends. So, what is different now to suggest that we may have backed off from the brink of economic disaster? At least two things have changed. First the Americans have contracted the 'British disease', and second the UK has had, since 1979, a government dedicated to restoring competitiveness.

American complacency – which to some extent must be condoned by virtue of the fact that it is the world's richest economy – was finally overcome by the publication of a paper entitled 'Managing our way to economic decline' by Hayes and Abernathy (1980). In drawing attention to the USA's declining competitiveness in international markets and the import penetration of domestic markets such as automobiles and electronics which it had 'invented', Hayes and Abernathy pointed out that in terms of economic growth, even the UK had outperformed the USA over the past two decades! Their diagnosis was an overemphasis on a financial/sales orientation, the key features of which can be summarized as follows.

1 The emphasis tends to be on short-range profit at the expense of growth and longer-range profit.
2 Budgeting and forecasting frequently pre-empt business planning.
3 Efficiency may outrank effectiveness as a management criterion.

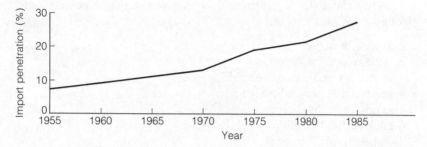

Figure 8.2 UK manufacturing import penetration. (*Source: Business Monitor MQ12, Import Penetration and Export Sales Ratios*. London: HMSO.)

4 Pricing, cost, credit, service and other policies may be based on false-economy influences and lack of marketplace realism.
5 The business focus is not on the customer and market but on internal considerations and numbers.

The impact of this pungent criticism (and others like it) stimulated an upsurge of interest in possible remedies (panaceas?) to cure the problem. One manifestation of this has been the enormous upsurge of interest in management books which has put several of them like *In Search of Excellence* (Peters and Waterman, 1982), *One Minute Manager* (Blanchard and Johnson, 1983), *Megatrends* (Naisbitt, 1984) and *Iacocca* (Iacocca and Novak, 1984) into the all-time best-seller lists. Significantly these books possess a number of common features.

1 They assert the superiority of American management and systems (particularly over the Japanese about whom Kenneth Blanchard – co-author of *One Minute Manager* – jokes: 'I often say that the second biggest mistake that the Japanese made after Pearl Harbour was to keep beating hell out of us about productivity');
2 They stress entrepreneurial values and the money-making ethic so strongly challenged by the consumerist movement of the 1960s and 1970s.
3 They are based upon the analysis of practice and procedure of firms or people who are leaders in their field and manifestly successful.
4 They reduce the ingredients of success to simple catechisms or formulae.
5 They emphasize that the essential catalyst and hero of the piece is the manager himself.

Perhaps the most influential of these books, and certainly the epitome of the genre, is *In Search of Excellence* (Peters and Waterman, 1982) in which they claim that excellent and innovative companies possess eight distinguishing characteristics:

1 a bias for action;
2 close to the customer;
3 autonomy and entrepreneurship;
4 productivity through people;
5 hands-on, value driven;
6 stick to the knitting;
7 simple form, lean staff;
8 simultaneous loose–tight properties.

Significantly, four of these factors relate to effectiveness and four to efficiency. To succeed (be effective) an organization needs to be pro-active, marketing oriented and risk seeking (points (1), (2) and (3)) and to build upon its distinctive competence or comparative advantage (point (6)). To optimize efficiency it needs to develop a structure combining the other four elements which are all concerned with *how* to manage – the creation of a corporate culture which will sustain the effectiveness factors.

While these proposals are intrinsically and intuitively appealing – hence the phenomenal success of the books – they possess significant weaknesses. The findings are overgeneralized and difficult to put into operation; the research from which the conclusions are drawn is usually based on non-representative samples of successful companies in growth industries (some of which have subsequently experienced major difficulties) with no control sample of less successful companies or consideration of mature and declining industries; the style is anecdotal and unsupported by hard data; key concepts like 'marketing oriented' are not clearly defined.

Despite these deficiencies (most of which are absent from more rigorous academic research into competitiveness (Baker et al., 1986) the belief persists that marketing and a marketing orientation offer the best promise of competitive success in the prevailing business climate. In an attempt to overcome the deficiencies noted above and identify whether there really are any critical success factors which distinguish between more and less successful firms Baker and Hart, with the support of the Economic and Social Research Council and Institute of Marketing, initiated a research project entitled Project MACS (Marketing and Competitive Success).

Project MACS

In Project MACS Baker and Hart deliberately set out to determine the presence or absence of a set of pre-identified factors and activities in a matched sample of both successful and unsuccessful firms. Conscious of the criticisms levelled against the management blockbusters, a classical approach to research design was followed comprising an extensive review of the literature, semi-structured depth interviews with a cross-section of opinion leaders and a structured interview with managing directors in 43 above-average and 43 below-average companies. Space limitations preclude a full description of the methodology and findings which can be found elsewhere (Baker and Hart, 1986), but five points are worth making here.

First, while our primary interest was in the contribution of marketing to competitive success it would be naive to impute success or failure to marketing alone. As our literature review confirmed, performance is the consequence of the interaction of at least five sets of factors as shown in figure 8.3. That said, we believe that it is possible to examine the elements of one construct through the elements of another. For example, the environment is often seen as a direct influence on the structure of an organization (Burns and Stalker, 1961). Similarly, Dunn et al. (1985), in a study of organizational culture, showed that a shared belief in informal communication has a marked impact on performance. In this case the culture of the organization was manifested, in part, through the style of

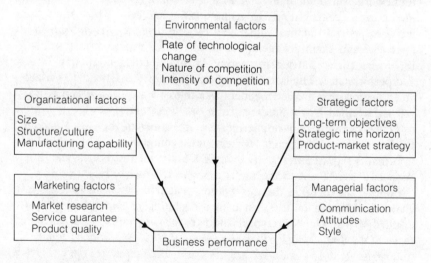

Figure 8.3   Factors contributing to business performance.

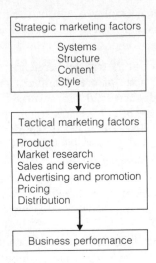

Figure 8.4   Marketing inputs to business performance.

its managers. However, in our opinion, marketing, defined as part of a company's total philosophy manifested as a strategic focus on the environment as well as a business function, should be detectable in the organizational, strategic and managerial factors in figure 8.3 and so is as good a medium as any through which to study competitive performance.

Second, to put this belief into operation we adopted the conceptual framework shown in figure 8.4 as a systematic approach to evaluating marketing's contribution to competitive success. This framework includes several factors subsumed by the five constructs shown in figure 8.3 and examines them from a marketing perspective. It contains three elements: strategic marketing factors, tactical marketing factors and performance. The last mentioned constitutes the dependent variable, and the first two are independent variables whose precise composition was determined by the findings from our literature review.

Third, our sample of opinion leaders (members of the CBI Marketing Committee and management writers) were complemented by several key informants representing the Economic Development Councils and Trade Associations relevant to the industries selected for study.

Fourth, based upon the observation that it is easier to succeed in a growth or sunrise industry than in a declining or sunset industry, we decided to sample both types. Industry growth rates were calculated from ICCs *Industrial Performance Analysis 1985/86*, which details 25 'industries' and 134 'industry sectors', and three measures were selected to measure performance – sales growth, average profit margin and average return on capital employed, all for the period 1981–84 – on the basis that these measures are readily understood and are usually available in published data. The composite sales growth for British industry was 11 per cent, the average profit margin was 4.65 per cent and the average return on capital employed was 13.5 per cent. The sectors chosen which outperformed these on all three measures were electronics, medical equipment and pharmaceuticals. Those chosen as below average on all three were agricultural equipment, paper and board, and sports and toys. Subsequently, a seventh above-average industry – food accessories – was added to ensure a sufficient database for analysis.

Fifth, data were collected by personal interview using a detailed questionnaire with three parts. Section A was concerned with organization and strategy, section B looked at various aspects of business practice and section C was a short self-completion section which examined the attitudes of managers to marketing. All interviews were conducted by a professional market research agency.

The findings

Without dwelling upon the detail, the key findings of the survey can be summarized as showing that successful companies in the sample have a number of operational differences from the less successful ones. These differences fall into one of the following categories: (a) differences in strategy; (b) differences in tactics. In above-average companies the marketing personnel meet significantly more frequently with the executive decision-making committee. These companies also exhibit a greater commitment to strategic planning: more of them carry it out, they quantify objectives to a greater extent and the period of time covered by strategic plans is generally longer. Additionally, the more successful companies pursue the achievement of their objectives by developing and adding value to their products to a significantly greater extent than their less successful counterparts.

Of the various tactical factors investigated, the more successful companies were more actively involved in market research and information gathering, market segmentation and promotion. The above-average performers carry out more in-house market research and employ more external agencies for specific studies. They conduct more customer surveys and field experiments than the below-average performers. The successful companies collate more types of internal information: they monitor stock levels, operational problems and the contribution of each product to overall sales volume to a far greater extent than the less successful companies. While there is little conclusive evidence to support the contention that successful companies segment their markets more than the less successful companies, successful companies were more active than the less successful ones in most methods of segmentation.

Finally, while both above- and below-average performers claim to engage in promotional activity, the former used sponsorship, catalogues, coupon drops, point-of-sale material, posters and sales aids to a far greater degree than the latter.

In a number of marketing tactics very little difference between the two groups of companies was detected. In some instances, distribution for example, the precise nature of a company's operations seems to be imposed by the structure of the market. In other instances (for example, maintaining quality) it is the size of the firm which tends to account for differences in method.

The results are obviously disappointing for those hoping for definitive evidence that there are clear and marked differences in the way in which successful and less successful firms go about their business. After all, comparatively few factors distinguish between the two groups. On reflection, and with the benefit of hindsight, this is unsurprising on at least two counts.

First, all the firms in the survey are successful to the extent that they have achieved the primary objective of the firm – survival – at a time when many others were going out of business.

Second, the enormous success of the management best-sellers belies the widely held belief that managers do not seek to improve their performance by taking new ideas on board. In consequence it is unsurprising that, managers in 'survivor firms' are aware of the claims made for critical success factors and rapidly adopt them. It follows that if every sample member possesses a given attribute, for example, uses long-range planning, this attribute alone will not enable you to discriminate between those possessing it unless you can develop quite sophisticated measures of the actual use made. (For our part we only used 'time horizon', but found that this did discriminate between successful and less successful firms). Further, we would predict that if our own findings enjoy any currency then these factors which we found to discriminate will rapidly disappear as less successful firms seek to emulate the performance of more successful firms. The problem is even further compounded on the grounds that many factors are situation specific and so cannot be generalized to industry as a whole. For example, a recent survey rank-ordering critical success factors in new product development placed 'design' sixteenth – for firms in which surface design is critical, e.g. fabrics and carpets, key decision-makers rank it first.

However, this is not an apologia for having done what was done. A structured and controlled survey like Project MACS was necessary to allay the criticisms of the anecdotal and partial analyses such as those in *In Search of Excellence*. In the event our findings are seen as lending support to these in the sense that ultimately it is clear that it is not so much what you do as how well you do it that matters. It is the quality of management and implementation which are determinant rather than the presence or absence of given techniques which, at best, are only aids to effective performance.

So what of marketing's contribution?

Conclusion

In this paper we have been concerned with the nature of competitive success and the contribution which marketing has to offer. It has been argued that success at the macrolevel implies maximizing the satisfaction to be derived from the consumption of the scarce resources available to a community. Implicitly it has been assumed that competitive markets offer the best opportunity of achieving this, with price acting as the lowest common denominator through which supply and demand will be brought into an equilibrium. Explicitly it has been argued that 'demand' reflects the satisfaction of myriad individual customers which will vary significantly in the particular and is subject to marked change over time. In pursuit of the economies of scale production becomes concentrated, and complex channels of distribution develop to serve rapidly growing markets. As a result of the separation of production and consumption the supplier's understanding of the precise nature of demand is liable to error, resulting in lost sales and profits and threatening the suppliers' survival.

In order to avoid this threat it is essential that producers first recognize that demand controls supply, and then organize themselves to ensure that they understand precisely what satisfaction customers are looking for and that their output matches these expectations. In that marketing is the orientation which starts with the identification of customer needs and insists that these condition all the firm's actions, it is self-evident that marketing is a necessary condition of competitive success. To be *effective* and succeed it is essential that firms, and all those that comprise them, adopt a marketing orientation. That said, it is clear that if all firms are marketing orientated they will still enjoy varying degrees of success with some performing better than others. Indeed, some marketing-orientated firms will fail because comparatively they are less *efficient* than their competitors.

Efficiency depends in part upon developing and deploying techniques and activities such as marketing research, long-range strategic planning, market segmentation and promotion, but these are only a part of the firm's total activity. Marketing is only one of several business functions, and it is the coordination and integration of R&D, production, finance and personnel with marketing which will finally determine the overall degree of success achieved.

What you do does matter but, ultimately, it is commitment and the quality of the execution which determines competitive success.

What next?

Given the preceding analysis and diagnosis, it is reasonable to inquire what the key research questions will be over the next decade? In that the modern marketing concept is firmly founded on the proposition that 'change is inevitable', as postulated in the theory of product life cycles with the practical consequences so eloquently spelled out by Levitt (1960), it is safe to predict that the management of change will continue as the central preoccupation of research in marketing. That said, it is also clear that this concern for the management of change will manifest itself in many different guises reflecting discrete subfields within the domain of marketing.

At the strategic level key issues are likely to include the following:

the nature of corporate culture and its influence on performance;
environmental analysis and technological forecasting;
the creation and maintenance of quality;
customer service levels;
the impact of information technology on exchange relationships.

In particular, the ability of advanced technology to enable almost infinite differentiation without significant cost penalty is bound to focus increasing attention on micromarketing. This emphasis will result in increased involvement and integration of marketing with R&D and manufacturing on the one hand and behavioural and information science on the other. To the extent that marketers can define unfilled customer needs with increased sophistication and precision, so they will increase the extent of their influence on the value chain from extraction through to ultimate consumption. The leverage in this system already lies with the marketing function and, in my view, will continue to grow as we approach the millennium.

These broad trends will both diminish and enhance the international aspects of marketing. In terms of communication and transportation/transfer of goods and services the world will continue to shrink to the extent that everything can be made available anywhere, anytime. However, the worldwide marketing of undifferentiated products proposed by the proponents of global marketing will be restricted to comparatively small segments in each national market as the full potential for differentiation is exploited by other competitors.

Finally, opportunities for extending and transferring the marketing concept and marketing techniques into other areas of activity, distinct from its commercial origins, will continue to be exploited. In the process is it pertinent to speculate whether it may become necessary to discover another new discipline concerned with the management of exchange relationships in place of 'marketing'? Fortunately, God (and the University Grants Committee) willing, I retire in 2000 AD!

References

Baker, M.J. and Hart, S.J. (1986). 'Project MACS: a conceptual framework for studying marketing and competitive success'. Scottish Enterprise Foundation: Ninth National Small Firms Policy and Research Conference, November 1986.

——, ——, Black, C.D. and Mohsen, T.M.A. (1986). 'The contribution of marketing to competitive success'. *Journal of Marketing Management*, 2(1), 39–61.

Blanchard, K. and Johnson, S. (1983). *The One Minute Manager*. Collins-Willow.

Burns, T. and Stalker, G.M. (1961). *The Management of Innovation*. London: Tavistock Publications.

Carson, R. (1963). *Silent Spring*. London: Hamish Hamilton.

Club of Rome (1972). *The Limits to Growth*. New York: Universe Books.

Dunn, M.G., Norburn, D. and Birley, S. (1985). 'Corporate culture: a positive correlate with marketing effectiveness'. *International Journal of Advertising*, 4, 65–73.

Hayes, R. and Abernathy, W. (1980). 'Managing our way to economic decline'. *Harvard Business Review*, July–August, **58**, 4, 67–77.

Iacocca, L. and Novak, W. (1984). *Iacocca: An Autobiography*. New York: Bantam.

Levitt, T. (1960). 'Marketing myopia'. *Harvard Business Review*, **38**, 4, 45–60.

Nader, R. (1966). *Unsafe at Any Speed*. New York: Pocket Books.

Naisbitt, J. (1984). *Megatrends*. New York: Futura.

O'Shaughnessy, J. (1984). *Competitive Marketing*. London: Allen and Unwin.

Packard, V. (1957). *The Hidden Persuaders*. Harmondsworth: Penguin.

—— (1960). *The Waste Makers*. Harmondsworth: Penguin.

Peters, T.J. and Waterman, R.H., Jr (1982). *In Search of Excellence*. New York: Harper and Row.

Schott, K. (1984). 'Economic competitiveness and design'. *The Royal Society of Arts Journal*, **132**, No. 5338, 648–56.

Schumacher, E.F. (1973). *Small is Beautiful*. London: Bland and Briggs.

9
Competitive advantage from relational marketing: the Japanese approach

Nigel C.G. Campbell

On both sides of the Atlantic, empirical and theoretical developments in marketing are leading to a greater study of buyer–seller dyads (Ford et al., 1986; Dwyer et al., 1987) and complex networks of relationships (Easton and Araujo, 1986; Arndt, 1984; Hakansson, 1987). Is Western research into these 'relational' aspects of marketing at last catching up with what the Japanese have been successfully practising for decades?

Nowadays few people cite the special characteristics of French or German approaches to marketing. In contrast, Japanese marketing has received much attention (Kotler et al., 1985; Lazer et al., 1985). Somehow the Japanese have combined manufacturing and marketing skills and captured dominant positions in many industries such as automobiles, motor cycles, watches, cameras, optical instruments and consumer electronics. This paper argues that the 'relational' marketing practised by the Japanese enables them to create and maintain internal and external relationships which help them to gain competitive advantage (Porter, 1985).

The first section of the paper will briefly trace the developments in marketing thinking which have led to the increased emphasis on the study of buyer–seller relationships and networks. The second section will review the literature on Japanese marketing. Against this background the third section will demonstrate the links between relational marketing and competitive advantage and illustrate them with examples of the practices and processes of Japanese firms. The final section summarizes the conclusions and suggests a new way of looking at competitive advantage that might link it better with the evolving marketing paradigm.

The ideas in this paper have been developed following in-depth interviews with 15 manufacturing companies in Japan and further meetings with their subsidiary companies in Britain. Ten companies made consumer products and the remainder were industrial.

The development of relational marketing

The recent literature reviews by Carmen (1980) and Hunt (1983) place strong emphasis on the concept of marketing as exchange, which was initiated by Bagozzi (1975; 1979). Exchange also plays an important role in Frazier's (1983) framework for inter-organizational exchange and in the unfolding political economy framework (Achrol et al., 1983; Arndt, 1983). This latter framework encompasses the concept of marketing as exchange and places it in an organizational perspective. To quote from Arndt:

> The political economy approach implies defining the identity, or character, of the focal social unit in terms of its exchange relations to other social units such as suppliers, customers, joint venture partners etc. Hence, the social unit is a part of the network, or social unit set, linked together over time by a system of structured exchanges. The ties may be of a technical, economic, social, political, emotional, informational, or competence nature. The role then for marketing is to develop, maintain and deepen the interorganisational network relations.

Arndt (1984) and Mattson (1984; 1986) have taken the concept of inter-organizational networks a step further. Arndt has proposed centrality, formalization and differentiation as the structural dimensions of the network, and Mattson has proposed that a firm's strategic position is dependent on both its micropositions (market share with a particular customer) and its macropositon (market share in the whole network).

The political economy paradigm also directs attention to the internal relationships of the marketing function (Arndt, 1983). Efficient implementation of marketing decisions requires dissemination of information to and from all internal groups. Other internal tasks are the development and maintenance of incentives, motivation and training systems for marketing performance. Bonoma (1985) also emphasizes the importance of internal relationships for which marketing managers with strong execution skills are required. Amongst the key skills Bonoma cites interacting, or the ability to manage oneself and one's interpersonal relations, and organizing, the ability to 'network' or create afresh an informal organization to match each different problem.

In parallel with these developments European researchers, carrying out empirical work on industrial marketing, have developed the interaction approach (Hakansson, 1982). This approach takes the buyer–seller relationship as the unit of analysis and argues that relationships are determined by the following four groups of variables: (a) the interaction process; (b) the participants in the interaction process; (c) the environment within which the interaction takes place; (d) the atmosphere affecting and affected by the interaction. Although this approach is largely confined to Europe, it has provided an important stimulus to theoretical and empirical research.

This brief summary suggests that relational marketing, defined as the management of both external and internal relationships, is becoming the focus of much research in marketing.

Japanese relational marketing

Japanese marketing has two opposing characteristics. The popular press frequently resounds with criticism of the aggressive pricing policies of Japanese firms. In the British electronics market Doyle et al. (1985) found that Japanese subsidiaries were more aggressive than comparable British firms. In the USA Kotler et al. (1985) found that the Japanese were very skilful in developing their market positions in a steady and sequential manner. Researching in Japan, Abegglen and Stalk (1986) comment on the aggressive financial and investment strategies which Japanese firms have used to overwhelm competitors in their own domestic market.

The opposite picture is of a management system which serves to create and strengthen external customer relationships. Weigand (1985) feels that the success of Japanese marketing is partly due to efforts to preserve harmony among trade partners, and Kelly and Hearne (1985) refer to the Japanese practice of finding peaceful solutions to conflicts with trade partners. Takeda (1985) emphasizes their attention to delivering on time and giving an excellent service. Others have commented on the Japanese willingness to invest in relationships as recommended by Johanson and Mattson (1985).

The Japanese attention to internal relationships comes out in their emphasis on implementation rather than strategy. Kotler et al. (1985) point out that the Japanese firms have made few original contributions to marketing theory and have obtained their success by the better application of marketing concepts developed elsewhere. Lazer et al. (1985), summarizing the views of academics and businessmen in Japan, agree that the Japanese generally have strength in implementing rather than formulating marketing strategy. Marketing activities are seen primarily as units of human activity rather than as impersonal costs or call reports. A greater emphasis is put on involvement and emotional commitment in implementing marketing programmes. Sagawa (1985) refers to the involvement of all management levels in product planning, and Ouchi (1981) suggests that one of the main ingredients of Japanese commercial success is their mastery of the internal tasks of marketing.

Thus Japanese relational marketing involves great attention to external relationships with customers and the trade, and great attention to the internal interactions within the company. How is this translated into competitive advantage?

Relational marketing and competitive advantage

Creating and sustaining competitive advantage is the only sure way of ensuring superior performance. Porter (1985) proposes that competitive advantage, in the form of lower prices or greater value, provided by the firm to its buyers cannot be understood by looking at the firm as a whole. Rather, it stems from the many discrete activities a firm performs in designing, producing, marketing, delivering and supporting its product. Each of these activities can contribute to a firm's relative cost position and create a basis for differentiation (greater value to the buyer). A value chain is a systematic way of examining all the activities and how they interact.

Figure 9.1 shows how the component parts of a firm's value chain fit together and appendix 9.1 gives a brief description of each of them. Of course a firm's value chain is neither isolated nor independent. It is embedded in a larger stream of activities, preceded by the value chains of suppliers and followed by those of channel members and buyers.

Logistics and operations

Although not strictly part of the topic of this paper, it is clear that many large Japanese firms have been particularly successful in applying relational concepts to both in-bound and out-bound logistics and to manufacturing operations themselves. The Kanban system, with its close

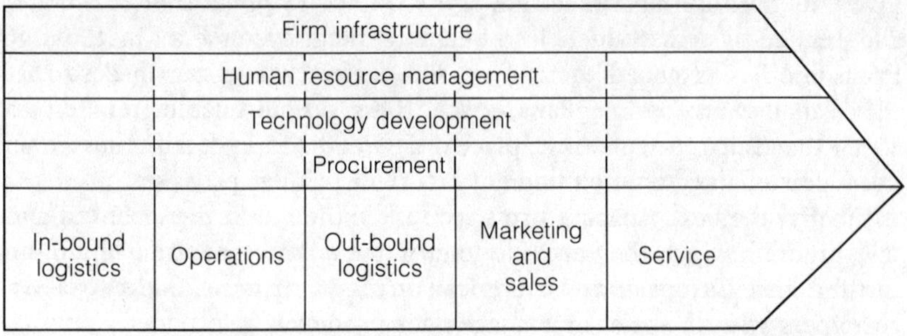

Firm infrastructure				
Human resource management				
Technology development				
Procurement				
In-bound logistics	Operations	Out-bound logistics	Marketing and sales	Service

Figure 9.1 The generic value chain (from Porter, 1985).

coordination between buyer and seller, is justly famous for its ability to reduce inventory and work in progress and to decrease manufacturing costs. Japanese firms use this system both to obtain supplies and to ensure timely delivery to their customers.

Within the manufacturing unit itself, Japanese firms use relational management to improve motivation and productivity. Team work is all important. At Nissan UK the foremen participated in the recruitment of their own teams and they maintain considerable autonomy in the allocation of work. Quality control circles are another important mechanism for creating participation and commitment.

Marketing, sales and service

The best Japanese companies seek to achieve partnership with their customers. Where the company's products are sold through a trade channel, the Japanese regard trade customers as the face the company shows to its ultimate consumers. Trade customers can greatly influence the consumer's buying behaviour, and they try to create strong bonds with trade customers so as to influence how the ultimate consumer is treated. In Japan, where distribution is very fragmented, many outlets are controlled directly or indirectly by the manufacturers.

Where Japanese firms cannot control their outlets, they use a mixture of both 'hard' and 'soft' relational marketing to achieve their partnership objectives. Hard relational marketing refers to the formal aspects of the relationship. In Japan salesmen call frequently (Campbell, 1985; Zimmerman, 1985). At IBM Japan, the sales force is larger and sales force costs are proportionately higher. It is more common in Japan than elsewhere for the supplier to loan salesmen to work for the customer. Seiko, for example, has three of its staff permanently working in a major Tokyo department store.

Similarly, the case studies suggest that Japanese firms are willing to invest in the information technology required to provide on-line order and service systems which link them to their customers. In the UK Panasonic has provided each of its 800 dealers with a terminal so that they can use the on-line Panaservice. This system enables retailers to check the availability of stock, place orders and obtain detailed advice on the repair of Panasonic equipment returned to their premises.

Finally, the best Japanese firms are very thorough in the technical and sales training which they provide to customers, and they are likely to go further than European and American firms in their readiness to assist customers with financial or management problems.

In addition to these hard relational marketing activities, Japanese firms, like the best American firms (Peters and Waterman, 1982), engage in a variety of 'soft' activities. When asked to compare the company's sales activities in the USA with those of other American firms, one Japanese electronics giant said that they felt that the selling activities of American firms were based on learning and following the sales manual, whereas they tried to train their salesmen to go beyond the manual and develop real empathy with the customers. In communicating with customers this company liked to use phrases such as 'we are in the same boat', 'we have to grow together', 'your problem is our problem'. Their philosophy is that trust has to be mutual and that it takes time to develop mature relationships.

The president of the UK subsidiary of the same company exemplified the willingness of senior Japanese executives to talk directly to customers. On one occasion he symbolized the importance his company attaches to customers by personally shaking the hand of every single customer who visited the firm's stand during a two-day trade show. He also regularly calls on trade outlets at random and agrees to sort out any difficulties, thus causing his staff headaches in implementing his promises! His example has helped the firm to understand the need to 'bend the system' to ensure that the customer obtains top-quality service. Bending the system to meet a customer's need can create goodwill of much greater value than the cost involved.

Successful companies in Japan and elsewhere invest in their relationships with distribution channels and ultimate customers. They gain competitive advantage through the superior value they provide, and the extra service costs are often offset by the reduced advertising and promotion required to sell where satisfied customers spread favourable opinions.

Procurement

The close management of supplier relationships is another well-known attribute of Japanese management. The origin of a Japanese firm's concern with suppliers is very simple. If the company's product does not perform correctly because of a supplier's failure, consumers will still think that the fault lies with the company. Therefore maintaining high quality from suppliers is important in ensuring the company's reputation for product reliability and quality. To achieve this Japanese firms seek to establish open communication with suppliers. They are willing to provide engineering support and technical advice. They expect to discuss costs and technical problems openly. The same pattern applies to relationships with advertising agents and other marketing consultants. Japanese companies like to bring them into the family so that they share the same values and philosophy.

Although old-established intimate relationships with suppliers are found in many Western firms, the Japanese seem to be more dedicated to this purchasing strategy. As Japanese firms have begun to manufacture overseas, they have frequently encouraged their suppliers to set up locally to maintain the relationships.

Technology development

Innovation is one of the fundamental driving forces in the Japanese domestic market (Campbell, 1986). In Japan consumers and retailers are constantly demanding new items, and firms have to develop their own products since staff do not move and taking over other firms is difficult. Japanese companies pursue innovation through relational activities with customers, suppliers and company members as well as through indirect relationships with government, research institutes, consultants and universities.

The close relationships with suppliers and customers frequently lead to joint developments. Technical knowledge is pooled to try and find a solution which will benefit both firms.

In consumer electronics the pace of new product introductions is such that companies do not have time to research what features consumers require. To cope with this situation, Japanese firms have developed an approach called 'successive creativity' (Tanomaru, 1986). The Japanese firm plans the first model change six to nine months after the initial launch. The changes incorporated in the new model result from fast feedback to the manufacturer from the trade. Japanese firms work with dealers to monitor consumer reactions and use the information to improve product performance. A similar approach, with a slower time-scale, is also a feature of industrial manufacturers.

In addition to their relationships with customers and suppliers, Japanese firms use their relationships with the large trading companies to gather valuable intelligence about new developments and competitive activity. They also have an intuitive understanding of the need to tap into other networks of relationships, academic or commercial, which could yield useful information (Hakansson and Waluszewski, 1986).

Internal relationships are also managed to promote technology development. This is achieved by quality circles, by persuading people to identify with the inventive traditions of a founding father and through loose and flexible organizations.

Human resource management

Human resource management is, of course, a relational activity. Japanese success in harnessing human resources is well documented. Higher productivity, leading to lower costs, and greater motivation, leading to better service, can both result in competitive advantage.

To achieve these benefits Japanese companies stress open and two-way communication fostered by open-plan offices, regular formal meetings, *ringi* decision-making, job rotation, and training and coaching on the job. They prefer overlapping responsibilities to tight job descriptions and managing by walking around rather than managing by memo. Informal meetings with staff are encouraged and social events are organized to help develop friendships between employees.

Firm infrastructure

As noted in appendix 9.1, Porter (1985) lists general management, planning, finance etc. as the main activities in this part of the value chain. Bonoma (1985) suggests less tangible activities – the creation and maintenance of policies of identity (marketing culture and theme) and policies of direction (marketing strategy and leadership). Marketing culture and theme generally tell the members of the marketing organization and the firm who the company is and what it does as regards marketing. Marketing strategy and leadership are policies of direction. They tell the firm, its management and its workers where the company is going and provide a general direction for all that is done in the marketing area. In Bonoma's view these activities are essential in achieving good marketing practice, value for the customer and hence competitive advantage.

Japanese companies are well known for the fervour with which they inculcate the company philosophy. They are equally active in developing marketing themes such as Sharp's 'New Life' programme to develop products which are both functional and convenient as well as aesthetically pleasing. The formulation of an explicit strategy is not a strong feature of Japanese marketing.

Linkages and interrelationships

The discussion so far has centred on individual value activities as the source of competitive advantage. In practice the value chain is not a collection of independent activities but a system of interdependent ones. Linkages can lead to competitive advantage through coordination. Much of the recent change in philosophy towards manufacturing and quality is a recognition of the importance of linkages. Better coordination leads to reduced inventory throughout the firm. By definition relational marketing encourages and exploits internal and external linkages. In Japanese companies internal linkages are fostered by the use of two-way communication, overlapping responsibilities, job rotation etc., in human resource management and by the team spirit which results from the sharing of common values and beliefs enshrined in the company philosophy. External linkages are fostered in the approach to procurement, customer service and technology development.

Interrelationships with sister companies are another source of competitive advantage. According to Porter (1985) there are two main types of interrelationship. First, tangible interrelationships, which arise from a sharing of activities in the value chain, are due to common buyers, channels, technologies and other factors. Second, there are intangible relationships which involve the transfer of management know-how and business intelligence between separate business units. Again, the Japanese seem to be well ahead in developing the structures and skills to achieve these advantages. The coordination and cross-fertilization between members of the large *zaibatsu* is well known, but the same spirit of cooperation pervades relationships between subsidiaries in many independent groups.

Conclusions and implications for future research

Kotler (1986) defines marketing management as

The analysis, planning, implementation and control of programmes designed to create, build and maintain beneficial exchanges and relationships with target markets to achieve organisational objectives.

The definition says that marketing programmes are designed to develop and maintain relationships, but there is little in Kotler's writing about how to achieve this. In contrast relational marketing highlights the management of a network of external relationships involving suppliers, advertising agents etc. as well as customers. Marketing success depends less on a succession of crisply executed programmes and more on the patient welding together of a group of firms who understand each other's requirements. To manage the multitude of links to the external network the firm itself must work as a team. An internal network must be created to serve and match the evolving external relationships.

Japanese marketing has this relational character, and its success springs from the way in which Japanese firms exploit the relational aspects of the value activities which make up a firm's value chain (see appendix 9.1). Their skill in using relational marketing helps them to lower the costs and/or improve the buyer value of those activities and so gain competitive advantage.

A focus on relationships and networks creates exciting new opportunities for research in marketing. Researchers now need to develop data-collection methods and analytical tools for describing and interpreting networks and individual relationships. This section focuses on the study of networks and describes some of the problems and research opportunities.

The first problem encountered in studying networks is one of definition. If a network consists of organizations which are linked together in some way, after a limited number of direct 'first-order' contacts the number of second- and higher-order contacts increases exponentially and ultimately spreads over the whole industrialized world.

Researchers must therefore focus on partial networks and limit the number of participants. In their key paper Aldrich and Whetten (1981) distinguish between an organization set (those organizations with which a given organization has direct links), an action set (those organizations which form a temporary alliance for a limited purpose) and a network (those organizations, chosen by the researcher, which are at least loosely joined together). In other words Aldrich and Whetten have explicitly recognized that researchers themselves must determine the scope of the network.

Hallen and Johanson (1988) define a product network as one which includes the exchange relations between the firms manufacturing, distributing and using the product or parts of it. Thus, for example, there are a number of firms manufacturing, distributing and using vehicle tyres. To limit a study in the tyre market a researcher might decide to investigate the network comprising the top 15 vehicle manufacturers and the 10 major tyre suppliers. Clearly, all 25 companies know each other well although they do not all trade with each other.

How best can the web of ties between the 25 companies in such a network be described? A conventional microeconomic analysis focusing on market shares, production volumes, transport costs and performance and service attributes will not reveal the pattern or quality of the relationships. To do this marketers must turn to the work of sociologists interested in network analysis. Mitchell (1969) has been a pioneer in this field with his work on the morphology or structure of networks.

The techniques of mathematical graph theory (Roistacher, 1974) can be used to represent network properties such as density (the extent and strength of the ties between organizations) and reachability (the existence and distance of a path between two organizations; for example, when A supplies B and B buys from C, A can 'reach' C). This yields insights into the existence of subsystems or cliques. Related techniques have been developed to assess the hierarchy and centrality of networks (Nieminen, 1973).

The main problem in performing mathematical analyses of networks is to decide what aspect of the relationship between two organizations to measure and how to quantify it. Aldrich (1976) used legal and contractual obligations between organizations. Fortunately, Mitchell (1987) has now developed techniques which allow data collected for a number of aspects to be integrated to give a composite picture of which organizations are 'structurally equivalent' to each other.

Data collection remains a problem. Although interval data are not required, thus allowing an aspect like closeness to be scaled as 3 for the closest relationships, 2 for intermediate relationships and 1 for the least close relationships, there is still the problem of completeness. Investigating the tyre network would require information from each of the 25 participants about each of the others. In larger networks such demanding data requirements can perhaps be overcome by survey techniques (Fischer, 1982) and the keeping of diaries (Cubitt, 1973).

This brief survey indicates the potential for a closer integration of marketing with the study of social networks to provide a powerful new stimulus for research. Important theoretical and methodological issues need to be resolved. How should researchers limit the networks they want to study? What aspects of relationships should be measured? How should the data analysis be performed? Empirical studies are needed of external networks – product networks (the relationships in a market), company networks (the relationships of one company) and technology networks (relationships linked by interest in a specific technology) – and internal networks (relationships in a marketing department or between marketing and other functions). Longitudinal studies are particularly needed to learn how networks evolve over time. A start has been made with the work of Smith and Easton (1986) and Hakansson and Waluszewski (1986) but much more needs to be done. Is it not time for marketing to shake off the shackles of economics and forge a new partnership with those who specialize in understanding human and organizational interactions?

Acknowledgement

The financial assistance of the Economic and Social Research Council is gratefully acknowledged.

Appendix 9.1   Value-chain activities (Porter, 1985)

Primary activities

In-bound logistics   Activities associated with receiving, storing and disseminating input to the product, such as material handling, warehousing, inventory control, vehicle scheduling and returns to suppliers.

Operations   Activities associated with transforming inputs into the final product form, such as machining, packaging, assembly, equipment maintenance, testing, printing and facility operations.

Out-bound logistics   Activities associated with collecting, storing and physically distributing the product to buyers, such as finished goods warehousing, material handling, delivery vehicle operation, order processing and scheduling.

Marketing and sales   Activities associated with providing a means by which buyers can purchase the product and inducing them to do so, such as advertising, promotion, sales force, quoting, channel selection, channel relations and pricing.

Service   Activities associated with providing service to enhance or maintain the value of the product, such as installation, repair, training, parts supply and product adjustment.

Support activities

Procurement   Activities associated with the function of purchasing, such as procedures for dealing with vendors, qualification rules and information systems.

Technology developments   Activities that result in improvements of the product and the manufacturing process. Examples would be telecommunications technology for the order entry system, office automation for the accounting department, basic research and product design, media research, and information systems for repair and servicing.

Human resource management   Activities involved in the recruiting, hiring, training, development and compensation of all types of personnel.

Firm infrastructure   Activities such as general management, planning, finance, accounting, and legal and government affairs.

References

Abbegglen, J.C. and Stalk, G. (1985). *Kaisha: The Japanese Corporation*. New York: Basic Books.

Achrol, R.S., Reve, T. and Stern, L.W. (1983). 'The environment of marketing channel dyads: a framework for comparative analysis'. *Journal of Marketing*, **47**, 55–67.

Aldrich, H.E. (1976). 'Resource dependence and interorganizational relations: local employment service offices and social services sector organizations. *Administration and Society*, **7**, 419–54.

—— and Whetten, D.A. (1981). 'Organization-sets, action-sets, and networks: making the most of simplicity'. In *Handbook of Organizational Design* (eds J. Nystrom and W.H. Starbuck). Oxford: Oxford University Press.

Arndt, J. (1983). 'The political economy paradigm: foundation for theory building in marketing'. *Journal of Marketing*, 47, 44–54.

—— (1984). 'The anthropology of marketing systems: symbols, shared meanings and ways of life in interorganisational networks. Paper presented at the International Research Seminar on Industrial Marketing, Stockholm School of Economics, 29–31 August 1984.

Bagozzi, R.P. (1975). 'Marketing as exchange'. *Journal of Marketing*, 39, 32–9.

—— (1979). 'Toward a formal theory of marketing exchanges'. In *Conceptual and Theoretical Developments in Marketing* (eds O.C. Ferrell, S.W. Brown and C.W. Lamb, Jr), pp. 431–47. Chicago, IL: American Marketing Association.

Bonoma, T. (1985). *The Marketing Edge – Making Strategies Work*. New York: Free Press.

Campbell, N.C.G. (1984). 'The structure and stability of industrial market networks: developing a research methodology'. Paper presented at 2nd IMP Research Conference on International Marketing, UMIST, 1–2 September 1984.

—— (1985). 'Buyer/seller relationships in Germany and Japan'. *European Journal of Marketing*, 19(3), 57–66.

—— (1986). 'Sources of competitive rivalry in Japan'. *Journal of Product Innovation Management*, 2(4), 224–31.

Carmen, J.M. (1980). 'Paradigms for marketing theory'. In *Research in Marketing*, vol. 3 (ed. J.N. Sheth), pp. 1–36. Greenwich, CT: JAI Press.

Cubitt, T. (1973). 'Network density among urban families'. In *Network Analysis: Studies in Human Interaction* (eds J. Boissevain and J.C. Mitchell), pp. 67–82. The Hague: Mouton.

Doyle, P., Saunders, J. and Wong, V. (1985). *A Comparative Investigation of Japanese Marketing Strategies in the British Market*. Bradford: Bradford Management Centre.

Dwyer, F.R., Schurr, P.H. and Sejo Oh (1987). 'Developing buyer–seller relationships'. *Journal of Marketing*, 51 (April), 11–27.

Easton, G. and Araujo, L. (1986). 'Networks, bonding and relationships in industrial markets'. *International Marketing and Purchasing*, 1(1), 8–25.

Fischer, C.S. (1982). *To Dwell among Friends: Personal Networks in Town and City*. Chicago, IL: University of Chicago Press.

Ford, D., Hakansson, H. and Johanson, J. (1986). 'How do companies interact?' *Industrial Marketing and Purchasing*, 1(1), 26–41.

Frazier, G.L. (1983). 'Interorganizational exchange behaviour. A broadenend perspective'. *Journal of Marketing*, 47 (Fall) 68–78.

Hakansson, H. (ed.) (1982). *International Marketing and Purchasing of Industrial Goods*. New York: Wiley.

—— (ed.) (1987). *Industrial Technological Development: A Network Approach*. London: Croom Helm.

—— and Waluszewski, A. (1986). 'Technical development in dense networks'. Paper presented at the 3rd International IMP Research Seminar on

International Marketing, Management Research Institute, Lyons, 3–5 September 1986.

Hallen, L. and Johanson, J. (1988). *International Business Relationships and Industrial Networks*. Greenwich, CT: JAI Press.

Hunt, S.D. (1983). 'General theories and the fundamental explanada of marketing'. *Journal of Marketing*, **47**, 9–17.

Johanson, J. and Mattson, L.-G. (1985). 'Marketing investments and market investment in industrial networks'. *International Journal of Research in Marketing*, **2**, 185–95.

Kelly, E.J. and Hearne, L.R. (1985). 'New rules for marketing leadership – today's and tomorrow's management in the international society'. *Marketing Journal, JMA*, 5(1), 55–70 (in Japanese).

Kotler, P. (1986). *Marketing Management: Analysis, Planning and Control* (5th edn). Englewood Cliffs, NJ: Prentice-Hall.

——, Fahey, L. and Jatusripitak, S. (1985). *The New Competition*. Englewood Cliffs, NJ: Prentice-Hall.

Lazer, W. (1985). 'On the marketing side in Japanese firms: management practices as viewed by an American'. *Marketing Journal, JMA*, 5(2), 54–62 (in Japanese).

——, Murata, S. and Kosaka, H. (1985). 'Japanese marketing: towards a better understanding'. *Journal of Marketing*, **49**, 69–81.

Mattson, L.-G. (1984). 'An application of a network approach to marketing: defending and changing market positions'. In *Changing the Course of Marketing: Alternative Paradigms for Widening Marketing Theory* (eds N. Dholakia and J. Arndt). Greenwich, CT: JAI Press.

—— (1986). 'Management of strategic change in a markets-as-networks perspective'. Paper presented at the International Research Seminar on Management of Strategic Change, University of Warwick, 14–16 May 1986.

Mitchell, J.C. (1969). 'The concept of use of social networks'. In *Social Networks in Urban Situations* (ed. J.C. Mitchell). Manchester: University of Manchester Press.

—— (1987). 'Network procedures'. In *The Quality of Urban Life*. Berlin: Walter de Gruyter.

Nieminen, U.J. (1973). 'On the centrality in a directed graph'. *Social Science Research*, **2**, 371–8.

Ouchi, W.G. (1981). *Theory Z: How American Business Can Meet the Japanese Challenge*. Reading, MA: Addison-Wesley.

Peters, T.J. and Waterman, R.H. (1982). *In Search of Excellence*. New York: Harper and Row.

Porter, M. (1985). *Competitive Advantage*. New York: Free Press.

Roistacher, R.C. (1974). 'A review of mathematical methods in sociometry'. *Sociological Methods and Research*, **3**, 123–71.

Sagawa, K. (1985). 'Product planning and market research in Japan'. *Marketing Journal, JMA*, 5(2), 36–43 (in Japanese).

Smith, P. and Easton, G. (1986). 'Network relationships: a longitudinal study'. Paper presented at the 3rd International IMP Research Seminar on International Marketing, Management Research Institute, Lyons, 3–5 September 1986.

Takeda, S. (1985). 'The international marketing of Japanese companies'. Tokyo: Dobunkan (in Japanese).

Tanomaru, H. (1985). 'Perspective of Japanese marketing'. *Marketing Journal*, JMA, 5(2), 26–38.

Weigand, R.E. (1985). 'Conflict solutions in Japan'. *Marketing Journal, JMA*, 5(1), 7–81.

Zimmerman, M. (1985). *Dealing with the Japanese*. London: Allen and Unwin.

10
Organizing professional work: the case of designers in the engineering industry in Britain

Arthur Francis and Diana Winstanley

Introduction

This paper attempts to serve two purposes. One is to discuss the organization and management of a particular important manufacturing activity – engineering design – in its own right. The other is to discuss this as an example of the more general and increasingly widespread phenomenon of the employment of people with high-level technical and/or professional qualifications within large-scale enterprises. The evidence cited here was collected during the first phase of a research project on the organization and management of engineering design which was funded by the UK Economic and Social Research Council's research programme on the competitiveness of British industry.

The organization and management of engineering design is of interest in its own right in the light of the considerable debate within the UK at the present time about how the quality of design (both industrial and engineering) might be improved, both by changes in the education and training of designers and by changes within firms. Reports commissioned by various Government agencies in recent years include the Corfield (1979) and Pilditch (1986) Reports for the National Economic Development Office (NEDO), the Finniston Report to the Department of Industry (1980), the Lickley Report to the Science and Engineering Research Council (1984) and a report on *Managing Design* sponsored jointly by the Council for National Academic Awards (CNAA), the Department of Trade and Industry and the Design Council (CNAA, 1984). This debate is notable for the number of prescriptions being advanced, but it is not underpinned by a great deal of research evidence about current practice and variations in this practice. One element of the research whose preliminary results are reported here is to provide empirical data to help fill this gap.

More generally, to the extent that engineering designers now have increasingly high technical qualifications but are usually employed in large engineering companies, they can be considered to exemplify what Child (1982), for example, notes as an increasingly common phenomenon. Occupations designated as professional and technical are constituting a growing proportion of total employment in the UK, in Western Europe as a whole and in the USA. Moreover, relatively more members of professional occupations are being employed in organizations. The employment of technical and professional people within large-scale organizations has attracted considerable interest over a long period because of the conflict that is seen to derive from the tension between the two contrasting principles of work organization normally assumed to be held by the professions on the one hand and managers of large-scale organizations on the other. A classic early statement of the problem is Hall's (1968) paper on 'Professionalization and bureaucratization', and this has been followed by more sophisticated theoretical reformulations of the issue (Child, 1982) and empirical studies of individual occupations. Engineering has been scrutinized on a number of occasions (Gerstl and Hutton, 1966; Ritti, 1971; Armstrong, 1972, 1987; Hutton and Lawrence, 1981; Child et al., 1983; McCormick, 1985; Whalley, 1986), and there have also been studies of accountants (Glover, 1986) and of doctors and scientists (for a review see Davies (1983)). A difficulty with this previous work is the extent to which the various occupations have been treated as though each was homogeneous. Within engineering, for example, there are many occupational groupings from diverse educational and training backgrounds. Because the study reported here looks at just one group, it may be able to identify more clearly the strategies adopted by that group and by management towards that group.

On the theoretical side the debate has until now focused almost solely on the dichotomous conflict between professional and managerial/organizational values, interests and modes of control (Child, 1982; Child et al., 1983). The contribution made in this paper is that of the development of a conceptual framework embracing four modes of organization which then allows an exploration of a variety of ways in which technical and professional work might be organized and managed.

The collection of the data on which this paper is based began in November 1986 with visits to 32 UK-based businesses which were active in mechanical engineering. Managers in charge of design activities were interviewed. The intention of this first phase in the research was to gain an overview of the range of practices within engineering design and not, at this stage, to collect the kind of data from which reliable conclusions might be drawn. In the second phase of the research, which began in Autumn 1987, detailed case studies are being conducted in three or four firms.

The first paper from our research (Winstanley and Francis, 1987) provides more detailed information about the particular engineering design practices we were told about and begins to set out our conceptual approach.

This paper attempts to set this out in more detail. It begins by noting a number of substantial changes taking place in the UK at the moment which are causing considerable reappraisal of the position of technical experts in industry. It then goes on to explore the various occupational groups involved in the design process and, at the core of the paper, identifies four alternative modes of organization (which are also strategies for interest groups to pursue) of complex technical work. It ends with a discussion of the British case.

Changes in the industry

A striking feature of our initial survey of design activies in 32 engineering companies was the amount of interest and concern expressed by practitioners in the topic of engineering design management. Design engineers themselves recognized that many changes were taking place within the industry, and that new forms of organization and management needed to be explored. Three major areas of change could be identified. There has, in the UK at least, been a substantial increase in the number of graduate-level technologists employed in the engineering industry; nearly all the firms we visited had invested substantially in computer aids for engineering and had plans for further investment, and they all felt a high level of competitive pressure on quality, performance, cost and lead times which intensified both the need for a high level of engineering design input and for efficient management of engineering design resources so that tight deadlines could be met reliably at reasonable cost.

Increased numbers

As early as 1963 the Feilden Report, considering the 'Present Standing of Mechanical Engineering Design', observed two major changes in the industry. One was the post-war development of the educational system, and the other was the rapid rate of technological progress. With regard to the former, the Feilden committee noted that until this post-war development

the shop floor was the main point of entry into engineering and engineering firms relied on their apprentice schemes to supply them not only with skilled trades-men, but with their drawing office staff, design engineers and managers . . . This system undoubtedly produced good engineers and its products are the mainstay of many firms, But they are a dying race.

On the latter point they noted that 'the design of modern engineering products requires an amount of scientific and technological knowledge which can only be acquired through formal study' and thus the industry had become increasingly dependent on the products of the universities and technical colleges. Although the Feilden Report gives no figures to back up this judgement, a recent report from the UK Engineering Industries Training Board (EITB) (EITB, 1986) provides startling illumination of this trend, although their data tend to suggest that the trend identified by Feilden began rather later than that Report suggested. The EITB figures indicate that the rise in the proportion of professional engineers in the engineering industry did not begin until as late as 1978 in the UK.

However, from this point on the changes are dramatic. The EITB figures show that, while overall employment in the UK engineering industry fell by 32.4 per cent between 1978 and 1985 the employment of 'professional engineers, scientists and technologists' increased by 46.5 per cent. This implies an increase of 217 per cent over seven years in the percentage of total employment in engineering represented by professional engineers. Moreover, whereas in 1978 there were nearly four technicians, including draughtspeople, to each professional engineer, scientist or technologist, by 1985 the equivalent figure was only two to one. However, it must also be noted that by 1985 professional engineers were still only 4.3 per cent of all engineering employees in the UK. It should also be noted that these figures relate to occupational categories in the industry as a whole and not just to the design function.

Even within the ranks of professional engineers there has been a very substantial shift upwards in the formal level of educational attainment. As the Finniston Report shows (1980, p. 48), over the three decades after 1945 the percentage of those with degrees amongst each cohort of qualifying professional engineers increased from under 30 per cent to about 80 per cent, with the balance qualifying via the HNC/HND route or by professional examinations only.

There may have been even more substantial changes within the design function and in particular sectors of the industry. In one very advanced engineering company we were told that in the 1950s one might have expected to have one specialist engineer (of graduate level) for every five designer/draughtspeople within the design function, but that today the ratio might well be reversed.

Computer aids in engineering

Although most attention seems to have been paid to computer-aided draughting (CADr) in discussions about the impact of computers in engineering, the use of computational aids in engineering analysis should not be overlooked. Such aids have a much longer history than CADr, going back at least to the early 1960s, and their impact may have been more pervasive than CADr equipment.

Computer-aided design at the engineering analysis stage (CADe) was, in its earlier stages, a numerical rather than a graphical exercise carried out via batch processing punched cards into mainframe computers. Only recently have developments in hardware and software enabled graphic simulations of engineering analyses to become common. CADe is concerned with such matters as stress analysis (finite-element analysis is now a particularly common computer-based activity), fluid-flow calculations and models of dynamic processes such as railway rolling stock.

Not only has CADe led to an increase in the number of graduate-level engineers employed at the analysis stage of engineering design, it is suggested that it has also had an impact further downstream with less experimental work now done in testing prototypes. New designs are tested in the computer rather than 'in metal', with consequences for employment in test departments (Wingert et al., 1984).

The way in which changes in the educational system and in technology have been handled organizationally was noted by Feilden in the following terms:

Industry has reacted to these two trends by dividing the design function into at least two parts; one of these concerns itself with the scientific aspects of design . . . the other concerns itself with depicting the shapes of the components within these limits. The first is frequently designated as an engineering department, the second as a design or drawing office.

The appropriateness of this division of labour will be the subject of discussion later in this paper.

Heightened competitive pressure

During the 18-month period 1979–81 nearly 20 per cent of all UK manufacturing capacity was lost, and the mechanical engineering industry was fully represented in this capacity reduction. The proximate causes of this epochal 'shake-out' were high interest rates, a high exchange rate and a world recession triggered by the second oil price shock (Aldington Report, 1985). At the time of our survey (winter 1986–7) the firms we visited were, in the main, recovering from this

1979–81 period and on a growth path from this low base. There was a strong feeling among a number of firms that they continued to be under threat from overseas competitors and that this competition was in terms of product characteristics, quality and the speed with which products could be brought to the market. Firms that supplied government were under pressure from fixed-price contracts which had now largely replaced the cost-plus contracts of a previous era. Some of our firms were newly privatized. A further competitive element was the change in procurement policy of several large UK organizations which had previously bought components and systems almost exclusively from UK suppliers and were now buying internationally. This had affected a number of the firms in our survey.

The occupational interest groups

The role of design in the mechanical engineering industry in Britain can only be fully understood in the context of how the industry itself has developed. The analysis presented here lends support to Stinchcombe's (1965) proposition, more recently given support from population ecology theorists (Hannan and Freeman, 1977), that structures become embedded in organizations at the time that those organizations are founded. What we see in the mechanical engineering industry is a set of organizational arrangements that owe their origins to artisan practices current at the time when steam power was first developed.

Traditional practice within mechanical engineering has been for design to be done within the drawing office by draughtspeople recruited from amongst the most able skilled craftworkers in the workshop. Cooley (1972b, p. 78) for example, claims that up until the 1930s the draughtsman 'was the centre of the design activity. He would design the component, draw it, stress it, select the materials for it, write the test specifications for it, liaise with the customer and usually liaise with the workshop floor for production'. Cooley goes on to suggest that towards the end of the 1930s and 'certainly during the war' all these functions were broken down into discernible separate jobs. Our own observations would support Cooley's view in the case of aerospace and aero-engine industries, each of which is dealing with the leading edge of technical developments and where the pressures for a high level of technical performance are most strong. In other sectors the division of labour is not always so elaborate. Nearly everywhere we found a trichotomous division of labour with a production engineering function having responsibility for liaising with the workshop floor and a division within design characterized by such categorizations as analysis versus synthesis, engineering versus design and development versus draughting.

However much there may have been an elaboration of the division of labour this has not resulted in an overall reduction of the level of technical qualifications of those involved in design-related activities. As noted earlier in this paper, the proportion of professionally qualified technical workers in the engineering industry has more than doubled. How, then, have graduate engineers become insinuated into the predominantly craft-based organizational culture and structure of engineering design activity? An interim stage has been the development of the technician role in the design process. Instead of recruiting draughtspeople from the shop-floor it has been the practice for some time to recruit school-leavers directly into the drawing-office and provide part-time training for technician-level qualifications, originally Ordinary and Higher National Certificates and Diplomas, and more recently for qualifications administered by the British Technician Education Council. Much of the technical expertise involved in engineering design has in the recent past come from those following this occupational route. Technicians in design have developed their own occupational interests through their own occupational association – the Institution of Engineering Designers.

The number of graduate engineers in design departments in the UK engineering industry still appears to be low, but on a rather fast growth path which seems to be quite recent. There does seem to have been a movement from the position of perhaps a decade ago when graduate engineers were mainly to be found either in a few very large companies which did highly sophisticated engineering (e.g. aerospace and power generation) or in niche positions in smaller companies where they were engaged primarily in analytical activities. Nowadays they are more likely to be involved in general development and possible conceptual design work in a broader range of companies.

As Child et al. (1983, p. 67) comments, concepts of professionalism (using the term as the antonym of managerialism rather than amateurism) have infused British management. It is a particular feature of the British social structure for occupational groups to attempt to lay claim to the title of profession, and for professional groups to enjoy higher status than those working without the benefit of a specialist occupational categorization in managerial capacities in trade and industry.

Graduate-level ('professional') engineers are served by the various 'professional' institutions, e.g. the Institution of Mechanical Engineers. None of these bodies has fully succeeded in establishing for itself as much power over the engineering occupation as equivalent bodies have for other occupations such as the law and medicine. In particular, there is no requirement for a licence to practice engineering and thus the role of the institutions in accreditation and control of entry to the profession is consequently weak. Nevertheless, following the publication of the Finniston Report on engineering in 1980 and the consequent setting up of an over-arching Engineering Council there have been a number of initiatives to establish standards, tighten up accreditation and exercise more control over the occupation. We shall return to the issue of the professionalization of engineering in the UK below.

There is another entirely separate tradition of design activity in the UK. From at least the middle of the eighteenth century there has been an interest amongst those primarily concerned with aesthetic design in the application of their work to functional objects. Labelled 'industrial design', the activity is taught within colleges of art and design and has in the past been mainly concerned with the appearance and ergonomic aspects of industrial products. More recently, the claim has been made that the basic techniques of industrial design can be applied to the more fundamental features of the design of industrial products. Many industrial designers would now claim an expertise in taking part in the fundamental conception of the product in asking what purposes the product was to serve, in conceptualizing (and sketching) a variety of possible solutions to how that purpose might be met, and in becoming involved in the details of materials choice, production method and so on. Within product markets traditionally served by the engineering industry the influence of industrial designers has been in the main, so far, through the use of design consultancy houses. Only one firm in our survey employed industrial designers in-house.

To the extent that changes in the educational system now mean, as Feilden observed, that there is not a ready supply of very able people going into the drawing office and that graduate engineers are trained primarily in analytical skills rather than in the kind of design skills taught within the design and art colleges, it can be argued that industrial designers are filling an important gap. Whether they will ever become generally acceptable to the engineering community, and whether their skills are those most appropriate for integrating the analytical skills of professional engineers and the draughting skills necessary for producing working drawings for the production department must for the moment remain open questions.

Various modes of organization

Coordination, control and the division of labour

The central concern of this paper is an analysis of the various ways in which complex tasks are organized in enterprises involving workers with high levels of expertise. A central problem within enterprises is the coordination and control of the division of labour, and there has been much sociological and organizational analysis of the processes which elaborate the division of labour and develop organizational arrangements to handle coordination and control (Francis, 1986, pp. 105ff). The previous sections have discussed some aspects of the division of labour within engineering design. What follows is an attempt both to conceptualize and analyse the coordination and control of these specialized workers.

Our point of departure is the distinction popularized by Williamson (1975) between market and hierarchy as mechanisms for conducting transactions between parties whose tasks need to be coordinated. From this dichotomy we generate four generic modes of organization which seem to accord with strategies being pursued by interested parties involved in engineering design as means of coordinating and controlling their work. One of these four modes is the pure market form. Two others are hierarchical and the fourth is a mixed case. The difference between the two hierarchical forms is the basis upon which the hierarchy is built – one is a form of hierarchical control based on the occupational group, and the other is based on a managerial hierarchy. The mixed case involves elements of market and both managerial and occupational hierarchical control and can be characterized as essentially corporatist.

Occupational control

The mediaeval guilds and the modern 'status' professions of law and medicine exemplify occupational control in its purest form. The defining characteristics of occupational control are that transactions between fellow members of the craft group are internalized and all other transactions are handled via the market. Secondary features are that control over work usually has a strong peer group element with norms of collegiality and, in many cases, a democratic basis to the selection of people to powerful positions within the occupational organization. Elevation to higher positions in the organization is frequently (although not necessarily) seen as being associated with higher levels of craft competence, and a series of lower positions may be specifically training grades.

The occupation maintains control over entry to the occupation, training requirements and jurisdiction over standards of work and behaviour of the occupational members. Equally important is control over the sole right of accredited occupational members to do the particular work of that occupational group. Such monopoly rights were often granted by royal decree in mediaeval times. More recently craft groups have had to rely on custom, practice and trade union strength to maintain their monopoly rights, but professional occupations still enjoy legal protection.

Although craft and professional occupations are similar in the extent and way in which many of them attempt to maintain occupational control, they do differ substantially on at least two related counts. One is in the relative social status which they each enjoy – craft occupations engage in manual work and are of working-class status, whereas professionals are, notionally at least, non-manual and are accorded very much higher social status. (In the UK the social position of the 'status' professions is related to the extent to which they were originally able to ally themselves with the landed classes and with their values and customs.) The other is that the institutional support for craft occupations has been on the wane for much longer than that for the professions. The high point of craft control was the Middle Ages. In the industrialized period craft groups have had to rely on custom, practice and trade union bargaining power to protect their occupational control. Moreover, for most of the industrialized period in the UK craftworkers in engineering have not sold their services on the open market. Not since teams of millwrights travelled the country building machinery for the cotton and wool mills has there been full occupational control in the sense defined above. For a long period (until well into the post-war period in some industries in Britain) certain craft engineering groups maintained a version of full occupational control by working in a subcontract relationship to employers within large engineering concerns, but even this appears to have largely disappeared. In contrast the 'status' professions in the UK have always operated as independent contractors and sold their services to clients. Although there has been some pressure in the National Health Service for doctors to become employees of the Service this has so far been resisted, and only in the last decade has there been significant erosion of legal support for the monopoly job rights of some professional groups. (Lawyers and opticians, for example, have each had their monopoly over certain of their activities removed by the post-1979 Conservative Government.)

Managerial control

In contrast with occupational control, in which only transactions between occupational members are internalized, the basis of managerial control is that all transactions related to the production of a particular good or service are internalized and it is the product of the managerially coordinated activity which is marketed. The boundary within which transactions are internalized is defined by the product or service rather than the occupation. More precisely, the boundary is usually defined in terms of a contractual relationship between employees and employer, the latter often being a legally constituted institution, i.e. the firm. Frequently, but not necessarily, managers are therefore acting on behalf of ownership's interests, i.e. capital.

The varieties of organizational forms of management control are well documented and do not need repetition here, although some of them are described below with specific reference to engineers.

The market

Except in the most comprehensively centrally planned economy all forms of internal organization eventually have their boundaries beyond which lies the market. Moreover, even within institutions in which occupational or managerial control dominates, some transactions are conducted via market mechanisms. The operation of internal labour markets is an obvious and relevant case. The point worth emphasizing here is that of the extreme case where the individual conducts all his/her occupationally related transactions in the market-place – the archetype is the sole practitioner in private practice. In its purest form that practitioner would have paid his/her own training costs in the expectation of earning a rent on the human capital.

Corporatism

Even economists recognize that markets sometimes fail, and sociologists would perceive market failure across a rather wider range of circumstances. A number of causes of market failure, and their relevance to the debate on markets and hierarchies, are enumerated and evaluated in Francis et al. (1983). The general point to make here is that, when occupational control fails, neither managerial control nor the operation of free markets can by themselves always satisfactorily solve a number of problems. For example, if firms organize the accreditation and training for an occupation they are open to the poaching of staff by free-riders. Also, a human capital approach to training, in which all the costs and risks of training are laid at the door of the individual, may result in a supply of trained members of an occupational group which is less than that demanded by employers. For reasons such as these there may emerge a set of organizational arrangements involving employers (managers), occupational members and state representatives to oversee the organization and funding of training, accreditation and the rights and obligations of occupational members at work.

The case of engineering in the UK

The demise of craft control

Craft control appears to have been on the ebb in British engineering companies for some decades. Within the design function we discovered numbers of firms who had switched from having the drawing office headed by a 'player–manager' (as one informant described it), typically known as the chief draughtsman, to one with a design office manager in charge who is not always recruited from the ranks of those on the drawing board. The take-up of CADr equipment reinforced this trend as in many cases firms appointed CADr managers, one of whose functions was to ensure high utilization of the equipment.

However, in a small minority of cases, where the firm and the drawing office were very large, there was a high level of union membership amongst designers, including graduates, and the union was exercising significant sanctions against a number of managerial initiatives, including the introduction of CADr and associated training. In one such case management's response was to use the introduction of CADr to decentralize and redistribute design activity away from the main drawing office locations as a means of bypassing union control.

Professional control

It does seem that from the very earliest days the mechanical engineers failed to achieve much significant control over their occupation (Watson, 1975). Although perhaps as many as half the civil engineers in the UK are in private practice within partnerships rather than as employees of publicly owned companies, virtually no mechanical engineers are so placed. Although from the earliest days there have been 'professional' institutions for each of the main branches of engineering and each institution has operated an accreditation system, it is only in the recent past that full institutional membership has required possession of a qualification equivalent to university degree level and, although full institutional membership now carries with it the status of chartered engineer, there is no associated requirement of a licence to practice.

Various forms of control via a management hierarchy

We observed a number of interesting variants of managerial control among the 32 firms in our study. A strong trend appeared to be the movement towards more formal lateral coordination within the firm.

Virtually all our firms had operated until the fairly recent past a conventional functional form of organization which included separate departments for design, development and production engineering. These departments in turn were quite separate from marketing/sales and production itself. A majority of the firms visited now took the view that rigid demarcations between departments and reliance on a combination of formal hierarchical coordination supplemented by *ad hoc* informal lateral communication was inadequate. A variety of solutions to this problem were being adopted. A radical attempt by one firm was that of obliterating functional distinctions entirely. The roles of design engineer and development engineer were being merged, and the distinction between development and design on the one hand and production engineering on the other was also being removed. The key notion was that of the multifunctional engineer. We have yet to gather detailed data on how such multifunctional engineers are being used and the extent to which particular types of expertise are still embodied in specific individuals as project teams for product development are set up. Certainly the company is investing heavily in in-service training to back up this changed policy with regard to the division of labour.

An equally radical move by another company was to set up project teams for product development which included industrial designers. The role of the industrial designer was that of conceptualizing new design possibilities, sketching options and acting as a channel of communication between members of the project team. This company had made no attempt to diminish particular technical specialisms and each project team would include a design engineer, a production engineer and someone with marketing expertise. It was claimed that the ethos of each team was egalitarian with no one given authority to make unilateral decisions to be imposed on the rest of the group, although the design engineer was said to have the most central role in terms of being likely to spend most time on any one product development.

Other firms had developed project team aproaches to a greater or lesser extent. No other company had egalitarian teams – everywhere else one person had managerial authority for the team – and in many companies there was less involvement in the team from marketing and/or production engineering. One company had considered setting up project teams but concluded that the time of so many specialists involved in project working was not justifiable and had taken the decision instead to relocate various offices physically so that the various functional departments were contiguous.

Within a handful of managerially organized firms we came across attempts to incorporate one element of professional organization, i.e. the ability of staff to continue to develop their technical expertise and be rewarded for it, without moving into a managerial position. In such companies the salary structure allowed individuals to be given higher status titles and salary increases up to the equivalent of quite senior managerial positions in order to retain valued technical staff who either lacked the preference or aptitude for management. Such strategies are also cited by, for example, Bills (1987) and Kanter (1984).

We did identify a major potential source of conflict between two sets of corporate objectives, however. One of these objectives was for flexibility with regard to the employment of individuals and the salaries they were to be paid and also with regard to the functions to be performed by the organization. A number of companies had undertaken radical organizational changes to enhance such flexibilities, one characteristic being that the role played by any one individual would in future be determined by his/her individual aptitude and level of performance and the work needing to be done. However, firms also have the objective of attracting and retaining appropriately qualified graduate engineers. In the past firms have enhanced their attractiveness to graduates by minimizing the individuals' career risks. There have been special ports of entry and career paths for graduates, and a demarcation in the work that is done by particular types and grades of staff. To the extent that it is in the interests of the members of an occupation to command professional status and full occupational control, people choosing a career are likely to be more attracted to occupations organized in their professional mode than to an organization in which their future is both uncertain and controlled by a managerial hierarchy. The firms' response has been that the existence of successful profitable innovative engineering firms will make engineering attractive to those school- and university-leavers making career choices. This remains to be tested.

The market

There does appear to be a re-emergence of the market in the conduct of design-related transactions and a new range of strategic decisions open to firms about where their designing should be done. For example, in a number of firms design work has been viewed as an overhead cost in the past but is now regarded as a chargeable cost. There are now elements of a market relationship between the design function and other parts of the firm. This extends outside the firm. Very many engineering products are assembled from an array of components manufactured by a large number of different suppliers. There is much variety of practice in the extent to which component design is done by the company responsible for the product as a whole or by the component producer. With high levels of complexity one organizational response has in the past been to give component suppliers a design brief and a space envelope and leave them to produce the design. Often the design, particularly for complex components, was done on a cost-plus basis. With the move to bidding for design work on a tendering basis and with potentially greater integration between firms because of computer-aided design (CAD) it is possible that component design may become more equally shared by contractor and supplier.

A second variant on this theme is the hiving-off in some large divisionalized companies of a projects division which can offer a design facility to the rest of the firm in competition with outside design contractors or a product division's own in-house design capability. An extension of this is the use by manufacturing firms of either subcontractors or specialist design consultancies. Conversely, in the electronics sector there are firms who do their own design marketing and subcontract manufacturing. Our overall impression is that, as firms are now facing a high degree of competition and as the nature of the design process is changing (with greater use of specialized technical expertise and computers), the opportunities for changing organizational forms are increasing and the pressures for switching to forms perceived as more effective are intensifying.

A third variant is that of a market relationship between a firm and the individuals providing a service to it. An example would be the use by large firms of individual consultants rather than having all work done by permanent employees. There has always been a certain amount of this in the engineering industry, in the case of both subcontract draughtspeople doing relatively routine work and technical experts, for example from the universities, providing highly specialized advice. There seems little evidence about trends either towards or away from this variant of the market relationship. However, with regard to the use of consultant experts, to the extent that in the past it has been firms engaged with more advanced technologies which have made more extensive use of technical consultants, one might hypothesize a growth in this organiz-ational form as more firms become more technologically sophisticated.

Corporatism

Although we have not yet systematically explored this particular area, it is clear that it is one in which there have been a number of developments. The setting up by the government of the Finniston Committee in the late 1970s and the formation of the Engineering Council can be interpreted as corporatism rather than professionalism because of the high level of involvement of those representing the engineering companies both in the deliberations of the Committee and the Council and in the surrounding political debate, although the power and influence of the Engineering Council, while not negligible, must not be overrated. What is unclear is the extent to which companies and the occupational associations are actively supporting these corporatist activities because they believe it is the best way forward or because it is a feasible political compromise.

Conclusions

A description of some of the processes which seem to be taking place within the practice of engineering design in the UK is set out above. These may be indicative of a more general set of processes within large-scale enterprises which employ workers with high levels of technical and portable expertise. Our argument is that the various interested parties are attempting particular strategies to establish and maintain particular organizational forms for coordination and control. Usually the dominant interested parties are the experts on the one hand and management on the other, and the major organizational forms are occupational control, managerial control, market mechanisms and corporatism, although the engineering design case is complicated by the historical role of craftworkers and therefore the presence of two types of occupational control. Each mode of organization has its costs and benefits for each of the parties and for the consumer. To the extent that these initial results from our study show a variety of ways in which the interested parties are negotiating accommodations for their different preferences they offer some support to the contentions of both Child et al. (1983) and McCormick (1985). The existence of a strong sense of occupational identity still exerts an influence on both occupational members and management, but there is also evidence of a considerable change in forms of work organization.

It is unlikely that it would be possible to specify an optimum organizational form or that market mechanisms will ensure that it is the best organizational form (in any sense) which ultimately emerges. The processes involved are politically and contextually bound. Nevertheless there is much that would repay further research, both in the engineering industry and with regard to the more general question of the employment of technical specialists within large-scale organizations. Within engineering design we found that most of our respondents were anxious to learn new ways of getting work done, and many experiments were being undertaken. There is not yet a new conventional wisdom about how things should be done, and certainly not a set of prescriptions, the efficacy of which could be tested by empirical research.

In our judgement there could be very valuable pay-off in terms of interesting new findings, and a possible agenda for research in this area for practitioners ready to pay attention to these findings is suggested below. This is set out in terms of research relevant to the general issue of technical specialists in large-scale organizations (what we will term the 'general' question) and that relevant to the specific question of graduate-level engineers in the innovation and design process (the 'specific' question).

There is need for further comparative research. There is still much to be learned from careful and detailed international comparative work. The debate between Child et al. (1983) and McCormick (1985) touches on many of the issues about which we need more data. Work of this kind would be of relevance to what we have termed above the general question. There is also much more to be learned from comparative studies across occupations. Much work in the past has focused on the relative status of various occupations, and in particular the allegedly low status of engineering in the UK, and has been conducted using survey methods. There is now need for work focusing on differences in the work organization of various occupations. This would more appropriately be done via case studies. These should also relate their findings to historical and institutional factors relevant to each occupation. Such research would be of particular relevance to what we have termed the specific question.

Some of the institutional factors to be taken into account should be the mechanisms used for conducting transactions, and within our own research programme into these issues we are intending to continue to explore and develop the model set out here, i.e. the categories of market, occupational, managerial and corporatist control.

The process by which scientific and technical knowledge is transferred from the laboratory to the design and production areas is also of much interest and great relevance. The dynamic of the relationship between these functions and the pattern of information flows between them are still not fully understood, although there are promising developments within the sociology of science in the conceptualization of this process (Whitley, 1987).

The marked change from non-graduate to graduate intake within engineering generally and the design function in particular needs further investigation, for example into the ways in which graduate career paths can be developed. Research into this topic would have considerable relevance more generally, not least to the question of graduate recruitment into general management, of which there is likely to be a very substantial increase over the next decade in the wake of the Handy and Constable Reports (1987). One problem for managers planning career routes for graduates in occupations where there is still a high proportion of non-graduates would appear to be that of avoiding the Scylla of demotivating and blocking the careers of the non-graduates without colliding with the Charybdis of holding back and therefore alienating graduates with high-flying expectations. Another will be that of instituting new career paths and patterns of work organization and thus breaking past traditions to which many in the organization may wish to cling.

Finally, if there is a general move increasingly to subject particular functions to market forces, as seems to be happening to the design function in, for example, the shift from cost-plus to fixed-price contracts, what are the costs and benefits? There is some patchy evidence that the UK was quite late in internalizing work within companies by reducing subcontract relationships – Mowery (1986) suggests that this happened during the 1930s, 1940s and 1950s – but there is a division of opinion as to whether there is a switch back to more subcontract relationships and very little empirical evidence cited to back up either view. To what extent is there a relationship between these shifts and the increases in the number of graduate employees? To what extent is subcontracting reconcilable with professionalization?

Such issues are highly relevant to policy questions of current note such as how the UK's economic performance can be improved through more effective design and innovation (Aldington Report, 1985). They are also consonant with some of the major themes under debate within management studies (Child, 1987). They constitute a research agenda for the 1990s which promises excitement and utility.

References

Aldington Report (1985). *Report from the Select Committee on Overseas Trade.* London: HMSO.
Armstrong, P. (1972). 'Professionalism and the industrial engineer'. MSc thesis, University of Bath (unpublished).
Armstrong, P. (1987). 'Engineers, management and trust'. *Work, Employment and Society*, 1, 421–40.
Bills, D.B. (1987). 'Costs, commitment, and rewards: factors influencing the design and implementation of internal labor markets'. *Administrative Science Quarterly*, 32, 202–11.
Child, J. (1982). 'Professionals in the corporate world: values, interests and control'. In *International Yearbook of Organisational Studies 1981* (eds D. Dunkerley and S. Salaman). London: Routledge and Kegan Paul.
Child, J. (1987). 'Information technology, organization and the responses to

strategic challenges'. 8th EGOS Colloquium, Antwerp.

Child, J., Fores, M., Glover, I. and Lawrence, P. (1983). 'A price to pay? Professionalism and work organization in Britain and West Germany'. *Sociology*, **17**, 63–78.

Cooley, M. (1972). *Architect or Bee*. Slough: Langley Technical Services.

Corfield, K.G. (1979). *Product Design*. London: National Economic Development Office.

Council for National Academic Awards (1984). *Managing Design – An Initiative In Management Education*. London: CNAA.

Davies, C. (1983). 'Professionals in bureaucracies: the conflict thesis revisited. In *The Sociology of the Professions* (eds R. Dingwall and P. Lewis). London: Macmillan.

Engineering Industry Training Board (1986). *Occupational Profile: Trends in Employment and Training of Professional Engineers, Scientists and Technologists in the Engineering Industry*. Stockport, Cheshire: EITB.

Feilden Report (1963). *Engineering Design: Report of a Committee Appointed by the Council for Scientific and Industrial Research to Consider the Present Standing of Mechanical Engineering Design*. London: HMSO.

Finniston Report (1980). *Engineering our Future: Report of the Committee of Enquiry into the Engineering Profession*. London: HMSO.

Francis, A. (1986). *New Technology at Work*. Oxford: Clarendon Press.

Francis, A., Turk, J. and Willman, P. (eds) (1983). *Power, Efficiency and Institutions*. London: Heinemann.

Gerstl, J.E. and Hutton, S.P. (1966). *Engineers: the Anatomy of a Profession: A Study of Mechanical Engineers in Britain*. London: Tavistock.

Glover, I., Kelly, M. and Roslender, R. (1986). 'The coming proletarianisation of the British accountant?' Presented at the Labour Process Conference, University of Manchester Institute of Science and Technology.

Hall, R.H. (1968). 'Professionalisation and bureaucratisation', *American Sociological Review*, **33**, 92–104.

Handy, C. (1987). *The Making of Managers*. London: National Economic Development Office.

Hannan, M.T. and Freeman, J.H. (1977). 'The population ecology of organizations'. *American Journal of Sociology*, **82**, 929–64.

Hutton, S.P. and Lawrence, P. (1981). *German Engineers: The Anatomy of a Profession*. Oxford: Clarendon Press.

Kanter, R.M. (1984). 'Variations in managerial career structures in high technology firms: the impact of organizational characteristics on internal labor market patterns' (ed. P. Osterman). Cambridge, MA: MIT Press.

Lickley, R. (1984). *Report of the Engineering Design Working Party: A Report to the Engineering Board of the Science and Engineering Research Council*. Report to the SERC (unpublished).

McCormick, K. (1985). 'Professionalism and work organization: some loose ends and open questions', *Sociology*, **19**, 285–94.

Mowery, D.C. (1986). 'Industrial research 1900–1950'. In *The Decline of the British Economy* (eds B. Elbaum and W. Lasonick). Oxford: Clarendon Press.

Pilditch, J. (1986). *Design*. National Economic Development Council paper (unpublished).

Ritti, R.R. (1971). *The Engineer in the Industrial Corporation*. New York: Columbia University Press.

Stinchcombe, A. (1965). 'Social structure and organizations'. In Handbook of *Organizations* (ed. James G. March), pp. 142–93. Chicago, IL: Rand McNally.

Watson, H.B. (1975). 'Organisational bases of professional status: a comparative study of the engineering professions'. PhD Thesis, London University (unpublished).

Whalley, P. (1986). *The Social Production of Technical Work*. London: Macmillan.

Whitley, R. (1987). 'The role of new knowledge in changing technical skills and practices'. Manchester Business School: working paper no. 144.

Williamson, O.E (1975). *Markets and Hierarchies*. New York: Free Press.

Wingert, B., Duus, W., Rader, M. and Riehm, U. (1984). *CAD im Maschinebau – Wirkungen, Changen, Risiken*. Heidelberg, Berlin: Springer-Verlag.

Winstanley, D. and Francis, A. (1987). 'Re-drawing the line – changing design practices in engineering design'. Presented to the BSA Annual Conference, Leeds. (Photocopy available from the Management School, Imperial College, London.)

11
'Qualitative' research and the epistemological problems of the management disciplines

Simon Archer

The arguments for qualitative research

Introduction

It is becoming common to call for 'qualitative' research in disciplines concerned with management. For example, in relation to accounting, eloquent pleas have been made by Tomkins and Groves (1983) and Kaplan (1984a,b), while Bonoma and Wong (1983) do the same in relation to marketing. In this respect such writers are following organizational sociologists, who have in recent years been showing considerable interest in 'qualitative methods'. For example, there are the papers by Van Maanen (1979) and the other contributions to a special 1979 issue of *Administrative Science Quarterly* (*ASQ*).

Various reasons can be advanced for the adoption of qualitative methods in management research, and various roles can be envisioned for such methods. In fact, three quite distinct (and, indeed, incompatible) positions can be found in the literature, regarding the role of qualitative research and the rationale for undertaking it. These can be summarized as follows.

1 *Complementarity on an equal footing* Qualitative methods can address aspects of research issues that are not accessible using quantitative methods. In particular, by using qualitative methods one can pay detailed attention to microlevel aspects that are barely accessible to quantitative approaches.
2 *Precursor and poor relation* Quantitative methods constitute the 'rigorous, hard' approach to research, but in some circumstances the state of theoretical development is such that they cannot be employed, and the 'less desirable, soft' qualitative approach can be used.

3 *The only true approach* In contrast with the 'pseudo-science' of quantitative methods, qualitative approaches permit access to the 'real' stuff of human interaction.

These different positions do not point to any generally accepted characterization of 'qualitative' as opposed to 'quantitative' research. The first position implies that the essential difference lies in the kind of phenomenon which the researcher is investigating. Relatively large numbers of observations of a relatively small number of variables lend themselves to a variety of quantitative (i.e. statistical or econometric) techniques of analysis, and research studies can be designed accordingly. Examples of such phenomena are security price movements and responses to opinion polls. In such cases the phenomenon can be likened to a commodity. With relatively small numbers of observations of large numbers of variables, the scope for using quantitative analysis techniques can be limited, and a research design based on the anticipation of using such methods is likely to be inappropriate. Examples are studies of complex decision-making processes involving a number of people. In this case the phenomenon can be considered as analogous to a complex custom-made product. From this standpoint, many phenomena lie between these two extremes and invite both kinds of research approach.

The second position implies that the essential difference lies in the quality of the knowledge produced. The assumed aim of research is to establish corroborated empirical generalizations, and in the end this calls for sufficient numbers of observations of variables to permit the use of quantitative methods. Phenomena that do not lend themselves to being treated as instances of empirical generalizations are not considered as being 'researchable' in a rigorous sense. According to this view, 'qualitative' research methods are essentially exploratory; the difference between them and quantitative methods concerns the state of knowledge of the phenomena that are under investigation.

The third position is, in a sense, the converse of the second, since it involves the view that the type of empirical generalization characteristic of the natural sciences is infeasible or inappropriate in the social–behavioural field. But, as we shall see below, there are at least three quite different positions which involve such a view, and each of these implies a different view of the distinction between 'quantitative' and 'qualitative' research methods.

Position 1 as outlined above might seem reasonable enough, and positions 2 and 3 somewhat dogmatic. Nevertheless, each of the latter is associated with one or more schools of thought in the philosophy of social science and has been adopted by influential writers. The philosophical presuppositions of these views will be examined at greater length in the next part of this paper, and will be mentioned only briefly here.

The 'precursor and poor relation' position can be seen in advice given to researchers by Abdel-Khalik and Ajinkya (1979). It exemplifies a view of science in which knowledge which can be expressed in terms of *measurements* is superior or preferable to knowledge which cannot (see the third section below).

The 'only true approach' viewpoint, however, can be associated with several rather different positions. For example, we have the view that 'the only valid and meaningful (or hard, scientific) evidence concerning socially meaningful phenomena we can possibly have is that based ultimately on systematic observations of everyday life' (Douglas (1971), quoted by Knorr-Cetina (1982, p. 7)).

Then there is the position of Winch (1958), that the quantitative methods applied in research in the natural sciences are associated with a view of reality that is ill-suited to the subject matter of the social sciences. According to this view, the role of social science is to offer insight and critique rather than to look for empirical regularities leading to causal explanations of phenomena.

These views can be compared with that suggested by Ravetz (1971, p. 374), namely that social and behavioural studies are in an immature or pre-scientific state, in which empirical research cannot go beyond 'a sort of [natural] history, conducted in a disciplined fashion and using all appropriate tools, whose objects of inquiry are those of a trained common sense'. By the same token, according to this view, theoretical development in the social and behavioural area cannot go beyond a sort of 'natural philosophy' analogous to the mixture of philosophy and theorizing about phenomena that took place before the development of the modern natural sciences.

For the proponents of this third view, therefore, the 'poor relation' (and possible precursor) is not qualitative research but, broadly speaking, present-day social and behavioural science as a whole. This would seem to be a very different position from that of Douglas, since from this perspective, to speak of 'hard scientific evidence' indicates a serious misconception regarding the epistemological possibilities of current research in the social and behavioural areas. However, unlike the position of Winch, the view suggested by Ravetz does not involve the 'anti-naturalist' claim that social and behavioural phenomena are inherently different from the objects of the natural sciences.

The comparison of natural and social–behavioural phenomena as objects of systematic study raises issues concerning the role of subjective beliefs, desires, meanings and intentions (in a word, of *intentionality*) in providing adequate explanations and predictions of the latter (Bateson,

1973; Searle, 1983). Suffice it to say here that acceptance of the unique explanatory and predictive role of intentionality in the social–behavioural domain (an *ontological* position) does not necessarily entail acceptance of the anti-naturalist view that knowledge of such phenomena is qualitatively different from that of natural phenomena (an *epistemological* position).

Where all these views grouped under position 3 above concur is in regarding quantitatively based studies using large databases (such as those obtained by the use of questionnaires) and intended to test hypotheses expressing empirical generalizations as 'pseudo-science'. To a large extent, this scepticism concerns the validity of the conceptual objects posited in the hypotheses being tested. As Ravetz (1971) puts it, 'Where the [conceptual] objects of inquiry have but a tenuous relation to the real things and events they purport to describe, and are, themselves ill-formed and unstable, an isolated investigation devoted to a supposedly 'empirical' test of some hypothesis about their relations is unlikely to yield worthwhile results'. (A similar judgement, with reference to management accounting research, is expressed by Kaplan (1984a) and will be discussed later.) A less radical, and arguably more constructive, criticism of certain quantitatively based studies is that they display a concern for multiplicative corroboration of research hypotheses at the expense of structural corroboration and cognitive refinement (Pepper, 1942). That is, the researcher in question is interested in multiplying the number of observations that are consistent with the hypothesis, rather than in developing a richer hypothesis that has a greater explanatory power, but also a greater chance of being refuted, and whose corroboration would therefore be more significant. The preoccupation with multiplicative corroboration is characteristic of a positivistic approach to research; the objections to positivism will be discussed later.

Distinctions and conflicts between the arguments

Given the disparities in the positions from which these critiques of quantitative research are being made, when we move from them toward consideration of how qualitative research is to be carried out it is (hardly surprisingly) not clear in what direction we are supposed to proceed. Although the proponents of the various positions agree on the need for qualitative research, they do so from quite different philosophical standpoints, which in turn point towards different conceptions of the appropriate methodology.

These philosophical standpoints will be examined in more detail later. However, one major set of differences may already be noted. Ravetz focuses on the state of epistemological development of the social and behavioural sciences relative to the natural sciences. Winch argues from a certain conception of the 'human sciences' as being essentially different epistemologically from the natural sciences, so that the kind of epistemological comparisons made by Ravetz are, for him, improper. Douglas argues that the appropriate kinds of systematic observations and analyses of small-scale microlevel social situations ('everyday life') can be 'hard and scientific', and that the epistemological problems of validity are raised by the abstractions of more general macrolevel theories.

The difference between the position suggested by Ravetz and that of Abdel-Khalik and Ajinkya relates to the value of *quantitative*, not qualitative, research. As will be shown in more detail below, this reflects very different views of the nature of knowledge, reality and science. These differences raise the question of whether the 'reasonable' position, that the two approaches to research are complementary, is tenable or philosophically coherent. This question is linked, in turn, to the issue of integrating microlevel and macrolevel approaches in social inquiry (Knorr-Cetina, 1981, pp. 25–42). It will be argued below that such complementarity and integration are coherently conceivable only in terms of a particular type of philosophical position, which we term 'post-positivist internal realism'.

If we return to the special 1979 issue of the *ASQ* mentioned earlier, we can see some of the differences noted above. Thus there is an evident difference between two kinds of researcher who are represented in the collection: the highly inductive such as Mintzberg (1979), for whom 'the field of organization theory has . . . paid dearly for the obsession with rigor in the choice of methodology' (Mintzberg, 1979, p. 583), and the considerably less inductive such as Miles (1979), for whom qualitative data have some attributes of 'an attractive nuisance' which can lead to 'injury', and who emphasize the need for 'well-formulated methods of analysis', 'guidelines for protection against self-delusion' and 'explicit preliminary frameworks' (Miles, 1979, pp. 590–1).

Miles, together with McClintock et al. (1979), seems to fit into the 'complementarity' position outlined above, while Mintzberg appears to be fairly close to Douglas's belief as the 'everyday life' approach, albeit without sharing his concern for being 'hard and scientific'. At the same time, the differing views of these writers about research raise more fundamental questions as to their beliefs about knowledge and reality. Miles, for example, acknowledges that inquiry is impelled by certain working hypotheses and background assumptions which are better made explicit, and that knowledge claims face the problem of validation, of 'analysis and how it can be carried out in ways that deserve the name of science'.

Mintzberg, however, appears to hold that his strategy of 'direct research' involves something close to pure description (unladen with theoretical presuppositions) from which conclusions are then drawn by means of inductive inferences in the form of 'creative leaps'. There is apparently little or no concern for the issues of validation.

Conclusions

The management researcher considering the possibility of employing 'qualitative' research methods might justifiably be dismayed by this lack of agreement on the part of its proponents as to which methods are appropriate. Disagreements between those who see themselves as 'quantitative' researchers seem to be of a technical and far less fundamental nature. What criteria exist, apart from the reputations of the various protagonists, to guide the choice of the would-be qualitative researcher? Is quantitative research as epistemologically unproblematic as its practitioners appear to assume? Given that no coherent view exists of what 'qualitative' research is supposed to be, how illuminating is the quantitative–qualitative distinction, and cannot better-founded and more useful distinctions be made? Other, but related, issues are raised by the frequent use in the management literature of terms such as 'positive' and 'normative' in ways which beg important philosophical questions.

It will be shown below that the so-called quantitative–qualitative distinction is more accurately characterized as a generally unarticulated, and somewhat old-fashioned, set of philosophical differences. Our views about how a piece of research may best be conducted presuppose philosophical positions (explicit or not) about the nature of 'knowledge' and 'reality', for presumably research is intended to study some aspect of 'reality' in order to contribute to 'knowledge'. Yet these are not unproblematical concepts, particularly in nascent or immature fields. Although, for example, modern accounting has been developing for several hundred years it is not a field in which research (as normally understood) has until recently been an established ongoing activity. Thus, accounting research must be considered as a nascent or immature field. Similar considerations apply to other management disciplines. Contemporary philosophy offers a perspective which allows us to identify the tendentious aspects of the 'quantitative' and the various 'qualitative' methodological positions, and to see how different research methods can be accommodated within a shared set of methodological considerations based on a robust yet subtle philosophical standpoint. Note that this is a different objective from that of Chua (1986), since she suggests an epistemological and methodological pluralism reflecting a variety of philosophical standpoints.

The remainder of this paper is structured as follows. The second section is concerned with indicating how contemporary philosophy, in the form of post-positivist internal realism, offers the perspective described above. The third section focuses on management disciplines, with particular reference to the epistemological problems that need to be addressed, not just in general discussions about methodology but in the actual design of research projects and choice of methods. The fourth section states the overall conclusions.

The philosophical background to management research

Introduction

Our first task here is to make explicit the assumptions about 'knowledge' and 'reality' that are presupposed by particular attitudes to management research. Thus the philosophical background to be considered here relates theories of knowledge (epistemology) to theories about existence or reality (ontology). The main purpose of this discussion is to indicate the pitfalls associated with some of the positions being espoused in the literature on methodology in management research, and to sketch out a philosophical position which avoids these pitfalls.

One major set of issues that needs to be addressed concerns theories about the relationships between facts and values in human knowledge. The 'positive–normative' and 'descriptive–prescriptive' distinctions are frequently mentioned in the literature on management theory and research methodology. The use of these terms in that literature presents the two distinctions as practically equivalent expressions of the basic fact–value distinction, with the qualification that 'descriptive' should be replaced by 'descriptive–explanatory–predictive' (Christenson, 1983). In addition, a certain amount of confusion is caused by the fact that the term 'normative' can be used in two senses, of which the first is narrow and the second is broader: (a) formally laying down a norm, rule or law which is the articulation of some value or set of values; (b) value-laden (the contrary of value-free), whether or not the value is articulated as a norm. The broader sense is used in this paper. In the literature of management disciplines, it is not uncommon to find a version of the narrow sense in which 'normative' is used to mean 'prescriptive'. This usage reflects one of the basic errors of positivism, since it suggests that only prescriptions are value-laden, while descriptions, explanations or predictions are 'positive' or value-free. The truth, to quote Putnam (1981, p. 201), is that 'every fact is value-loaded and every one of our values loads some fact'.

There is, however, a distinction which is relevant for management and other applied disciplines, namely that between descriptive–explanatory–

predictive theory (science) and theory used prescriptively (technology). In the first place it should be recognized that implicit in any technology is some (normative) value-commitment to the instrumental goals stated in the prescriptions, even though the prescriptions themselves may be formally value-free in the sense that they do not logically imply or presuppose any commitment to either the goals or the means that are stated. Thus an engineer who produces a design (prescription) for a 150 miles per hour gas-guzzling automobile is implicitly subscribing to a goal just as much as an accountant who produces a design (prescription) for a financial control system.

In the second place, however, it may be relevant that in our present state of knowledge the automobile is more likely to perform to specification than the accounting artefact is. For example, it can be argued that engineering is based on 'known facts' to a much greater extent than accounting, and that the natural sciences (physics, chemistry and biology) which are available as a basis for engineering prescriptions have a much higher 'fact-to-value ratio' than the social and behavioural sciences (economics, psychology and sociology) which are available as a basis for prescriptions in disciplines such as accounting, marketing and other social technologies.

Nevertheless, it should also be noted that engineering prescriptions usually incorporate unambiguous goals which are taken for granted (such as fast and prestigious driving), whereas accounting prescriptions are typically not linked to any such unambiguous goals. Not just cause-and-effect relationships ('known facts') but also goals themselves are typically more uncertain in social technologies. Because of this, the social technologies and sciences themselves problematize normative issues in a way that engineering and the natural sciences do not (this is part of their 'reflexivity'. However, that does not mean that the former are more normative than the latter as Whitley (1984a) points out. If anything, the opposite might be true, since the former reflect more on their values than the latter do.

Theories of knowledge and theories of reality

In this section we briefly (and therefore, of necessity, rather crudely) characterize the various philosophical positions in epistemology and ontology. These are then examined in more detail below.

Positivism is an epistemological position characterized by the view that fact and value are logically and epistemologically distinct, and hence that value-free knowledge is possible. This view is based on the formal logical impossibility of deriving normative conclusions (conclusions expressing a value judgement) from only positive premises (premises expressing no

Table 11.1 Combinations of epistemological and ontological positions

	Ontology: theories of reality		
	External realism[d]	Internal realism[e]	Subjective idealism[f]
Positivism[a]	AD	AE	AF
Non-positivism[b]	BD	BE	BF
Normativism[c]	CD	CE	CF

[a] Facts and values are distinct, and scientific knowledge consists only of facts.
[b] Facts and values are intertwined and hard to disentangle; both are involved in scientific knowledge.
[c] Scientific knowledge is ideological and inevitably conducive to particular sets of social ends.
[d] Reality exists independently of our construction of it.
[e] Reality-for-us is an intersubjective construction of the shared human cognitive apparatus.
[f] Each person constructs his or her own reality.

value judgement). *Non-positivism* rejects the epistemological distinction, while a more radical view, termed *normativism* below, rejects the fact–value distinction completely.

While positivism, non-positivism and normativism are *epistemological* viewpoints about the nature of 'knowledge', realism and idealism are *ontological* viewpoints about the nature of 'reality'. Traditional (or 'external') *realism* is the view that reality exists objectively and independently of the perceiving subject. This view can also be termed objectivism.[1] It is associated with the view that a proposition is true if and only if it corresponds to this objective reality – the Correspondence Theory of Truth (Putnam, 1981, chapter 3). *Idealism* is the contrary view that reality is a product of the cognition of the individual knowing subject. *Internal realism* (described more fully in the next section) considers reality as we can know it to be a product, not of the cognition of the individual subject, but of the shared human cognitive apparatus; it is thus independent of the individual knowing subject.

Simple visual aids often help in examining complex issues. Of course, such visual aids are inevitably reductionist; many potentially important nuances have to be omitted. However, certain points may be conveyed more easily and economically. Table 11.1 presents a tabulation of ontological versus epistemological positions. A particular attitude regarding research methodology reflects a combination of ontological and epistemological positions, and the disagreements between proponents of 'quantitative' and 'qualitative' methods can be related to the different combinations which are representative of their explicit or implicit philosophical positions.

Thus, those such as Abdel-Khalik and Ajinkya (1979) for whom rigour in research requires the testing of hypotheses against multiple observations using statistical tools can generally be identified with a combination of positivism and external realism. The reality to be researched is considered as existing independently of the research community that studies it (external realism), and the observations made by researchers ('facts') are considered as being independent of the beliefs and values to which the researchers adhere (positivism); rigour depends on maintaining such independence. There is considerable emphasis on the generalizability of research findings, which tends to be seen in terms of statistical generalization rather than analytical generalization (the extension of theory).

In contrast, those who advocate the superiority of 'qualitative' approaches tend to see rigour as requiring the close and intimate observation that can only be given to a small number of examples at any one time. Such observation does not readily permit the independence between researcher and researched, or between fact and value, to which positivistic external realists attach great importance. Some advocates of 'qualitative' methods consider the concern for such independence as fundamentally misguided; in fact, they reject the idea of generalizability, not just statistical but also analytical, in matters of human behaviour, except in the very weak sense that insights into human behaviour may be generalizable by analogy. According to this view, one should not distinguish the way in which research reports can be 'true' from that in which great works of fiction can be said to show the truth. The combination of ontological and epistemological positions occupied by this latter standpoint is subjective idealism and normativism: the former because of the unimportance accorded to intersubjectivity (except in the weakest sense) in the construction of reality, and the latter because of the lack of interest in the distinction between fact and value.

One would have thought that there was ample room between these two extreme positions for research approaches which accepted the validity of both multiple-observation statistically based studies and those involving more intimate study of a small number of examples. However, the philosophical positions which are involved often seem to be tenaciously held, and may indeed be bound up with a set of personal values and beliefs about the relationships between knowledge and society (Mitroff and Kilmann, 1978). Yet from a strictly philosophical standpoint, there are some fairly strong objections to positivistic external realism and to normativistic subjective idealism. These are examined in the following sections, where the arguments will be stated for an intersubjective view of reality and a non-positivist view of knowledge.

The case for 'internal' realism

Research methodology raises issues concerning the nature of the 'reality' to be researched. According to external realism, this reality is independent of perceiving subjects. As far as social reality is concerned, this position has been criticized for ignoring the reflexivity inherent in the fact that social reality is constructed by social actors (Knorr-Cetina, 1981). The philosophical position of internal realism involves the recognition that, in an important sense, physical reality is also constructed by social actors. For example, Ravetz (1971) explains in considerable detail how the objects of natural science are conceptual rather than simply natural objects.

The term 'internal realism' was coined by Putnam (1981) in delineating an ontological position first developed by Kant (1787) in response to the subjective idealism of Hume (1748), whose work had 'aroused him from his dogmatic slumbers'. For Kant, the work of Hume had demonstrated the untenability of traditional external realism. The traditional ontological debate concerned attributes of objects, which were divided into 'primary' and 'secondary' qualities. The former comprised the spatio-temporal attributes of objects, while the latter included attributes such as colour, smell, taste and temperature. The ontological status of the secondary qualities was the subject of a debate between the realists and their opponents, the nominalists. While the realists held that objects exist quite independently of perceiving subjects, nominalists argued that 'secondary' qualities do not belong to objects as such but are assigned to them by perceiving subjects. The more radical British philosophers, including Berkeley (1710) and Hume, extended this logic to the primary qualities and hence to objects-in-themselves. Hume thus reached a position of subjective idealism: logically speaking, we have no warrant for asserting the existence of objects independently of the perceiving subject, who is himself or herself no more than a 'bundle of perceptions'.

The objection to subjective idealism is that it leads to solipsism (Putnam's (1981) 'brains in a vat'), namely that an individual cannot vouch for the reality of anything beyond his or her immediate thoughts and sensations. Berkeley proposed an ingenious solution: the ontological status of reality is assured by the all-perceiving deity. This answer, however, did not recommend itself to the less theologically inclined.

Kant developed a different line of reasoning. He focused on the preconditions for human knowledge and argued that the extension of nominalism to include primary qualities should be interpreted differently from Hume's arguments. If objects-in-themselves are considered apart from all their qualities, secondary and primary, then it is the case that we cannot know objects-in-themselves but only what the human cognitive apparatus makes of those objects. However, this does not imply (as Hume argued) that objects-in-themselves do not exist. Rather, the situation is that human knowledge cannot deal with objects-in-themselves, but only with those objects as apprehended by the human cognitive apparatus. Thus, not merely the 'secondary' qualities, but also the spatio-temporal individuation ('primary qualities') which we ascribe to objects, are a function of our shared cognitive apparatus and cannot be considered as inherent in objects-in-themselves. The latter can be regarded only as constituting an indeterminable substrate for our experiences of reality.

This ontological position has epistemological implications which concern the tenability of positivism, for if human knowledge cannot apprehend objects-in-themselves then the Correspondence Theory of Truth (see above) is non-operational. Facts cannot be defined by reference to an external reality that is 'objective' in the sense that it can be known to exist in a given form independently of perceiving subjects. However, human beings share certain characteristic ways of construing reality, in terms of which human cognition can discover intersubjectively validated facts.

The argument for rejecting traditional realism has recently taken a 'semantic turn' in the work of philosophers such as Dummett (1978) and Tennant (1987). As Tennant (pp. 11–12) puts it:

For Dummett, that old [external] sense of realism was not philosophically fruitful . . . [T]he substantive issue now lies with the nature of truth-determination . . . [O]ntological hagglers are invited to address themselves to a new sort of question. Insofar as the old realist questions of existence had any residual value, they would be cashed in terms of that in virtue of which statements are true, when they are true.

Thus, it is not fruitful to consider ontological issues independently of issues of meaning (semantics) and knowledge-criteria (epistemology).

As both Ravetz (1971) and Popper (1972, 1975) have pointed out, scientific knowledge, like other forms of knowledge, is socially produced. A distinguishing feature of scientific knowledge is the nature of the social processes involved. Far from scientific knowledge being 'value-free', as writers such as Stigler (1976), Watts and Zimmerman (1979) or Lipsey (1980) seem to believe, the ethos of a community of scientists is crucial for the type of knowledge that they produce. For example, the point about Popperian 'rationality of science' is that it derives from the collective purpose and values of the scientific community as such.

It is these considerations which lead writers such as Feyerabend (1975b) to the normativist position that science is indeed a kind of ideology. This is not a position with which internal realists agree. To be sure, many of Feyerabend's strictures on a certain scientific mentality may seem to be well justified, but the charge that some, or even many, scientists display a dogmatic belief in their ability to lay down rules for society concerns their attitude towards the application of scientific knowledge and not their criteria for its production. Again, it can be pointed out that analytical methods exist for examining any body of ideas and laying bare the normative or ideological content, a process which has been termed 'deconstruction'. The criteria as to what constitutes fact as opposed, for example, to wishful thinking or political propaganda are, potentially, a matter of intersubjective agreement. However, the term ideology becomes vacuous if, as normativists appear to claim, fact and value are not just intertwined but indistinguishable.

Note that this is not an argument against research as the basis for social critique. But critique becomes mere propaganda if the desire to change society, or to prevent change, is allowed precedence over the issue of what constitutes a valid (or rationally acceptable) knowledge-claim. Of course, in certain situations the production and dissemination of propaganda might be a more effective means of promoting (or obstructing) immediate social change than the dissemination of research findings produced with a scrupulous concern for the validation of knowledge-claims; but that is quite a different issue.

The epistemological and ontological position of internal realism can therefore be distinguished from those of positivists, normativists, internal realists and subjective idealists as follows. While accepting (as against positivists) that epistemological criteria are culturally situated, external realism does not consider this to be an argument for normativism and still less for methodological anarchism. On the contrary, the study of the social conditions of knowledge production, while unsupportive of more formalistic approaches to methodology, points to the importance of shared epistemological norms within research communities (Ravetz, 1971). On the issue of realism, the internal realists occupy a position deriving from that first developed by Kant's indefatigable logic: our shared perceptual and cognitive experiences presuppose the existence both of our shared perceptual and cognitive capabilities and of something of which we can have perceptions, but this does not imply that our perceptions and cognitions could characterize reality in any absolute sense.

In contrast with the Correspondence Theory of Truth characteristic of external realism, internal realists adopt what has sometimes been termed a Coherence Theory. As Putnam (1981, pp. 49–50) puts it:

'Truth', in an internalist view, is some sort of (idealized) rational acceptability –

some sort of ideal coherence of our beliefs with each other and with our experiences as those experiences are themselves represented within our belief system – and not correspondence with mind-independent or discourse-independent states of affairs.

For the researcher in management and related social and behavioural fields, internal realism offers a number of benefits when compared with other philosophical positions. Most significantly, internal realism provides a bridge between the practitioners of two different types of research design, both of which are popular within the management disciplines and have the potential to complement each other in important ways, but whose proponents are kept apart by the methodological schism mentioned above.

The bridge consists of a post-positivist epistemology which allows this methodological schism between positivistic external realists and their normativistic opponents to be seen for what it is – a failure to absorb the more recent developments in logic and epistemology. (For example, the work of Popper is sometimes cited by positivists in support of their views, yet Popper's later work (Popper, 1972, 1975) shows a keen and very non-positivist awareness of the socially situated character of knowledge production. However, we find writers such as Donaldson (1985, p. 49) referring to Popper as 'one of the leading exponents of positivism'.) This recognition allows both groups to accept that each of the two styles of research raises questions that only the other can address – the kind of conversation mentioned by Morgan (1983, pp. 374–81), but without requiring the transcendental ability to encompass several epistemologies which he envisages.

Second, the notion of truth as the ideal maximum degree of rational acceptability focuses on the crucial role of research methods in conferring warranted assertability on research findings. At the same time, recognition that all our observations are inevitably theory- and value-laden provides important guidance for the design of research studies so that such theories and values are made as explicit as possible.

Thirdly, internal realism offers a way out of the so-called 'naturalism' controversy as to whether epistemological criteria need to be different in social science as compared with natural science, which continues to affect the consideration of epistemology in the management disciplines. This was always an unsatisfactory debate owing to the difficulties of locating a boundary between natural and social (or human) sciences. (For example, on which side of it would the various branches of psychology belong?) In fact, the situation is a good deal more complex. Studies in the history and sociology of knowledge indicate that the conceptual objects of disciplines may vary in epistemological footing, both over time and between disciplines at the same time, and are related to the sociocultural and material conditions of knowledge production (Foucault, 1969; Ravetz 1971). The attempt simply to separate natural and social or human sciences from an epistemological standpoint will not do.

However, as writers such as Bateson (1973) and Searle (1983) have argued, explanatory notions such as causality need to be considered differently in the social and behavioural sciences as compared with the natural sciences. As Bateson points out, this is what distinguishes psychology from physiology. Likewise, Searle develops his concept of intentionality so as to distinguish natural from intentional causes. In this respect, there is a distinction to be made between the social–behavioural and natural sciences. It does not follow, however, that they differ in some systematic way as regards epistemological criteria for the validity of research findings. Nor does it follow that the social and behavioural sciences are inherently more normative than the natural sciences, as Whitley (1984a) points out. In fact, the social sciences tend to problematize normative issues in a way that the natural sciences do not, but that does not mean that they are more normative than the latter. If anything, the opposite might be true, since the former reflect more on their values than do the latter.

Conclusions

Various writers, including Mitroff and Kilmann (1978), Burrell and Morgan (1979), Morgan (1983) and Chua (1986), have alluded to the epistemological and ontological bases underlying the methodological controversies in the management disciplines and related fields, and to the problems that this state of affairs raises in the development of research strategies in these disciplines. In general, the type of solution proposed is one which seeks to accommodate widely differing epistemological and ontological positions within the research culture of the field of management. The hope is that conversations of some kind may be possible between the different schools of thought.

However, widely different ontological positions seriously inhibit such 'conversations', not just because the potential participants may well not share the same sets of conceptual objects but even more because they will tend to differ in their views as to what kinds of conceptual objects are valid. For example, external realists will be accused of reifying their constructs in claiming that they are representative of 'external reality'. They will in turn protest that their nominalist opponents are indulging themselves in the creation of arbitrary conceptual schemes that do not have to pass the test of being representative of anything. But the differences in epistemological position would probably be even more serious than this, for 'positivism' has become quite literally a term of abuse in certain circles while remaining a sought-after accolade in others.

The argument presented here is that those concerned with methodology need to devote more attention to philosophical fundamentals and to the more recent developments which allow the traditional controversies over ontology and epistemology to be considered from a new perspective. Following Putnam, who has taken a leading role in developing this perspective, we have termed it 'internal realism'. It is suggested that this, rather than eclecticism or transcendental–dialectical accommodation, would provide a basis for the methodological *rapprochement* so urgently needed in the management disciplines. Internal realism, then, provides the philosphical background to the remainder of this paper.

The development of knowledge in the management disciplines

In considering the implications of the above discussion for the management disciplines, one can note the positions taken by a number of writers on these issues. However, in general, these writers do not acknowledge the science–technology distinction which was made above and which is important in the context of such disciplines. For example, the debate in the accounting literature between Chambers (1973) and Sterling (1979), on the one hand, and Stamp (1981), on the other, conflates several issues which need to be distinguished.

(1a) To what extent is the existing practice (technology) of accounting science-based?

(1b) To what extent could the technology of accounting become substantially more science-based than it is?

(2a) What kind of science contributes to the basis of existing accounting technology?

(2b) What kind of science might provide the basis for accounting to become substantially more science-based than it is?

(3a) What kind of research is needed to develop the science which might provide that basis?

(3b) What is an appropriate methodology for such research?

As for question (1a) few, if any, writers would wish to assert that existing accounting practice is substantially science-based (as, say, engineering practice and, albeit to a lesser extent, medical practice are). Questions (1b), (2a), (2b) and (3a) are addressed in relation to management acounting by Kaplan (1984a,b), while very similar questions in relation to marketing have been considered by Bonoma and Wong (1983). These papers, however, have not gone on to consider question (3b), and it is this lacuna which has largely motivated the present paper.

In the next section there will be a number of references to the author's own discipline of accounting, although the issues concern the management disciplines in general and the focus on accounting is abandoned in subsequent sections.

A potential scientific basis for accounting?

Some years ago, a number of writers sought scientific foundations for accounting in an axiomatic or postulational approach to the explication of accounting concepts. This approach is exemplified by Chambers (1955), Mattessich (1957, 1964), Kosiol (1978) and, to some extent, Moonitz (1961) and Ijiri (1975). It would seem to suggest that, in contrast with what has been argued above, accounting could develop its own scientific basis from logic and mathematics rather than looking to other social and behavioural science disciplines. This approach, which can be likened to analytical positivism in legal theory (Lloyd, 1979), is to some extent being continued in the attempt of the US Financial Accounting Standards Board (FASB) to articulate a conceptual framework for financial accounting.

It is also clear that the thinking of FASB researchers in this area has been considerably influenced by economics. This is only to be expected, since work such as that of Edwards and Bell (1961) illustrated the links between accounting concepts and those of economics. Moreover, the developments in theory and empirical research in accounting since 1960 have emphasized the links not just with economics, but also with psychology and sociology, as sources of both hypotheses for testing and research methods.

Yet, as Kaplan (1984a) argued, this combination of theorizing and empirical investigation does not seem to have contributed substantially to improving the effectiveness of accounting practice, at least in management accounting. He points to the ossification of management accounting around concepts and techniques which originated in the early part of this century, and whose effectiveness is, for various reasons, increasingly questionable. As he indicates, this ossification is shown both in the preoccupation with a 'widget-costing' approach to manufacturing operations and in the emphasis upon short-term financial-accounting based measures of divisional performance. According to Kaplan:

the references in today's management accounting literature are to economists . . . , contemporary researchers' knowledge of managers' behavior is based not on studying decisions and procedures of actual firms, but on stylized models of managerial and firm behavior that have been articulated by economic theorists who, themselves, have limited first-hand knowledge of the behavior they have modeled.

Kaplan cites information economics, agency theory and transaction cost theory as examples of recent theoretical developments which, because they are difficult to operationalize and to test in realistic settings, have not yielded the major empirical developments which are necessary if academic management accounting is to be useful in devising administrative processes or performance and control measures. In Kaplan's view, then, the development of knowledge in management accounting now requires not an increased effort to operationalize, test and develop existing theories, but the adoption of a substantially different research strategy employing field-based small-sample methods and an inductive approach to theory development.

Kaplan's view of these issues calls for some modification in view of the absence of any mention by him of the numerous references in today's management accounting literature to psychology and sociology in addition to economics. Sociology, particularly in the form of functionalist theories of organizations as 'open systems', has played a major part in the development of organization theory and of the contingency approach to analysing management accounting requirements. Dermer (1977) provides an example of a textbook on management planning and control systems in which this type of organization theory plays a crucial role. From the 1950s, a considerable number of publications have appeared in which theories from psychology or sociology, rather than economics, have been applied or tested in empirical situations. Early examples were Argyris (1952) and Stedry (1960), followed by Hofstede (1968), Hopwood (1973, 1974), Otley (1978) and numerous others.

Implications for research philosophy and methodology

Kaplan's critique therefore needs to be reinterpreted as a criticism not of economics as a source of ideas for management accounting research, but rather of the existing mainstream approach in management research. This approach is characterized by its adherence to positivistic external realism, as exemplified both in the economic theories which Kaplan mentions and also in the sociological functionalism and psychological behaviourism which have generally been favoured in such research. More specifically, all these theories consider human behaviour in a manner which excludes, as potential explanatory variables, the subjective beliefs, desires and other intentional states related to situations and actions by actors in the research site. This ignoring of the subjective rationalities of social actors in favour of some postulated objective rationality of an essentially mechanistic nature can be termed objectivism, to distinguish it from the interpretive approach which pays attention to intentionality.

For the objectivist researcher, social facts exist independently of the research community that studies them, and they can be observed in the form of empirical relationships which can be captured by appropriate research design and statistical inference that are considered to be value-free. This approach tends to focus, at the organizational level, on states rather than social processes, the latter being less easy to accommodate within an objectivist perspective (e.g. differing accounts of them typically exist). For the interpretive researcher, social facts are be considered in the intentional contexts intersubjectively constructed by the social actors whose interactions constitute such facts. This approach is more sensitive to the dynamics of social processes, as it is able to accommodate more than the account of a process.[2]

The problem of reconciling interpretive and objectivist approaches in studying organizations and social systems generally is well known to social theorists (for an examination of this problem and a suggestion for reconciliation at the theoretical level, see Giddens (1981)). The methodological implications of Giddens's suggestions remain to be developed (Knorr-Cetina, 1981). They are also overlooked by Chua (1986), whose conception of the interpretive approach owes more to Dilthey and the *Verstehen* school than to Weber.

The appeal of objectivism is widely recognized: it lies in its assumed affinity with the research methods of the natural sciences. Its weaknesses, however, are far from widely recognized, although some writers have held the predominantly objectivist character of management accounting research largely responsible for the 'schism' between academics and practitioners (Tomkins and Groves, 1983). While this may be somewhat overstating the position, it certainly seems likely that research approaches which ignore the vocabularies and subjective rationalities of managers in research sites, and impose a theoretical framework which is alien to their reasoning, create an epistemological schism which constitutes a major barrier to the sharing of ideas (and may lead to a degree of antipathy).

More significant for the present discussion is the fact that the objectivist approach systematically ignores a whole category of potential explanatory variables, namely beliefs, desires and other intentional states, making various assumptions intended to operationalize standardized concepts such as 'utility maximization'. To be sure, scientific models start off as highly simplified abstractions dependent upon very restrictive assumptions (or idealized conditions) and reflecting only a very partial (but hopefully crucial) understanding of the phenomena, e.g. frictionless mechanics. However, empirical testing of such models becomes feasible only when enough of the restrictive assumptions can be relaxed so that the model can be operationalized as a testable theory in some set of real-world (experimental or quasi-experimental) conditions. Thus, 'quantitative' research design as typically required by the objectivist approach can properly be applied only when (putative) theoretical understanding has developed to the point where this can be done. (As Kaplan (1984a) suggests, this may not yet be the case for the Agency and Transactions Cost Theories). These problems entail a major pitfall of objectivism in practice; the researcher is offered a choice between carrying out pseudo-tests of inadequately operationalized theories and atheoretical 'brute empiricism' (Foster, 1978, p. 277) leading to *ad hoc* theorizing from the results of data collection and analysis.

A related point, which emerges from Kaplan's writings, concerns the fruitlessness of a situation in which the researcher has hardly any personal familiarity with the phenomena being studied, i.e., to press the mechanical analogy, the researcher does not even know that there is such a phenomenon as 'friction', let alone have a model of how it operates mechanically. Kaplan's complaint is that far too much research into management accounting is being undertaken by individuals who have minimal personal familiarity with the empirical domain to which the theory they are 'testing' is supposed to relate.

If the two points noted above are put together, the situation to which Kaplan is objecting can be characterized as follows: in too many instances we have theories which are not really in a state to be operationalized being 'tested' by individuals whose familiarity with the relevant empirical domain is inadequate for them to realize the implications of this.

A feature of this situation is that theorists and would-be empirical researchers tend to be two different sets of individuals possessing rather different skills. Such a state of affairs is acceptable (and perhaps necessary) in a developed field like modern physics where theory has achieved a degree of comprehensiveness such that the conditions of empirical testing can be rigorously specified. However, in a developing applied social science field such as management, this kind of division of labour between 'theorists' and 'experimentalists' is much more problematic. Here, indeed, lies the strength of the case for a 'grounded theory' approach which is discussed below. But the question remains whether such an approach can avoid the pitfalls of 'brute empiricism' and *ad hoc* theorizing to which excessive inductivism inevitably leads.

Kaplan's proposals, while sharing the rationale of the 'grounded theory' approach, place particular emphasis on the preparation of the 'ground' in the form of case studies. As already argued at length above, however, case studies cannot be theory- or value-free, and a failure to articulate key assumptions involved in a case description will vitiate it as a research report. The 'case for case studies' requires more careful consideration than its proponents have given it (see, for example, the most informative monograph by Yin (1984)).

Case studies and the need for epistemological bootstrapping

Both Kaplan (1984b) and Bonoma and Wong (1983) refer to the role of case studies in the earlier stages of epistemological development of a discipline. But they fail to pay adequate attention to the pitfalls in research which result from the interactions between the way in which case studies are written and the state of epistemological development in a field.

In any empirical research the researcher requires a set of taxonomic categories as a basis for classifying data and some concepts of relevance in deciding what to ignore. The taxonomic categories and the concepts of relevance are linked to the content of existing theory. Thus there is a link between an *interpretive theory*, which 'provides the facts', and the current state of development of an *explanatory theory*, which does not merely seek to explain them but also influences how they are currently understood. This link is what Lakatos (1970a,b) called the *positive heuristic* of the research programme: the researcher is thereby given a fairly coherent idea of what to look for in order to test and develop further the explanatory theory.

However, this link barely exists in a nascent discipline. Explanatory theory is too underdeveloped to suggest anything at all clear and unambiguous in terms of taxonomic categories and concepts of relevance. For these, the researcher is still largely dependent upon conceptions which are pre-theoretical, in the sense that they derive from the taken-for-granted background understandings whose very limitations provide the stimulus for seeking to develop the nascent discipline.

Thus the nascent discipline faces a problem of 'epistemological bootstrapping'. In computer parlance, a *bootstrap* is a program which prepares the computer to receive (other) programs. A program has to be read in as data, under the control of another program, before it can be executed. The particular function of the bootstrap program requires that it must read itself in. But, unlike the case of the computer, which merely uses the bootstrap to read in other programs (which then handle the data), the 'epistemological bootstrap' constitutes a proto-interpretive theory which is used to read in data and loads those data with its own assumptions.

To a certain extent, this epistemological bootstrap is provided by basic understandings about the world which all human beings develop during childhood and which were much studied by Jean Piaget (e.g. Piaget, 1970). Even these, however, may differ in part from culture to culture. For one thing, these understandings are associated with the acquisition of language. Noam Chomsky (e.g. Chomsky, 1968) has devoted many years' work to seeking an underlying generative structure for human languages. But disagreement continues, both as to the extent to which cognitive development is guided by that of language and related sociocultural tools (or vice versa) and as to the innateness of certain universal structural principles of human language. To borrow from computer parlance again, where fundamental cognitive abilities are concerned, there is no clear boundary between shared *biological* '*hardware*' (whether innate or dependent upon neurophysiological development during childhood) and *cultural* '*software*', which is not necessarily shared by people with different childhood experiences.

The problem, then, is that the 'epistemological bootstrap' (or proto-interpretive theory) may present the 'facts' in terms of a view of the world that begs some of the important issues with which the nascent discipline is concerned. How can we escape from this vicious circle of tendentiousness? Kaplan (1984b, pp. 27–33) brings a 'knowledge-tree' model from Roethlisberger (1977) to bear on this issue, prior to discussing the role for case studies in research (see table 11.2).

Roethlisberger's stages in the possible evolution of a body of knowledge, with their quasi-medical terminology ('clinical', 'syndromes'), are quite similar to those enumerated by Foucault (1969, chapter 6), whose view of the emergence of scientific knowledge was also strongly influenced by his study of the history of medicine. Foucault focuses on the steps or thresholds which a body of knowledge must cross if it is to progress towards scientific status. The first threshold is for a body of knowledge to be recognized as a distinct subject. The second is what Foucault terms 'the threshold of epistemologization'. At this stage, 'there separates off [from the extant body of knowledge] a distinct set of statements, which claims to assert (not necessarily successfully) *certain rules of verification and of consistency*, and exercises a dominant role (of model, critique or verification) (pp. 243–4, my translation, emphasis added). This is the threshold that demarcates 'clinical knowledge' from mere 'skill'.

Foucault's next threshold is that of 'scientificity', when 'the epistemo-logical form thus delineated obeys certain formal criteria, and its [component] statements reflect not merely some culturally given rules of formation, but also certain laws governing the construction of propositions' (Foucault, 1969, chapter 6). This is the step from 'clinical' to 'analytical' knowledge. The final threshold, that of 'formalization', is the one which gives access to the very top of Roethlisberger's tree of

Table 11.2   The knowledge enterprise

Levels	Characteristic statements (theories)	Method	Products
Analytical (scientific) knowledge	General propositions	Creative and inductive leap of imagination	Deductive systems
	Empirical propositions	Operational definitions Rigorous measurement	Statements of the form x varies with y under given conditions
	Elementary concepts	Definition of concepts and variables Elementary measurement	Statements of the form x varies from y
Clinical knowledge	Conceptual schemes	Observation Interviewing Classification	Descriptive cases and syndromes Taxonomies
Skill	Knowledge of acquaintance	Practice and reflection The phenomena	How-to-do-it state-ments and aphorisms

For the development of knowledge, read from the bottom up; for the practice of knowledge, read from the top down.
From Roethlisberger (1977, p. 393).

knowledge – formal deductive systems.

The analysis provided by Foucault is of interest here, both for his historical perspective and because of his comments on the two intermediate thresholds (of epistemologization and scientificity) which are of particular relevance to the social and behavioural sciences. For to say, as Kaplan does (quoting Roethlisberger), that 'going from the bottom [of the knowledge tree] up involves sweat, tears, toil, a great deal of imagination, and little deductive logic' begs a crucial question.

The language employed by Roethlisberger and Kaplan strongly implies that the top section of the 'tree', incorporating formal deductive systems, is epistemologically superior to the section immediately below it. Such a view ignores the powerful arguments of Georgescu-Roegen (1971) regarding the distinction to be made between 'arithmomorphic' and 'dialectical' concepts. The former are capable of precise quantifi-cation and correspond to extensive properties. The latter are surrounded by a 'penumbra', so that the borderline between the extension of the property and that of its opposite or negation is not clearly delineated, and precise quantification is problematic. Georgescu-Roegen argues that a number of crucial scientific concepts in social science, biology and also physics are dialectical in this sense.[3]

In any event, the issue for the social and behavioural sciences, and for the related management disciplines, is not the attainability of the threshold of formalization but rather the development of knowledge capable of leading across the thresholds of epistemologization and scientificity. Ravetz (1971, p. 185) considers this issue in a way that is particularly relevant to case-based research:

Two properties . . . are necessary for an assertion [in a research report] to become a fact. These may be called 'significance', in that it must be noticed by someone if it is not to fall into oblivion; and 'stability', in that it must be capable of reproduction and use by others, if it is not to be refuted as spurious. . . . In addition, it must have a [third] property of 'invariance'. . . . When . . . new work is done on its basis, then the objects of investigation will necessarily change, sometimes only slightly, but sometimes drastically. . . . There is then the question of whether it can be translated or recast so as to relate to the newer objects descended from the original areas, and still be an adequate foundation for a conclusion. If not, then the original conclusion is rejected as dealing with non-objects, or as ascribing false properties to real objects.

By the same token, if case studies are to provide a basis for 'clinical' knowledge, something more than accounts based on commonsense naturalistic observation is called for. To speak of 'direct research' (as does Mintzberg) is to ignore the epistemological analysis which shows that 'if commonsense accounts are not taken as intellectually problematic there seems little reason to expect scientific knowledge to be produced' (Whitley, 1984b, p. 387). Crossing the threshold of epistemologization entails the establishment of an intellectual standpoint in terms of which commonsense accounts can be examined and questioned. Until it has been crossed, it is hard to see how research, in a scientific sense, can take place. Thus, the arguments for Mintzbergian 'direct research' can be seen to be quite naive (or disingenuous). Yet Kaplan (1984a) seems to accept these arguments, and his later more detailed paper (Kaplan, 1984b), while considering epistemological issues much more explicitly, contains nothing which indicates awareness of the crucial role of research methodology in establishing the stability and invariance of assertions that are candidates for factual status.

A commentator on a previous version of this paper made the following point:

[With regard to] the establishment of the science of mechanics by Galileo and Newton . . . [m]any of the facts in this field were well, if imprecisely, known for millennia when they begun their work: the tendency of bodies to fall toward earth, the periodic motions of the heavenly bodies, etc. The accomplishment of the new science was to coordinate these facts in a rational framework, and in the process, to 'correct' many of them.

Let us divide the 'facts that were well, if imprecisely, known for millennia' into two categories: those that were evident to any intelligent and observant member of society, and belong to what may be termed 'general knowledge', and those that were known only to specialists (engineers, astronomers etc.) and can be termed 'specialized knowledge'. Many of the latter will in fact be more refined versions of the former. Now the task of the researcher (Galileo, say) is somewhat different in the two cases. As an educated member of society, he presumably would not need to discover 'general knowledge' for himself or to report on it, although he may end up by 'correcting' it. But he might well need both to discover and to report on the specialized knowledge. It is the latter that would call for particular study in the first instance, e.g. by visiting shipyards and other places where the application of the relevant specialized knowledge can be observed. This is the analogue for a form of case-based research which aims to capture the knowledge of specialized practitioners with a view to building upon it. But the methods used to produce research reports of this kind need to be such that (a) if certain relevant beliefs or practices of specialists are observably instantiated in several research sites, the research will record them as such, and (b) another researcher replicating the observations within the context of the same research programme will record substantially similar findings.

Nor do Bonoma and Wong (1983) appear to recognize what is at stake. They mention that case studies may contain quantitative as well as qualitative data, claiming that this can provide an element of 'triangulation' in the research. They also provide a discussion of the trade-offs to be made between the external and internal validity of a research study in social and behavioural science, i.e. between the applicability of its findings to other non-experimental settings (which they term 'generalizability') and the researcher's ability to control error and bias in the data ('data integrity'). However, their discussion, and particularly their use of the term 'generalizability', blur the issue clearly spelled out by Ravetz: how can a research programme be organized so as to produce descriptive assertions which are not merely significant, but which also have a chance of exhibiting the stability and invariance required of candidates for factual status? We return to these questions below. First, however, the problems of both Mintzbergian 'direct research' and 'grounded theory' will be examined in more detail.

The dangers of inductivism and the fallacy of 'direct research'

Mintzberg seems in some respects to think like a positivistic external realist, since researchers are assumed by him to be able to produce unproblematic descriptive accounts of organizational reality based on naturalistic observation. Such accounts are evidently not supposed by him to be either theory- or value-laden to any significant extent. This suggests that, according to Mintzberg, such observation concerns a reality which exists independently of the observer and which the latter can research 'directly'. He makes no concessions to antipositivism, appearing to think that, provided one is not 'setting out to prove some prescription', then one's descriptions can avoid being theory- and value-laden (or, at least, one does not need to worry whether they are or not). Yet, as Tudor (1982, p. 155) remarks, 'crude claims about "staying close to the phenomena" and thus ensuring better "evidence" have tended merely to substitute one unquestioned interpretative theory for another'.

Paradoxically, however, positivistic external realism is a viewpoint which (as we have already noted) has led, in organizational research, to precisely the concern to use quantitative methods which Mintzberg criticizes so effectively.

The type of case research advocated by Mintzberg might have a clear rationale in just one scenario, namely that in which it was accepted that the social science disciplines concerned in management research are far from their threshold of epistemologization and are, as Ravetz (1971) termed it, pseudo-sciences. For then research could not realistically aspire to be of a different type from that carried out in the natural science areas before they crossed that threshold, in other words, the production of natural history.

But this would not appear to be Mintzberg's view of the social sciences. Even if it were, 'natural history' should not be confused with 'clinical research' of the type that Kaplan and Bonoma and Wong are advocating. For as Roethlisberger's 'tree of knowledge' makes apparent, the 'clinical' stage of knowledge involves conceptual schemes and taxonomies which constitute an intellectual standpoint that transcends more naturalistic observation.

What distinguishes Mintzberg's 'direct research' approach from the hypothetico-deductive orthodoxy characteristic of positivistic external realism is that he appears to share with Glaser and Strauss (1967), whose views are examined at greater length below, a completely inductivist view of theory construction.[4] In Bateson's (1973) words, they

were trained to think and argue inductively from data to hypotheses but never to test hypotheses against knowledge derived by *deduction* from the fundamentals of science or philosophy . . . [they] believe that progress is made by study of the 'raw' data, leading to new heuristic concepts. The heuristic concepts are then to be regarded as 'working hypotheses' and tested against more data. Gradually, it is hoped, the heuristic concepts will be corrected and improved until at last they are worthy of a place in the list of fundamentals (pp. 23–5).

Lakatos (1970a,b) identified the reasons why inductivism fails to produce theoretical advances: purely inductive hypotheses are *ad hoc*. For a hypothesis to lead to theoretical advance, three conditions must be satisfied. The hypothesis must be (a) theoretically progressive, (b) empirically progressive and (c) part of a coherent preplanned programme of research.

Theoretical progressiveness involves predicting some new hitherto unexpected fact, while empirical progressiveness is achieved if the existence of this fact is corroborated. A hypothesis which is not theoretically progressive is *ad hoc* in one sense, while one which merely makes predictions that are uncorroborated is *ad hoc* in a second sense. But a hypothesis which meets these criteria will still be *ad hoc* (in a third sense) if it does not form an integral part of a coherent preplanned research programme. 'Serendipitous' discoveries do not lead to coherent theoretical development.

Foster (1978, p. 277) uses the term 'brute empiricism' to refer pejoratively to quantitative research (in finance) that is grossly *ad hoc* in Lakatos's sense. The kind of 'direct research approach' advocated by Mintzberg is a different form of 'brute empiricism' (perhaps we could term it 'crass empiricism').

In contrast, other papers in the same special 1979 issue of *ASQ* are concerned with the role of an explicit conceptual framework (if only a rough one) in the early stages of fieldwork (Miles, 1979), how to do field research on organizations that 'transcend story-telling' (Miles, 1979) and how to produce material that is both 'thick and generalizable' (McClintock et al., 1979). These contributions do not subscribe to the myth of theory- and value-free descriptions, and they acknowledge the intersubjective nature of the validation of knowledge-claims. For the development of knowledge in the management disciplines, research approaches that exhibit this kind of *epistemological awareness* may demand more of researchers, but they also offer more. We return to these themes below.

The ambiguities of 'grounded theory'

One detailed set of methodological proposals for conducting research in a nascent field is set out in *The Discovery of Grounded Theory* by Glaser and

Strauss (1967), to which reference has already been made above, in a comment on its inductivism. For example, their heuristic concept of 'social loss' (Glaser and Strauss, 1967, p. 23) appears to exemplify the kind of inductivism criticized by Bateson (1973, pp. 21–31). It is nevertheless a serious and carefully thought-out work which undoubtedly contains many valuable ideas on how to conduct research in a nascent discipline (for example, chapters 3 and 5 on 'theoretical sampling' and 'the constant comparative method') and which cannot be casually dismissed. However, it needs to be recognized as a product of its circumstances, and particularly as a reaction – an *over*reaction – against the objectivistic abuses of inadequately operationalized 'grand theory' in research design (cf. Kaplan's present-day concerns, as discussed above). Moreover, like many seminal works, it contains serious ambiguities which are conducive to a garbling of key concepts. Some of these ambiguities are particularly evident in their important chapter 3. For example, 'the basic question in theoretical sampling . . . is: *what* groups or sub-groups does one turn to *next* in data collection? And for *what* theoretical purpose? . . . Our criteria are those of *theoretical purpose and relevance* (Glaser and Strauss, 1967, pp. 47–8). The crucial word in that quotation is 'next'. For how is one to apply these precepts to the *initial* acquisition of data?

The picture given by Glaser and Strauss (GS) is that of a research programme (in Lakatos's sense) gradually taking shape through successive, and increasingly theoretically focused, samplings of data. This might be a reasonable enough view, were it not for the problem of the initial motivation of the research in their model of the research process. In urging a prospective researcher not to 'commit himself exclusively to one specific preconceived theory' (p. 46), GS overlooked two important considerations. First, some specific conjecture or putative insight is required to motivate a piece of research. Second, it is a question not of a researcher committing himself or herself exclusively to any specific preconceived theory but of testing out a specific conjecture or putative insight.

A cynical reading of GS might suggest that the only initial motivation required in their model is the desire to 'generate theory' as a means to career advancement, avoiding the Cinderella role of testing other people's theories (pp. 4, 10). But a fairer reading suggests that the motivation is supposed to come from being a trained sociologist, possessing a 'general, sociological perspective' and sufficient 'theoretical sensitivity'; in other words, it seems to be a somewhat obscure matter of professional mystique. 'Only sociologists are trained to want . . . to look for . . . , and to generate . . . sociological theory from their work' (pp. 6–7). Thus equipped, the sociologist may begin the research with a partial framework of 'local' concepts, designating a few principal or gross features of the situation that he will study . . . These concepts give him a beginning foothold on his research. Of course, he does not know the relevancy of these concepts to his problem – this problem must emerge . . . (p. 45).

The authors do not state what the would-be researcher should do if he or she (despite being a 'trained sociologist') does not possess enough knowledge of the field to be able to put together this 'partial framework' or proto-theory. Apart from that, the passage seems to describe the process of 'epistemological bootstrapping' that must precede research in a nascent discipline. However, there is another difference between this picture and the role of epistemological bootstrapping as presented in this paper: for GS, the bootstrapping is part of the research, which is essentially a process of personal discovery, whereas the argument here is that such bootstrapping is a precondition of empirical research, which is essentially a process of trying to establish accounts of phenomena that are candidates for factual status.

Turning to their equally important chapter 5, we see that, while they appear to depict the establishment of a robust taxonomy as the cornerstone of theoretical development (a position which is consistent with the analysis presented here), they also state that 'the constant comparative method is not designed . . . to guarantee that two analysts working independently with the same data will achieve the same results . . . [but to] aid the creative generation of theory' (p. 103).

The crucial interdependence between theory and taxonomic categories has already been noted. Where GS differ from the position which is argued in this paper is in their relative lack of interest in the intersubjective validation and acceptance of a taxonomy, as opposed to its use by the researcher who developed it, for the further generation of theory. They understandably reject the view that 'whatever qualitative research has been done is . . . merely a . . . preliminary providing of categories to use in the ensuing quantitative research' (p. 234). However, this rejection misses the point that, once a taxonomy has been generally accepted as reasonably robust by the research community, the process of generating further theory based on that taxonomy can proceed on a wide scale.

A powerful example of this is provided by the development of modern biology. Linnaeus (Carl von Linné) worked out his classification of living things about 100 years before Mendel propounded his laws of genetics and Charles Darwin developed his theory of the origin of species. Linnaeus used comparative anatomy to develop a comprehensive and robust taxonomic framework (biosystematics) in which the concepts of species and genus occupied key positions, but it was left to his successors to develop powerful explanatory theories of the evolution and transmission of the characteristic properties of species. Thus, although Linnaeus did not set out to propose a theory of speciation, his work was able to serve as a basis for later research which did so and which, in turn, generally served to confirm the robustness of his classifications.

It is instructive to consider this example of knowledge accrual in biology at a time when it was relatively immature in evaluating the methodology proposed by GS. Their proposed model of knowledge accrual focuses very much on the individual researcher or small research team who develop their taxonomy and proceed to seek their own 'complex theory that corresponds closely to the data . . . '. According to GS, 'This method . . . especially facilitates the generation of [developmental] theories of process, sequence and change' (pp. 113–14).

Whitley (1984a) has characterized the research culture in certain areas of social and behavioural science as a 'fragmented adhocracy': *fragmented*, because individual research teams act in relative isolation from one another and tend to be small; *adhocracy*, because the development of theory proceeds in a predominantly *ad hoc* inductive fashion rather than being impelled by a positive heuristic consisting of issues raised by some existing theory, or of conjectures or putative insights arising out of some proto-theory. The implication of Whitley's analysis, in common with those of Ravetz and Lakatos already mentioned, is that 'fragmented adhocracy' is a model of research that is not conducive to the development of intersubjectively valid knowledge-claims.

This tendency of GS towards a particularistic view of research is also apparent in their consideration of 'the credibility of grounded theory' (chapter 9). GS are, of course, aware of a researcher's need to convey his or her findings to professional peers and other potential actors in the process of intersubjective validation. But there are ambiguities here also. Thus they state that

in this book we have suggested that criteria of judgement be based [not on the canons of rigorous quantitative verification, but] instead on the detailed elements of the actual strategies used for collecting, coding, analyzing, and presenting data when generating theory and the way in which people read the theory (p. 224).

The statement just quoted would be exceptionable, were it not for the last dozen or so words. What is meant by those words is amplified when GS write that 'the researcher's task of conveying credibility is actually like that of a realistic novelist' (p. 229n). For them, the distinction between credibility and mere plausibility is not evident: in a nascent discipline, discovering plausible theory, rather than establishing candidates for corroborated factual status, is for them the essential goal of research.

This brief analysis of GS's methodology of 'grounded theory' should be sufficient to indicate why their work, while full of interesting ideas reflecting a wealth of research experience, is unlikely to provide a basis for the development of knowledge-claims which are intersubjectively valid.

Conclusions

Implications for research methods in the management disciplines

The failure of facts to be achieved is an effect of undetected pitfalls . . . false assessments of the quality of evidence or insufficiently strong inferences . . . caused by insufficiently strong criteria of adequacy (Ravetz, 1971, p. 156).

In applied fields such as the management disciplines, research must draw on ideas and methods derived from various more fundamental fields, in our case those of social and behavioural sciences, many of which are relatively immature and unstable. Even in an established scientific discipline, research method involves a tacit element of craft skills that have to be 'learned on the job'. In a nascent discipline, skills remain to be developed and there exists the problem of epistemological bootstrapping described above.

It is (notoriously) not possible to state a set of sufficient conditions for the production of knowledge. At most, we may hope to articulate a number of necessary conditions which signpost major pitfalls. The list below draws on the work of Miles and Huberman (1983, chapter 2) as well as other works cited above and the writer's own experience.

1 A research programme, to be recognizable as such, requires an initial conceptual framework or proto-theory, which, even if it is tentative and hazy, at least suffices to set forth initial taxonomic categories and criteria of relevance. The taxonomic categories can be thought of as 'labels we put on bins containing a lot of discrete events and behaviors' (Miles and Huberman, 1983, p. 28). This initial framework should be explicitly articulated in writing or, perhaps even better, in diagrammatic form.

2 This proto-theory contains a crucial insight or conjecture (in Lakatosian terminology, a 'hard core') which constitutes the original intellectual motivation of the research programme. The function of this 'hard core' is not so much to be corroborated (by withstanding attempted disconfirmation) but rather to be fruitful in raising issues whose investigation leads, as the research progresses, to findings which can themselves be corroborated and which thus

become candidates for factual status. In other words, the purpose of a proto-theory is not to offer formal hypotheses for disconfirmation, but to provide an epistemological bootstrap in the quest to establish facts.

3 Thus, 'it is a direct step from the elaboration of a conceptual framework to the formulation of research questions' (Miles and Huberman, 1983, p. 33); in Lakatosian terminology, to the 'positive heuristic' of the research programme. These initial research questions should not be too numerous and may not be very precise at first, but they will serve to make the assumptions of the proto-theory more explicit and to sharpen up the criteria of relevance by identifying what the researcher (or research team) wants to know *most* or *first* (Miles and Huberman, 1983, p. 34).

4 The articulation of this proto-theory will require at least some minimal familiarity with the field to be researched. If this has not been gained as part of the would-be researcher's life experience, then it can be achieved by a combination of studying the extant literature (if any) and personal exposure to the field (which may well involve some informal data collection).

5 It may be preferable not to characterize this essential self-education process as 'research'. In fact, it is a prerequisite to research, as it is the phase during which the proto-theory which is the springboard for the research programme is developed. It is also an informal individualistic process.

6 Factual status is achieved through a social process of intersubjective validation, the first step in which is replication to test for stability. Therefore it is crucial that the research is carried out in such a manner as to permit a sufficient degree of replication for stability to be tested, for otherwise there is no hope of establishing any facts.

7 Particularly in case-based research, we are concerned with such questions as 'using the same basic field notes, could another researcher write a case study that was plausibly similar to the original?' (Miles and Huberman, 1983, p. 16).

8 It is becoming increasingly important to compare research hypotheses and findings at the macrolevel and the microlevel. Macrolevel research using quantitative techniques is not necessarily incommensurate with microlevel research using qualitative techniques; however, it must be recognized that each will display (if successful) a different facet of reality, that these facets cannot be left unreconciled and that the modelling of human rationality in quantitative research designs tends to be crude.

9 The accommodation of different research designs (say, question-

naire-based surveys and case studies) within the same research programme requires a shared epistemological basis other than brute or crass empiricism. Such a basis needs to be non-positivistic and to avoid the ontological pitfalls of the realism–idealism debate.

10 The interrelationship between the establishment of facts and the development of theory means that, while case studies are no panacea for the problems of a nascent discipline if they are properly used within a research programme as described here, they have a potentially crucial role in the application of epistemological bootstrapping and hence in the evolution of a body of knowledge from 'skill' to 'clinical knowledge'. The danger is that, since to use them in that way is relatively demanding, they can be chosen as an 'easy way out' (crass empiricism) and thus contribute mere stories rather than progress towards the establishment of facts.

It may be protested that the necessary conditions just articulated are 'more Lakatosian than Lakatos', in that Lakatos (1970a) stated that he did not claim that a research programme needs to be undertaken strictly according to his methodology, but only that it must be such that it can be 'rationally reconstructed' *ex post* to fit that methodology. In other words, the concepts just enumerated clearly imply that research, 'qualitative' or otherwise, cannot simply involve jumping in at the empirical deep end. Yet, perhaps a person (or even a team) who had indeed 'jumped in at the deep end' could subsequently present the research as having been conducted along 'Lakatosian' lines.

There are, however, severe limitations on the extent to which this could happen. It is not simply that analytical tools are required. Equally if not more crucial is the proto-theory which initiates the research and raises the issues to be investigated.

This leads to the question: 'But doesn't the development of the proto-theory itself require research?' The answer suggested by the above analysis is that a certain intellectual capital must exist, apart from the learning of analytical tools, before research can start. Research, properly speaking, cannot begin from a basis of little or no personal familiarity with the field in question. There is a danger, in a nascent field, that a great deal of work consisting of a would-be researcher's initial familiarization with the field may be passed off as research and published as such, even though it offers virtually nothing of substance to the reader. This danger exists whether quantitative or qualitative research methods are being applied. Moreover, there is not a great deal to choose, epistemologically speaking, between a purely inductive approach in which no proto-theory is articulated prior to data acquisition (brute or crass empiricism) and an approach in which the proto-theory is merely a naive attempt to operationalize theory found in the literature that is not yet sufficiently developed so as to be operationalizable (by a novice in the field, at any rate).

Concluding remarks

With characteristic (if somewhat sexist) wit, Feyerabend (1970, p. 229) pokes fun at those whom he sees as methodological pedants:

Scientific method, as softened up by Lakatos, is but an ornament which makes us forget that a position of 'anything goes' has in fact been adopted. . . . Such a development, far from being undesirable, changes science from a stern and demanding mistress into an attractive and yielding courtesan who tries to anticipate every wish of her lover. Of course, it is up to us to choose either a dragon or a pussy cat for our company. I do not think I need to explain my own preferences.

These preferences may well be shared by proponents of 'direct research' such as Mintzberg, or those for whom the writing of case studies appears to be a fairly unproblematic way of opening up a poorly known field to research. But others are likely to find Feyerabend's muse sluttish rather than seductive. The alternative need not be a neopositivist dragon: cannot a muse who recognizes that the development of intersubjectively valid knowledge-claims requires certain conditions and offers guidance on how one can meet them, be an equally attractive and more rewarding companion?

Acknowledgements

I am grateful to Peter Brownell, Graeme Macdonald, Stuart McLeay, Ken Peasnell, Roy Payne, Paul Taylor and Richard Whitley for helpful comments on earlier drafts.

Notes

1   Some writers (e.g. Tudor, 1982, p. 4) use the term *positivism* to refer to the view that 'there is a single, observable, factual reality, and all else fails the test of knowledge'. But this usage needlessly conflates external realism (an ontological position) with positivism (an epistemological one).
2   For example, Georgescu-Roegen (1971) criticizes the 'arithmomorphism' of contemporary economics on the grounds that it takes no account of the direction of 'time's arrow', since its mathematical models are derived from those of classical mechanics and thus imply processes that are reversible (unlike many economic processes).

3 The idea of 'dialectical' concepts discussed by Georgescu-Roegen parallels the rejection by modern intuitionist logicians of the classical law of the excluded middle (i.e. the law that for any proposition p, either p or its negation must be true (Tennant, 1987)).

4 Hypothetico-deductivism is a position which can be traced to the earlier work of Carl Hempel (Hempel and Oppenheim, 1948). It can be briefly characterized as follows: 'the explanation of a finding . . . is the process of showing that the finding follows as a logical conclusion, as a deduction, from [a theory that states] one or more general propositons under specified conditions' (Homans, 1967, quoted by Tudor, 1982, p. 93). Conversely, according to this view, observation of the finding gives support to the theory. This, however, is the logical error pointed out by Popper: the fact that the finding logically follows from the theory means that if the theory is true, the finding must also be true (by the logical rule of *modus ponens*); it also means that if the finding is false (does not occur), the theory must also be false (by the logical rule of *modus tollens*). But the truth (or occurrence) of the finding has no logical bearing on the truth or otherwise of the theory, since a false antecedent can imply a true consequent. At best, one can point out that the theory survived attempted falsification. The strength of such a claim will depend on how rigorous the attempt at falsification was.

References

Abdel-Khalik, A.R. and Ajinkya, B.D. (1979). *Empirical Research in Accounting: A Methodological Viewpoint*. American Accounting Association, Accounting Education Series, vol. 4.

Argyris, C. (1952). *The Impact of Budgets on People*. New York: Controllership Foundation Inc.

Bateson, G. (1973). *Steps to an Ecology of Mind*. London: Granada.

Berkeley, G. (1710). *A Treatise concerning the Principles of Human Knowledge* (reprinted 1971). London: Scolar Press.

Bonoma, T.V. and Wong, K.B. (1983). 'A case study in case research'. Working Paper 9-784-036, Harvard Business School, Boston, MA.

Burrell, G. and Morgan, G. (1979). *Sociological Paradigms and Organizational Analysis*. London: Heinemann.

Chambers, R.J. (1955). 'Blueprint for a theory of accounting'. *Accounting Research*, January.

—— (1973). 'Accounting principles or accounting policies'. *Journal of Accountancy*, May.

Chomsky, N. (1968). *Language and Mind*. New York: Harcourt Brace Jovanovich.

Christenson, C.R. (1983). 'The methodology of positive accounting'. *The Accounting Review*, January.

Chua, W.F. (1986). 'Radical developments in accounting thought'. *The Accounting Review*, October.

Dermer, J. (1977). *Management Planning and Control Systems*. Homewood, IL: Irwin.

Donaldson, L. (1985). *In Defence of Organization Theory*. Cambridge: Cambridge University Press.

Douglas, J.D. (1971). 'Understanding everyday life'. In *Understanding Everyday Life* (ed. J.D. Douglas). London: Routledge.

Dummett, M. (1978). *Truth and Other Enigmas*. London: Duckworth.

Edwards, E.O. and Bell, P.W. (1961). *The Theory and Measurement of Business Income*. Berkeley, CA: University of California Press.

Feyerabend, P.K. (1970). 'Consolations for the specialist'. In *Criticism and the Growth of Knowledge* (eds I. Lakatos and A. Musgrave). Cambridge: Cambridge University Press.

—— (1975a). *Against Method*. London: New Left Books.

—— (1975b). 'How to defend society against science'. *Radical Philosophy*, Summer 1975. Reprinted in Hacking, I. (ed.) (1981). *Scientific Revolutions*. Oxford: Oxford University Press.

Foster, G. (1978). *Financial Statement Analysis*. Englewood Cliffs, NJ: Prentice-Hall.

Foucault, M. (1969). *L'Archéologie du Savoir*. Paris: Gallimard.

Georgescu-Roegen, N. (1971). *The Entropy Law and the Economic Process*. Boston, MA: Harvard University Press.

Giddens, A. (1981). 'Agency, institution and time–space analysis'. In *Advances in Social Theory and Methodology* (eds K.D. Knorr-Cetina and A.V. Cicourel). London: Routledge and Kegan Paul.

Glaser, B. and Strauss, A.L. (1967). *The Discovery of Grounded Theory*. Archive Publishing.

Hempel, C. and Oppenheim, P. (1948). 'Studies in the logic of explanation'. *Philosophy of Science*, 15. Reprinted in Hempel, C. (1965). *Aspects of Scientific Explanation*. London: Collier-Macmillan.

Hofstede, G. (1968). *The Game of Budget Control*. London: Tavistock Publications.

Hopwood, A.G. (1973). *An Accounting System and Managerial Behavior*. London: Saxon House.

—— (1974). *Accounting and Human Behaviour*. London: Haymarket.

Hume, D. (1748). *A Treatise on Human Nature*. Oxford: Clarendon Press, 1967 (reprint).

Ijiri, Y. (1975). *Theory of Accounting Measurement*. SAR No. 10. American Accounting Association.

Kant, I. (1787). *Kritik der Reinen Vernunft* (Critique of Pure Reason) (translated by N. Kemp Smith). London: Macmillan, 1950.

Kaplan, R.S. (1984a). 'The evolution of management accounting'. *The Accounting Review*, July.

—— (1984b). 'The case for case studies in management accounting research'. Working Paper 9–785–0001, Harvard Business School, Boston, MA.

Knorr-Cetina, K.D. (1981). 'Introduction'. In *Advances in Social Theory and Methodology*. London: Routledge and Kegan Paul.

Kosiol, E. (1978). *Pagatoric Theory of Financial Income Determination*. Urbana, IL: Center for International Education and Research in Accounting, University of Illinois.

Lakatos, I. (1970a). 'History of science and its rational reconstructions'. In *PSA 1970 Boston Studies in the Philosophy of Science* (eds R.C. Buck and R.S. Cohen). Dordrecht, Holland: D. Reidel.

—— (1970b). 'Falsification and the methodology of scientific research programmes'. In *Criticism and the Growth of Knowledge* (eds I. Lakatos and A. Musgrave). Cambridge: Cambridge University Press.

Lipsey, R.C. (1980). *Positive Economics* (5th edn). London: Weidenfeld and Nicolson.

Lloyd, D. (1979). *Introduction to Jurisprudence* (4th edn): Stevens.

McClintock, C.C., Brannon, D. and Maynard-Moody, S. (1979). 'Applying the logic of sample surveys to qualitative case studies: the case cluster method'. *Administrative Science Quarterly*, 24, 612–29.

Mattessich, R. (1957). 'Towards a general and axiomatic foundation of accounting'. *Accounting Research*, October.

—— (1964). *Accounting and Analytical Methods*. Scholars, 1977 (reprint).

Miles, M.B. (1979). 'Qualitative data as an attractive nuisance'. *Administrative Science Quarterly*, 24, 590–601.

—— and Huberman, A.M. (1984). *Qualitative Data Analysis, a Sourcebook of New Methods*. Beverly Hills, CA: Sage.

Mintzberg, H. (1979). 'An emerging strategy of "direct" research'. *Administrative Science Quarterly*, 24, 582–90.

Mitroff, I.I. and Kilmann, R.H. (1978). *Methodological Approaches in Social Science*. Beverly Hills, CA: Sage.

Moonitz, M. (1961). *The Basic Postulates of Accounting*. Accounting Research Study No. 1, American Institute of Certified Public Accountants.

Morgan, G. (1983). *Beyond Method*. Beverly Hills, CA: Sage.

Otley, D.T. (1978). 'Budget use and managerial performance'. *Journal of Accounting Research*, Spring.

Pepper, S.C. (1942). *World Hypotheses*. Berkeley: University of California Press.

Piaget, J. (1970). *L'Epistémologie Génétique*. Paris: P.U.F.

Popper, K.R. (1959). *The Logic of Scientific Discovery*. New York: Basic Books.

—— (1972). *Objective Knowledge*. Oxford: Oxford University Press.

—— (1975). 'The rationality of scientific revolutions'. Reprinted in Hacking, I. (ed.) (1981). *Scientific Revolutions*. Oxford: Oxford University Press.

Putnam, H. (1981). *Reason, Truth and History*. Cambridge: Cambridge University Press.

Ravetz, J. (1971). *Scientific Knowledge and its Social Problems*. Oxford: Oxford University Press.

Roethlisberger, F.J. (1977). *The Elusive Phenomena*. Boston, MA: Harvard University Press.

Searle, J.R. (1983). *Internationality, an Essay on the Philosophy of Mind*. Cambridge: Cambridge University Press.

Stamp, E. (1981). 'Why can accounting not become a science like physics?' *Abacus*, June.

Stedry, A. (1960). *Budget Control and Cost Behavior*. Englewood Cliffs, NJ: Prentice-Hall.

Sterling, R.R. (1979). *Toward a Science of Accounting*. Scholars.

Stigler, G.J. (1976). 'Do economists matter?' *Southern Economic Journal*, January.

Tennant, N. (1987). *Anti-Realism and Logic*. Oxford: Clarendon Press.

Tomkins, C.R. and Groves, R.V. (1983). 'The everyday accountant and researching his reality'. *Accounting, Organizations and Society*, 8(4).

Tudor, A. (1982). *Beyond Empiricism: Philosophy of Science in Sociology*. London: Routledge and Kegan Paul.

Van Maanen, J. (1979). 'The fact of fiction in organizational ethnography'. *Administrative Science Quarterly*, 24, 539–51.

Watts, R.L. and Zimmerman, J.R. (1979). 'The demand for and supply of accounting theories: the market for excuses'. *The Accounting Review*, April.

Whitley, R.D. (1984a). 'The fragmented state of management studies: reasons and consequences'. *Journal of Management Studies*, July, 21(2).

—— (1984b). 'The scientific status of management research as a practically-oriented social science'. *Journal of Management Studies*, October, (21)3.

Winch, P. (1958). *The Idea of a Social Science*. London: Routledge and Kegan Paul.

Yin, R.K. (1984). *Case Study Research Design and Methods*. Beverly Hills, CA: Sage.

Index

Index by Geoffrey Jones